I'll miss you 5th ~

BLACK SCARS

BLACK SCARS

A rigorous investigation of the effects of discrimination, with an appendix on the Southern white

BERTRAM P. KARON

Foreword by **SILVAN S. TOMKINS**

SPRINGER PUBLISHING COMPANY
New York

Copyright © 1975

Springer Publishing Company, Inc.
200 Park Avenue South
New York, N.Y. 10003

75   76   77   78   79   /   10   9   8   7   6   5   4   3   2   1

Library of Congress Cataloging in Publication Data

Karon, Bertram P
    Black Scars.

    First published in 1958 under title: The Negro Personality.
    Includes bibliographical references.
    1. Negroes—Psychology. 2. National characteristics,
American. 3. Negroes—Social conditions
I. Title.
E185.625.K35   1974   301.45'19'6073   74-79412
ISBN 0-8261-0302-2

Printed in the United States of America

570341-7 DES 6-17-76

Contents

Foreword   vii

The Perspective from 1975   ix

Preface to the first edition   xv

I
Introduction   1

II
The American Caste System   7

III
The Psychology of the Black   41

IV
The Picture Arrangement Test   52

V
Design of an Experiment   73

VI
The Differences Between Blacks and Whites   113

VII
The Differences Between Northern and Southern Blacks   137

VIII
Northern Versus Southern Blacks—Further Studies   144

IX
The Personality Characteristics   157

X
Conclusions   165

Appendix   172

References   193

Index   197

Seventeen years ago Bertram P. Karon demonstrated that black Americans lived under the threat of violence, to which they responded with an anger whose expression was muted and indirect. At the time these findings were far from obvious; events have since confirmed the reality of black anger.

The effects of oppression on blacks are not likely to be forgotten. There remains, however, the question of the cost to the oppressor and to society as a whole. Using the same research methods, Dr. Karon now demonstrates that whites in the Deep South have paid an enormous price for the maintenance of an oppressive society, and that enforcing passivity upon black Americans has resulted in increased passivity in white Americans as well. This passivity, as Dr. Karon's data makes clear, manifests itself in an unwillingness and inability to work or to sustain work, and in submissive authoritarianism and negativism. These effects represent deep erosions of the American ideal of an independent, active person, cooperative but not submissive to authority.

The addition of this new data contributes to the longitudinal study of American society, white and black, as it struggles toward the realization of its own ideals.

Silvan S. Tomkins
1975

Seventeen years ago I wrote a book about the psychological aspects of the problems of American blacks as a consequence of the special pressures imposed on them by the white majority. Its virtue was the certainty with which its conclusions were drawn. Many things have changed since then, but much has remained the same. It is impossible to review all of the changes, but some aspects of black-white relations require discussion.

Words have changed. "Negro" is no longer an acceptable description to blacks; "Afro-American" and "black" are used instead. (The changes in usage occurred shortly after publication of my book.) According to present-day usage, the Negro is the dehumanized black person.

Perhaps the original title, *The Negro Personality*, may still be appropriate insofar as it deals with the specific effect of the destructive pressures of discrimination. The title did mislead some readers into thinking that the book maintained that there was a distinctive basic personality common to all black people, but the text clearly dispels that notion. Nonetheless, the new title is more accurate.

The word "caste," which is used (and precisely defined) in my book, as in older anthropological works, is sometimes considered inappropriate now because, it is claimed, "caste" implies acceptance by the so-called "lower caste" of the appropriateness of their status. Of course, the unambiguous definition in my book implies nothing of the sort; indeed, I made clear that American blacks have never really accepted their lower status as appropriate. Those who quibble with the word "caste" argue that one must go to India to find a real caste system. But recent events in India have indicated the resentments of the lower castes; acceptance of one's status is a psychological variable that must be empirically investigated and cannot be assumed. Acceptance by the so-called lower caste of the appropriateness of their lower status seems, to the best of my knowledge, always to be in large part a fiction perpetuated by those people enjoying upper caste status.

There has been much real change in the United States. In some ways, the clear regional variations on which this study was based have diminished. In many ways, the South has become less severely caste-like in its social, political, and economic organization. On the other hand, the northern city has in many ways become a worse place for black people to live.

This retrogression of the northern ghetto was not planned by whites; indeed, most northern whites are unaware that it has even occurred. Nor was it expected by northern blacks. It is the unintended and unforeseen consequence of the continuing pattern of migration of southern blacks and southern whites into northern cities.

The southern white brought with him a more extreme attitude about race relations than was characteristic of the northern city. Nevertheless, this was probably a minor element in making the northern city worse. More important was the sheer increase in population. Every northern city has had a population explosion, and expanded outward to its suburbs. In this outward expansion, whites moved, but blacks could not because of housing segregation. Thus, new housing in the suburbs was segregated white. Areas in the central city that had long been desegregated now became black as the whites moved out, leaving the blacks behind.

It is generally held that, when the oppressed receive some benefits, their aspirations rise, the aspirations outstrip their advancement, and violence and revolution become possible. Such a view misses an essential element.

The process leading to violence may be schematized as follows: first, let a group sense a legitimate grievance. Second, tell them that you recognize their grievance and intend to do something about it. Third, begin to do something about it so that they believe that the situation will get better; thus, their aspirations rise. Fourth and finally, however, by delaying improvements or reversing the improvements, take their hope away, and that is when the lid blows off.

It is not merely the fact that aspirations rise, but that an attempt is made to put the lid on, or that the gains are reversed whether or not anyone intended to reverse them, that makes the situation intolerable. These are the situations where violence, and in some cases revolution, may be precipitated.

Violence in the northern cities in the 60's was precipitated in just such a fashion. Blacks have had legitimate grievances. They have been given the feeling that the situation was improving and would improve. Their aspirations have risen, but hope for a better life has then been taken away. The reason that violence occurred in the North and not in the South is that, while the South has generally been more severe in its treatment of blacks, it has also been growing in the direction of improvement in the past ten years. It is in the North that the situation has worsened.

For blacks in the northern ghetto, subjected to population pressure and to the resegregation of the center-city area, the enforced housing segregation has caused a population problem of serious proportions. When the population of a suburban or rural area increases, one sees new housing going up. Immediately one asks, "Where will the schools come from for the children in those houses? Where will the hospitals come from? Where will the sewers and the police and fire services come from? Where will all the services these new people require come from?"

In the center city, however, when the population increases rapidly, there are few new buildings and no one asks where the services—the schools, the police, the firemen, sewage, and rat control—will come from. As the population grows, all one can see is that the neighborhood seems to be run down. But when the population of a given area becomes greater, with no new housing and no new services, it means that services are being taken away, not because anyone intends to do this, but because in fact the same services must be shared by a much larger group of people.

Paradoxically, rents and house prices go up as a neighborhood deteriorates. For the unscrupulous real estate operator there is a financial windfall in a slowly expanding black ghetto. Such operators, known as "block-busters," buy houses cheaply from whites and then sell to blacks who, because of the unavailability of housing, must pay premium prices for substandard housing. This windfall profit is, of course, one of the reasons why most real estate interests oppose the creation and enforcement of fair housing laws that would interfere with their profits. That decreased profits would be accompanied by a decrease in human misery is, they feel, no concern of theirs.

Surprisingly enough, most whites are unaware that what blacks pay to buy or rent substandard dwellings would buy adequate housing outside the black area. Whites believe that the value (i.e., price) of a house goes down in a black neighborhood, but in fact it increases. The neighborhood may become more unpleasant because of crowding and because of the unfair proportion of income that must be devoted to housing, but rents and the price of houses go up. The windfall profits described above depend upon the ignorance of most whites. Blacks, on the other hand, are often surprised if they learn that whites do not know that ghetto rents and house prices are disproportionate, and find it hard to believe that most whites are so ignorant of the suffering endured by ghetto residents. Indeed, if whites know and tolerate the situation, one can only conclude that they approve— an angry but logical conclusion to which many blacks have come.

To return to the problem of the unrealized effects of increased population, it may help to cite the following example. In one northern city the white conservatives on the city council regularly argue that the city hospital should be maintained at its previous level of services; they mean that there should be no increase in the hospital budget. The liberal whites on the same city council fight for the preservation of the same services, which they interpret as meaning the same number of hospital beds and the same number of doctors and nurses. This, of course, requires an increased number of dollars to offset the rise in costs and salaries. Typically, after a prolonged battle, the liberals win.

However, this hospital is now serving a larger number of center-city blacks, whose hospital services are now curtailed. Other public services are similarly curtailed (on a per person basis) while being "increased" (on a total cost basis). But the whites in power, conservative or liberal, have no awareness that they have been taking anything away from the blacks, and are startled when, in their city with its "good" race relations, a violent riot erupts.

Even the black, who is more likely to know what is happening, may not be fully aware of what is happening in his community and to him. He may be aware only that "I always had to wait a long time, only now I just don't seem to be able to take it as much, it irritates me more." Ten years ago he waited three hours in the emergency room to see a doctor; now he waits ten to fourteen hours. Even if he is not exactly aware of what has happened, his reaction, "It makes me angry now," is appropriate to a worsened situation.

This is the situation in the North. It has developed since the publication of the first edition of my book. It is a situation of which most northern whites are not aware, but which they must begin to see if we are not to become a country divided into two armed camps.

But conditions have also changed in a more complex way. It is no longer possible to characterize in a meaningful way the patterns of discrimination by region, by state, or even in many instances, by city. The southern "etiquette of race relations" no longer exists. Within a few miles of each other in any region of the U.S. the patterns of racial relations differ drastically. Not only do the patterns vary markedly between different industries and educational institutions in the same area, but different departments in the same industrial plant, or different schools in the same system, or different departments in the same university will be found to be at opposite ends of the spectrum of race relations.

There is no question that, on the whole, blacks have made enormous progress—economically, socially, and psychologically. But the gains are spotty. For example, a city may have a black mayor but at the same time may have a predominantly white police force, which is distrusted, feared, and hated by the black population, unfortunately, often with good reason. The economic position of some blacks has improved enormously, while others have been left behind. For those left behind, the situation may be even more intolerable because they hear how easy it is for blacks to make it, how many blacks are making it, and, even though there is no easy road available to them personally, they feel there ought to be, and their sense of personal inadequacy is paradoxically increased. Unfortunately, it is those blacks at the bottom of the socio-economic structure whose situations have least improved or have even become worse.

In some employment and educational settings blacks, particularly if they reach a certain level of education, now even have a competitive edge over equally qualified whites because of measures taken to counter discrimination. These blacks are highly visible to whites, and tend to obscure the plight of the less fortunate. Whites, impressed with the apparent advantage of this highly visible minority, tend to feel there is no longer a problem of anti-black discrimination.

There are other paradoxes. It used to be that dating between black men and white women was rare, and dating between white men and black women frequently occurred, but often on an exploitative basis. Now there are settings in which white men are almost never seen with black women, while black men are more often seen with white women, a kind of personal demonstration of the breakdown of the old taboos. But this has created a special problem for black women in these settings—a problem of isolation and consequent frustration. A still more important paradox is that of birth control. Most Americans, black or white, find that a large family is a hindrance to upward mobility. The black ghetto family with eight, nine, ten or more children is not rare. Contraceptive advice is needed to avoid misery, and yet some black groups have called this genocide—an attempt by whites to destroy blacks. Interestingly enough, black sociologists have pointed out that those black leaders most vociferous on this issue almost always have small families themselves, indicating that they themselves practice birth control, and that the voices are almost exclusively male. Recently, black women have become more vocal on this issue, and the birth control equals genocide equation has been appropriately called into question.

The past decade has witnessed the emergence of black pride. It has at times been called "black power," "black history," "pan-Africanism," even "black separatism," but its essence has reflected the inevitable development of an increased sense of identity and self-determination. Although this era of black pride has unquestionably been valuable and important, the aspect of separatism has also created new problems—for example, blacks' increasing ignorance of whites. Thus, a black patient in psychotherapy cannot discuss fellatio because "white people don't do that sort of thing," or considers the universal (in our society, at least) phenomenon of adolescent rebellion to be specifically black and indicative of the inadequacy of black parents; or a black psychologist talks as if the fact that the victims of black homicides are largely relatives or close friends of the murderer were a black phenomenon (when this is true of homicide in all American ethnic groups). There are even black psychologists who state flatly that only the effects of white discrimination need to be dealt with in psychotherapy, and that the encouragement of black identity and social action are the only remedial steps that are necessary, denying explicitly that blacks are affected by the dynamics of their specific individual family experiences, or that they have unconscious fantasies and defenses—errors at least as great as ignoring the realities of discrimination and their impact.

Surprisingly enough, the intelligence controversy has been raised anew, but the new data are, in essence, the same as the old data, and the discussion in the book is still relevant.

So much for what is new. What remains unchanged is that the basic problem is anger and the way in which this anger is expressed. Insofar as people are hurt, they will be angry. This anger will come out in one way or another—as a symptom, as a protest, as an act of violence. It is still true that when a person can face the reality of what has happened to him, he wards off some of the destructive effects of an oppressive experience.

The appendix, a new and important addendum to this edition, is an empirical analysis of the effects on the southern white of the 1950's of his supposedly privileged position. It will come as no great surprise to find that, rather than benefiting from being the so-called upper caste, the southern white has suffered destructive psychological consequences.

It is my belief that this book, updated by these notes and the appendix, remains relevant. In trying to make real one's values and ethics concerning the way in which one human being should treat another, it is valuable—indeed necessary—to start with a concern for those facts that are ascertainable by scientific investigation.

Bertram P. Karon, Ph. D.

If there is any point to a science of man, it is that those matters that are closest and most important to human beings are as resolvable by scientific investigation as are the secrets of the physical universe. It is therefore fitting that this investigation should concern something about which people have, for a long time, held strong convictions—but convictions based upon emotional and not rational necessities.

This is a book about blacks, but it does not merely describe a number of people with dark skins who were living in the United States in the 1950's. It describes what happens to human nature when it is subjected to certain kinds of pressures from society. Before I began these researches, it might have been said that this would be a book about what happens to the nature of blacks, rather than human nature in general, but the findings themselves dictate that no such restriction is warranted. Perhaps that is what is most important; the conclusions about the nature of man are not determined by what you or I or anyone else believes or wishes to believe but by a careful examination of the real world.

Men have always speculated upon the relationships between themselves and the societies in which they live, but within the last fifty years we have acquired the tools—psychological, sociological, and statistical—for scientific investigation. While this book represents a step in the direction of increased scientific rigor, and therefore of an increased degree of surety with which its conclusions about the relationships are drawn, it is safe to predict that its successors will improve upon its model in the development of the science of man and society.

Because this book deals neither with man nor with society but with the relationship between the two, it is possible not merely to describe what exists, but to predict what will exist as society changes. Society, of course, does change continually. The social institutions described in this book produced the black personalities of today; the black personalities of tomorrow will be determined by the changes in these social institutions that have occurred even while the book was being written, and by the changes that will occur in the succeeding years.

I am indebteded to many people for their help. I should especially like to thank:

Dr. Silvan S. Tomkins, the least of whose contributions consisted in making the PAT files available. Whatever merit this book may have is to a large extent the result not only of his guidance through many of the complexities (and perplexities) of the psychological theory and methodology directly involved, but also of the impact of his characteristic demands of his students that they attempt to resolve for themselves the theoretical dilemmas of psychology.

Dr. John W. Tukey, without whose statistical advice this book would have been impossible. It was only after being faced with methodological problems I was unable to solve myself and after being told by others I consulted that there were no known solutions, that I consulted him; it is a tribute to his remarkable abilities that, after the solutions are explained, they are so simple and "obvious."

Dr. Irving E. Alexander, whose guidance, advice, and criticism have proved invaluable. Mr. Donald P. Estevan, who not only made available to me his critical judgment but invested many hours of his own time in helping me complete the research. Dr. Harold O. Gulliksen, under whose supervision I had the privilege of taking part in the Psychometric Fellowship Program of the Educational Testing Service, as part of which I began these researches. Drs. Hadley Cantril, Frederic M. Lord, David Saunders, and Ledyard R. Tucker, each of whose help and advice I called upon on many occasions.

The Educational Testing Service, which financially supported my research and let me use its facilities while I was a Research Fellow in Psychometrics and even after I was no longer officially connected with that institution. The United States Public Health Service, whose grant made possible the completion of the research reported in this book. Princeton University at which the research was carried out.

Bertram P. Karon, Ph. D.
1958

East Lansing, Michigan

Acknowledgments

For arrangements made with various publishing houses and authors, whereby certain copyrighted material was permitted to be reprinted, and for the courtesy extended by them, acknowledgments are gratefully made. Full bibliographic data will be found at the end of the book.

To W. W. Norton & Company, Inc., for passages from *The Mark of Oppression* by Abraham Kardiner and Lionel Ovesey, and *Mental Health and Mental Disorder* by Arnold Rose.

To the Macmillan Company for the passage from *The Negro in the United States* by E. Franklin Frazier.

To Harper and Brothers for a passage from *The Negro in America* by Arnold M. Rose.

BLACK SCARS

Chapter I

INTRODUCTION

"You live in a city all your life, but you're never home. Maybe that's what it means to be black."

We were in a town in the Northeast. My car had broken down, and, since it would take a few hours to have it repaired, I stopped at a small restaurant nearby for coffee. Soon I joined in the friendly conversation between the owner and several of the local citizens; in the course of this conversation it came out that I was a psychologist and was, at that time (1954), working on a study of the personality problems of blacks.

After a while a young black man in his 20's asked to speak to me privately. We went to his shop, a small place which afforded him a living. He began by telling me about his girl friend who he felt needed psychotherapy. He asked me what professional help might be available in the vicinity and I made several suggestions. But it became obvious there was something else on his mind. Finally, after asking whether or not I minded his talking about it, he started to tell me how it felt to be black. He seemed relieved that he could talk about it to someone.

"I got this letter from a friend of mine. He's gone to Paris and he says, 'Come over here. You need a rest from being black.' I never told him it bothered me, but he's right. I do need a rest from being black. But a bunch of expatriates living in France is no answer, it's got to be solved here. . . .

"Down South I was a pretty bright boy; I graduated high school at the top of my class. Then I came North to college. First day in class the instructor called on a white boy and he didn't know the answer. I was shocked. I didn't know the answer, but I thought white boys knew.

"Down South they hadn't taught me things I needed. Even things that were down on my record. Like geometry. I had to teach myself geometry while I was taking calculus. But it was more than that. There was a difference between northern blacks and me. It wasn't that they were more intelligent. More sophisticated, I guess that's what you'd call it—they expected to be able to learn, and I didn't. . . .

"When I had this trouble with my stomach, they sent me to a psychiatrist or psychologist, I don't know which, but he was a good man. I liked him, and he helped me a lot. But one day he asked me how this being black affected me, and I never went back. I didn't want to believe my problems were due to being black, I wanted to believe they were mine.

"I'd like to think that I'd have my problems no matter what I was, and sometimes I believe it. But sometimes I think it's all because I'm black. I can't be sure. I just don't know. Maybe you could tell me what it really means to be black."

It was a problem for which I had no answer. To some extent I could tell him what experiences were typical of blacks in the United States, or were more typical of blacks than of whites. In turn, this young man could tell me about his own life and about experiences like those I had described. He could also tell me how he felt about them. But neither of us could tell how these experiences had affected him, what the cumulative impact of such lifelong pressure might be. This book represents the result of my attempt to find an answer to this question.

In the United States, insofar as blacks are allowed to marry only blacks, insofar as an individual is classified as a black on the basis of whether his parents were blacks, and insofar as blacks are treated as social inferiors, to that extent they are treated like a "caste."

The social institutions whose function it is to perpetuate a black caste—so that blacks will marry only blacks, the children of blacks will be treated as blacks, and, especially, all blacks will be treated as inferior—are termed "caste sanctions." Social institution, as used here, refers not merely to something to which we can point, such as a court of law or a legal code, but also includes what you and I do when we meet a black person on the street, and even what we think about that person, provided that there is some regularity among people in our society.

The experiences whose effect upon blacks are the focus of this book obviously represent either the caste sanctions themselves or the consequences of the caste sanctions. The effects of the caste sanctions may be felt by the black child from the moment he is born. It is because of the caste sanctions that there are so many broken homes among blacks; that black homes are so frequently overcrowded; that black parents are often so overworked that they have little time to show affection for their children.

Insofar as his parents have learned in their own lives that a dark skin is a bad thing, an American black child may find himself liked or disliked by his parents on the basis of whether his skin color is a little lighter or darker than that of his brothers or sisters. Thus, he learns at an early age, and in a manner difficult to unlearn, that skin color is important, and that, as compared with whites, he is inevitably "bad." As soon as he comes into contact with people outside his own family, he may find himself excluded, disliked, or physically assaulted for being a "nigger." (Goodman found that, by the age of four, black children are aware of being blacks, and that being black is a problem.) The black child may find himself expected to show deference in the face of insults. He will be presented with a humiliating picture of blacks as dirty, violent, lazy, happy-go-lucky, smelly, ignorant, treacherous, superstitious, and cowardly, and he may find himself expected to live up to this. He may find himself offered inadequate and segregated schooling, and he may find himself forced to leave school and work for a living at an early age.

As an adult he may find himself excluded from opportunities for vocational training, or from jobs, even if he has obtained training, and from decent housing and recreational facilities. He may find himself unable to provide for his family. He may find himself cheated, robbed, or physically assaulted and have no recourse or protection from the law. He may find himself deprived of the right to vote, and to serve on juries. He may find himself confined to segregated and inadequate facilities. Even where segregated facilities are equal (and this is rare), the separation from white facilities seems to imply his inferiority. And all of this may be written into the public law, so that he cannot even have recourse to the feeling that it is just "bad people who do these things to me."

A black man may escape any one of the restrictions considered by itself, but no black American is able to escape all of the caste sanctions no matter how fortunate he may be. The problem with which we are concerned is the effects of these social institutions upon his personality.

The problem of culture and personality

The interrelationship between the social institutions and the personality structures of the individuals in a given society has been one of the most important theoretical issues in modern psychology. Despite the difficulties involved in investigating this type of problem, a good deal has been accomplished (cf. Erikson, Kardiner, Kardiner and Ovesey, Kluckhohn and Murray, Parsons et al., Whiting and Child, Rose, 1955, etc.). However, one of the limitations of research in this area has been that it has largely concerned itself with primitive societies (i.e., nonliterate societies) of limited complexity. The attempts to approach the institutions of western society have generally been based on relatively little direct empirical observation of individuals, or, at best, on observations of a small and relatively homogeneous group of individuals in a society which is itself heterogeneous.

It is therefore of considerable general theoretical interest to investigate a set of social institutions (such as the caste sanctions enforced against blacks in the United States) which operates in a modern complex society and which should have considerable consequence for the personality structures of the individuals in that society, particularly members of the "lower" caste.

As Kardiner and Ovesey have pointed out, it would be a mistake to think of a group like black Americans as having, as a result of the caste sanctions, a single "basic" personality. Inasmuch as the United States is a complex society, there is no single "basic" personality common to all Americans, and black Americans share in the diverse American personality structures. Grafted upon these are the special problems involved in adjusting to the caste sanctions.

The North and the South of the 50's

One way to investigate the effects of the caste sanctions is to compare the personality structures of blacks living in different areas, since the sanctions varied widely both in their severity and nature from region to region. Although it would be possible to subdivide the United States into many gradations on the basis of local differences in the application of the caste sanctions, there was such a large difference between the "South" and the "North" in this respect that it is not unreasonable to treat each of these regions as a whole.

The sanctions in the North may be briefly summarized as being largely social (personal animosities, exclusion from social organizations and privately owned facilities) and economic (exclusion from some occupational opportunities and from decent housing). The lines are less sharply drawn than in the South, and the sanctions are more a function of individual behavior than of the official policy of the government. The general principles of equal political rights and equal protection under the law are accepted, as well as the idea that public facilities should be made freely available, even if, in actual practice, there is a good deal less than full equality in these respects in many instances.

In the South the situation was quite different. The sanctions were often embodied in state law. To the social and economic sanctions of the North were added segregation in public facilities, disenfranchisement, often a lack of police protection, and a code of etiquette designed to demonstrate the inferiority of all blacks to all whites.

The implications for society

The investigation on which this book is based was undertaken to gain a scientific insight into the general problem of culture and personality. No social institution in any western society has been described as thoroughly as the caste sanctions against blacks in the United States. Relevant data on the personality structures of the individuals who feel the effect of these sanctions became, for the first time, readily available in the data gathered by Tomkins and Miner when they standardized the Tomkins-Horn Picture Arrangement Test. It was obvious that a solution of the remaining statistical and experimental problems would contribute to psychological theory.

Nevertheless, it is nearly impossible to investigate the nature of human beings without the results of that investigation being relevant to human beings. The problems of blacks are not only of interest to blacks and to those psychologists, psychiatrists, and social workers whose job it is to deal with the psychological problems of blacks, but also to any of us who are affected by the changes which are now taking place, or have been proposed, in the status of blacks in this country. The status of blacks in the United States has become the focus of controversy in the arena of practical politics. Public opinion has been stirred by the Supreme Court decision that, in the case of segregated schools, separate facilities for blacks and whites were, by the very fact of being separated, unequal and, therefore, unconstitutional. This decision reversed the famous Plessy vs. Ferguson doctrine of separate and equal facilities, which forms the legal basis for Jim Crow laws. Thus, the stage was set for a far-reaching revision, which has partially taken place, in the social institutions affecting the status of blacks.

The Supreme Court decision has been hailed by many as a long overdue affirmation of the basic rights of human beings guaranteed by the American Constitution. But from the South came the cry that the court had arrogated to itself powers beyond those which were legitimate, that it was serving a legislative function, that it was ignoring precedent, and that implementation of the decision must be fought in every possible way. It was objected that the court decision was based not on law, but on a social science which had no real evidence; the Supreme Court had mentioned in its decision that sociologists and psychologists support the Court's opinion that separate facilities are, by that very fact, unequal. Many of the objections were forced, or hysterical, or mere rationalizations, and much of the impetus behind the protests came from the need to preserve vested interests in the political, economic, or social exploitation of blacks. Nevertheless, many of the protests were sincere.

To most people outside the South the language of the Fourteenth Amendment seems unequivocal; so, according to historians, was its intent. The Plessy vs. Ferguson decision permitting segregation appears clearly to contravene both the wording and the intent of the amendment; the explanation may be found in the political expediencies of the 1890's—any decision which outlawed segregation would not, and could not, have been enforced at that time. But the political expediencies of the 1890's are hardly a sound basis for long-term policy, and the recent decision merely reinstates the original intent of the amendment, which was to guarantee to blacks equal political rights as Americans. Thus, as long as the Fourteenth Amendment is not repealed, which is hardly likely, the legal issue would seem to boil down to whether or not blacks are hurt by legally enforced segregation. If they are hurt by the practice, then it is obviously unconstitutional.

Does segregation hurt blacks? What is the evidence, and how good is it? Isn't it possible that the caste sanctions have no real effect on the black personality, that blacks blame these sanctions for whatever problems they have, even though they would have the same problems if they weren't blacks? How do we know that whatever special problems they have may not be hereditary, that they were not born inferior?

Rather than segregation and the other caste sanctions of the South being bad for blacks, isn't it equally plausible that southern blacks live in a culture which is consistent and the caste sanctions are, therefore, not a problem for them? Isn't it reasonable to believe that the caste sanctions would become a problem only for northern blacks, who live in an inconsistent culture and who "do not know their place"? Perhaps whatever differences there are in personality problems are due to variables other than caste sanctions. How do we know? How can we be sure?

The peculiar merit of the study on which this book is based is the degree of certitude with which it allows us to answer these questions. Each of them was investigated thoroughly. The conclusions of the investigation were tested rigorously and repeatedly, and the findings were found to be consistent. Objective and rigorous answers are now available.

Chapter II

THE AMERICAN CASTE SYSTEM

A prerequisite to any consideration of the possible effects of the caste sanctions enforced against blacks in the United States is a description of these sanctions, that is, a description of the special restrictions enforced against blacks and the special experiences which blacks undergo as a result of these restrictions.

The United States is a large, complex, industrialized society which may be subdivided into a great many sub-cultures. Sociologically speaking, its dominant culture has been characterized (Parsons, pp. 107-108) as the best empirical example of the Universalistic-Achievement oriented society. Of all known societies it is the one in which most frequently people deal with each other on the basis of general standards and in which a person's status is most frequently determined by what he does, can do, or has done, rather than who he is (or was born). It is clear that insofar as the caste sanctions prescribe differential treatment for people solely on the basis of whether their parents were black or white, they represent elements of the society which conflict with the major orientation. In a Universalistic-Achievement oriented society, the activities and functions of people occupying different positions in the social structure differ from each other markedly. (A good brief description of characteristics of such a social system is to be found in Parsons, pp. 182-191.) Consequently, a good deal of diversity in the personality structures and problems of the individuals within this society is to be expected. Inasmuch as blacks share in the diversity of social institutions and roles, they will share in the diversity of resultant personality structures. This book, however, is concerned only with those institutions which differentially affect blacks and the related facets of the black personality.

Fortunately, there is a considerable body of sociological literature concerning black-white relations in the United States. Although supplementary material has been derived from the other volumes listed among the references, Myrdal's encyclopedic work, Rose's (1948) summary of Myrdal, and two volumes by Frazier (1939 and 1949) form the main basis for this chapter. The survey which follows is, of course, by no means exhaustive, and the reader is referred to the above sources for a fuller account.

To begin with, the position of blacks in the American culture is in many respects very much like that of other minority groups. Blacks are differentiated from other minority groups in this country by (1) their relative ease of identification (although there are some cases of blacks "passing" as whites, this is not even a possibility for most blacks), (2) their large incidence in the population—one out of ten Americans is black, (3) the fact that almost all blacks came to this country against their will for the sole purpose of being economically exploited as slaves.

Inasmuch as slavery was most profitable in the South, it is not surprising that most blacks were imported into the South. The lesser economic utility of slaves, plus the lack of large numbers of blacks, allowed humanistic feelings to be reflected in the abolition of slavery in the North, beginning with Vermont, which abolished slavery in 1775. By 1784 Massachusetts and New Hampshire had followed Vermont's lead, while laws providing for gradual emancipation rather than immediate abolition had been adopted by Connecticut, Rhode Island, and Pennsylvania. The Northwest Territory was closed to slavery in 1787 and by 1804 all of the original thirteen states north of Delaware and Maryland had either abolished slavery or provided for its gradual elimination. By 1861 every state north of the Mason-Dixon line had abolished slavery (Davie, p. 21).

This difference between the North and South was most dramatically exemplified during the Civil War: the North was fighting for, among other things, the freeing of the slaves; the South fought for, among other things, the preservation of the slave status.

The slave status

Utility is the predominant value of the cultural institution of slavery. The slave owner attempts to maximize the economic utility of the slave. In this process of exploitation, the original African culture of American slaves was smashed. In order to make slave rebellions more difficult, American slave owners sent slaves from the same tribe to different plantations so that the slaves would have no language in common other than that of the slave owner. It is thus not possible to explain the characteristics of the American black subculture as it now exists on the basis of an evolutionary development of his previous way of life, but only as an adaptive reaction to those aspects of the American culture which were literally forced upon him; according to Frazier (1957, pp. 3-21), black Americans show less evidence of "survivals" from their previous cultures than any other group of blacks in the New World.

According to Kardiner and Ovesey (p. 47), the major effects on the black slave of being a slave include loss of self-esteem, destruction of his culture, and forced adoption of foreign, that is, American, culture traits. The unity of the family was destroyed to facilitate the buying and selling of individual slaves. Women assumed the central role in the slave culture; this relative enhancement of the woman's status was due to her value as mammy to the white children and as a sex object for white men, while male slaves were useful only for their labor. The possibility of close social interrelationships among blacks was eliminated by their inability to have any culture of their own. The master was idealized, but this idealized master was hated as well as revered. These mixed feelings necessarily led to deep-seated conflicts in the black personality.

When slavery was finally abolished, the changes in the status of blacks were far more apparent than real. As Kardiner and Ovesey have pointed out (pp. 50-51), the change in status from slave to free man required changes which were not slight in the inner worlds of both blacks and whites.

The whole range of adaptations by blacks to the demands of life, and especially their reactions to whites, had to be revised if they were to take their place as equals. It would have been interesting to see how quickly and how well such a readjustment could be made—but the simple fact is that, whether or not blacks could have learned to interact as equals with whites, no real opportunity was ever given them to do so. Only a modicum of equality was offered; whites from Emancipation on, kept placing blocks in the way of blacks; whites were not ready to deal with blacks on any basis of equality. Whatever the difficulty may be for blacks in shifting from thinking of themselves as inferior beings to thinking of themselves as equals, the blocks are much greater for whites who must shift from thinking about a piece of property to thinking about a human being with the self-same properties reserved to themselves. Whites have never fully made the shift, but merely made various compromises between treating (and thinking of) blacks as slaves and as equals. The movement toward equality has been made grudgingly. And, of course, the South, where the exploitation of blacks had been most rewarded economically, was the place where resistance to change in social and emotional status of blacks was greatest.

At the end of the Civil War promises were made to blacks which were never kept. The issue of the status of blacks was subject to violent fluctuations, but no amount of effort by blacks could induce the white man to keep his word. Emancipation brought only a partial change in status. The caste situation which obtained is evidence that the drive for "white supremacy" in the South has, on the whole, been successful and blacks have been subordinated by force. The usual American accounts of the period after the Civil War grossly exaggerate the gains of blacks and the evils of Reconstruction while minimizing or ignoring the terrorism and brutality with which blacks have been subjugated. Whites have protected their own position by imposing restrictions on blacks and blacks have then had to adjust to them.

The North and the South of the 50's

The difference between the North and the South, which is the focus of this book, has already been mentioned. The conditions under which blacks live are, and always have been, more favorable in the North than in the South. Although there is considerable discrimination in the North, blacks nevertheless enjoy far more security as citizens, greater economic opportunity (even though that economic opportunity may come in the form of relief payments when jobs are not available), and, most important of all, greater freedom as human beings.

The South differs in many ways from the rest of the United States, and, as Myrdal has pointed out, almost all of these have to do directly or indirectly with the relationship between blacks and whites which characterizes the region.

The South is still more agricultural and rural than most other segments of the country, and many parts of the South are relatively isolated. Until recently it has lagged considerably in the development of industry. The pattern of migration is unique: almost all migration is from one place to another within the South, or from the South to someplace outside. The number of people who migrate into the South from a foreign country or from another part of the United States is not appreciable.

Economically, the South is a poor area. There are more poor people and they are poorer, on the average, than in the North. However, since a larger proportion of the poor in the South are blacks, the gap in economic position between whites in the South and the North is by no means as large as the general economic differential. Indeed, at least for urban areas, the southern whites as a whole have roughly the same average income as do northern whites, and well-to-do whites form roughly the same proportion of the population, if the few tremendous fortunes are excluded—the latter being more numerous in the North than in the South.

The tradition of the small independent farmer is a northern one; tenant farmers are a predominant pattern in the South as a carry-over from the plantation system. Also surviving from the plantation system is the tradition of aristocracy. The stereotypes of "the southern gentleman," "the southern lady," "southern hospitality," etc., reflect the widespread survival of part of this tradition.

The beliefs that hard work, inventiveness, or making oneself indispensable is the road to success represent ideas which are natural to a mercantile and industrialized society. The relative lack of industry in the South plus the survival of the traditions of the plantation aristocracy lead to radically different notions—namely, that the way to get and remain rich is to find someone weaker than yourself and exploit him. From the southern standpoint blacks are the ideal choice for such treatment.

To the average southerner, change seems more hazardous than it does to most Americans. This is due not only to the racial issue but to the fact that the southerner is imbued with such traditions as states' rights. He feels the need to preserve legal restrictions against blacks which conflict with the legal code of the rest of the country. Southern education for *both* blacks and whites is inferior as compared with the North, but is worse for blacks than for whites.

In the North, the racial issue is merely one of many problems. Rapid change attendant upon a high degree of industrialization characterizes the North. The tempo of life is speeded up, and there is a feeling of progress. Northern farmers have been vociferous in their demands, and so have labor unions in the North. There have been labor problems and strikes, as part of the development of large-scale heavy industry. There has been a steady stream of immigrants from abroad into the North, bringing with it the problem of how to assimilate the newcomers into the economy. Local problems of poverty and maladjustment have resulted from the influx of people. The immigrants offered possibilities for exploitation and, in many instances, these possibilities were seized upon. The conflicts of interest, the attempts to exploit and the rebellions of the exploited, the struggles for power, money, or status in the North have all been reflected in frequent clashes of political opinion and open controversy in the struggle for political office. In such a milieu, the problem of black-white relations was not distinct. Wherever it existed in the North, it was a local problem, one of a multitude but neither unique nor focal.

The contrast with the South is striking. There the racial issue is *the* problem. The entire culture of the South may be said to be determined by this one issue. Every other issue for the southern white is cast in its terms—whether political, economic, or broadly cultural in content, and whether local, regional, or national in scope. Moreover, in the South private opinions were marshaled in a solid phalanx of support for the suppression of blacks and for whatever steps may be necessary to attain that end. In the North, public opinion shows no such unanimity. There is no "Solid North" either for or against blacks as there was a "Solid South" against their advancement.

One of the factors which made black-white relations less of a problem in the North is the simple fact that there are fewer blacks in the North. The bulk of the northern black population is concentrated in the large cities. In the smaller cities of the North, blacks form only a small element of the population, and race has never been much of a problem in these small urban areas. The problem of race relations in the North lies in the large cities. In the metropolitan centers of the North one typically finds separate neighborhoods for different races, ethnic groups, or economic groups; this pattern of spatial segregation prevents the presence and problems of any one element of the population from obtruding itself upon the others. The impact of whatever contacts do occur between various groups is minimized by the anonymity of casual contacts in any large city. The arrangements that protect the northern white from being concerned about any underprivileged group shielded him from being aware of the problems of blacks until recently.

The caste system still exists in the North, but there are big holes in it. Not only do the legal codes of the North guarantee equality before the law to blacks, but in actual practice blacks exercise the right to vote. Consequently, elected officials cannot be entirely oblivious to their needs. Indeed, in areas where blacks predominate, the racial issue may be the fundamental one in political campaigns. Like any relatively uneducated group of immigrants, blacks, of course, have often been exploited, and the political gains they were promised frequently failed to materialize.

Nowhere in the North was there an elaborate racial etiquette of personal relations governing the actions of blacks and whites when they meet, such as the code prescribed by the South. Economically, blacks are better off in the North. More jobs are open to them. Nevertheless, in general they are kept out of the better jobs available in the North.

Reports of how blacks fare in the South did filter up to the northern white, who generally reacted to these reports with a feeling of reassurance about how good things were in the North. One might expect such accounts to give rise to an urge to reform the South; such is not the general case. Most frequently, they led to smug self-satisfaction—look how much better off the black is here than he'd be down South. If there are problems, why get excited? After all, nothing can be done about the South. The South is thus useful to the northern white. As long as it exists, he can smother any guilt feelings he may have over his own treatment of blacks, and, in fact, congratulate himself that he does not mistreat them more.

The First World War marked the beginning of a mass black migration to the North. It was inevitable that this migration would eventually rouse the resentment of northern whites who felt that it was unreasonable for southern blacks to come into northern communities: "Their place is in the South; why should we have to take care of them? Our communities cannot afford this. Any improvement in our welfare policies will encourage more blacks to come here, but they will stop coming North if they are not encouraged." It is this attitude of northern whites which, according to many authorities, seems to be the biggest block to the development of sound welfare policies. What is unknown to most northerners is that the black has no alternative to migration. He is being inexorably pushed off the farmland by government agricultural policies which place the heaviest burden on the black farmer and farm laborer, as well as the shrinking demand for southern agricultural products.

Basically, however, the northern white, through the 50's, did not hate or even resent blacks; he just did not know anything about them, nor did he want to know anything about them. While the southern white was continually concerned with how to deal with blacks, the northern white dealt with the black-white problem by pretending it did not exist. Most northerners were generally quite successful in their pretense, and the problem of race relations did not obtrude itself into their awareness. True, the southern white also ignored much of this problem, but his was a much more specific and directed ignorance, one which allowed him to live with himself while actively carrying out the pattern of suppression he felt necessary in dealing with blacks. When the blinders of the northern white are lifted, he is usually disturbed by what he sees; the effects of the things that he himself—as part of his unthinking way of life—has done to blacks are repugnant to him when brought to his attention.

It is easy to exaggerate the difference between the North and the South even in the 50's. In the South, too, many whites were shaken when they began to face the facts. The younger generation of the South were less thoroughly convinced of the rightness of the caste situation than were their fathers. Although they were less heavily committed to the ideology of slavery, even in its watered-down form, improvement in the situation was forestalled by the fact that they were likely to have even less familiarity with blacks than did their forebears. The social barriers which had been erected not only to keep blacks in their place, but also to keep southern whites from becoming aware of the embarrassing fact that blacks are persons, had become ever harder to breach. Even the latest generation, when they lack the contact that might make understanding possible, are often irritated by what they see of black people but cannot understand.

Geographical distribution

A basic aspect of the cultural milieu of blacks is their geographical distribution in the United States; Table II-1 gives the number of blacks and the percentage of the population who were blacks for each state in 1940, 1950, 1960, and 1970. From this it is clear that the large majority of blacks still live in the South, but that there is a continued migration northward. According to Myrdal (p. 965), roughly three out of five blacks now living in northern states were born in the South.

Interpersonal relations

The most dramatic aspects of discrimination in the United States are the restrictions on face-to-face contacts between whites and blacks.

From the white man's standpoint, the most important restriction was the ban on intermarriage. It was the restriction about which whites felt most strongly, and was supported by many whites who would not support other kinds of discrimination. Consequently, the spectre of intermarriage was apt to be raised by the advocates of "white supremacy" in defending any suppression of the rights of blacks. Any advance in the status of blacks, the argument runs, will eventually lead to intermarriage, and "Would you like your sister to marry one?"

From the standpoint of blacks, this restriction was the least important of all the patterns of discrimination in the United States because of the rarity of intermarriage, or even the desire for intermarriage. Far more important are physical security, economic well-being, and the chance to advance socially and economically (including educational opportunities).

Laws forbidding intermarriage were found not only in all southern states, but in most states west of the Mississippi river. Of the non-southern states east of the Mississippi, only Indiana forbode intermarriage between blacks and whites. Of course, the Supreme Court declared all such laws unconstitutional. Where intermarriage was permitted, few marriages between blacks and whites actually occurred until recently, because any such white person takes upon himself the burden of discrimination encountered by blacks. This is nearly intolerable to most whites, even to that small group who had enough social contact with blacks and are unprejudiced enough to consider marrying blacks.

By the 1950's the black community, too, had increasingly ostracized such mixed couples, leaving them with no social circle, except other mixed couples, that accepted them. The development seemed to be a function of the fostering of "race pride" among blacks as a reaction to the white attitude of depreciation. The ostracism by the black community was even more pronounced toward mixed couples who were not married. That is, towards illicit pairings of white men and black women, since such relationships mainly represent an exploitation of the black by her white partner. Extramarital relations between black men and white women were extremely rare in the North and practically nonexistent in the South, through the 50's. The few extramarital relations of this sort in the North seemed to be confined to sexual experimentation in nonconformist circles. There was also some white prostitutes whose clientele was black.

The practice of white men to keep black concubines was rare in the North of the 50's and becoming rare in the South, but illicit sexual liaisons between white men and black women were by no means rare in either section. These relationships were usually kept secret, since public opinion generally did not favor them, although they were tolerated.

In discussing the treatment of the black, the southern white was more apt to invoke states' rights than lust, but it was nonetheless true that the sexual advantage of the white was one of the major motives upholding the caste sanctions. In the South, a sexually inadequate, insecure, or unattractive white man might force his attentions on black women, who could neither defend themselves nor expect defense from anyone else. This privilege of sexual abuse and exploitation was jealously guarded; the black man was prohibited from protecting his woman against a white man's importunities. Myrdal cites, for example, the case of a black minister in the South who merely protested against interracial liaisons in a sermon and was, as a result, approached and warned by a group of white businessmen.

Outside of overtly sexual relationships, the activities that are considered most intimate are, naturally, those which imply sex; they were never tolerated between white women and black men in the South through the 50's. For a black man in the South to flirt in any way or to the slightest degree with a white woman was to endanger his life. Dancing between blacks and whites, whether between black men and white women or between white men and black women, was forbidden throughout the South, and only seldom occurred in the North. For blacks and whites even to swim together was universally tabooed in the South, apparently because it involves exposure of large parts of the body. In the North, this taboo was strong but not universally inviolate.

Table II-1 BLACK POPULATION BY STATE AND AS PERCENT OF STATE POPULATIONS, 1940–1970

U.S. Bureau of the Census

	1940		1950		1960		1970	
	Total	%	Total	%	Total	%	Total	%
New England								
Maine	1,304	0.2	1,221	0.1	3,318	0.3	2,800	0.3
New Hampshire	414	0.1	731	0.1	1,903	0.3	2,505	0.3
Vermont	384	0.1	443	0.1	519	0.1	761	0.2
Massachusetts	55,391	1.3	73,171	1.6	111,842	2.2	175,817	3.1
Rhode Island	11,024	1.5	13,903	1.8	18,332	2.1	25,338	2.7
Connecticut	32,992	1.9	53,472	2.6	107,449	4.2	181,177	6.0
Middle Atlantic								
New York	571,221	4.2	918,191	6.2	1,417,511	8.4	2,168,949	11.9
New Jersey	226,973	5.2	318,565	6.6	514,875	8.5	770,292	10.7
Pennsylvania	470,172	4.7	638,485	6.1	852,750	7.5	1,016,514	8.6
East North Central								
Ohio	339,461	4.9	513,072	6.5	786,097	8.1	970,477	9.1
Indiana	121,916	3.6	174,168	4.4	269,275	5.8	357,464	6.9
Illinois	387,446	4.9	645,980	7.4	1,037,470	10.3	1,425,674	12.8
Michigan	208,345	4.0	442,296	6.9	717,581	9.2	991,066	11.2
Wisconsin	12,158	0.4	28,182	0.8	74,546	1.9	128,224	2.9
West North Central								
Minnesota	9,928	0.4	14,022	0.5	22,263	0.7	34,868	0.9
Iowa	16,694	0.8	19,692	0.8	25,354	0.9	32,596	1.2
Missouri	244,386	6.5	297,088	7.5	390,853	9.0	480,172	10.3
North Dakota	201	—	257	—	777	0.1	2,494	0.4
South Dakota	474	0.1	727	0.1	1,114	0.2	1,627	0.2
Nebraska	14,171	1.1	19,234	1.5	29,262	2.1	39,911	2.7
Kansas	65,138	3.6	73,158	3.8	91,445	4.2	106,977	4.8

South Atlantic								
Delaware	35,876	13.5	43,598	13.7	60,688	13.6	78,276	14.3
Maryland	301,931	16.6	385,972	16.5	518,410	16.7	699,479	17.8
District of Columbia	187,266	28.2	280,803	35.0	411,737	53.9	537,712	71.1
Virginia	661,449	24.7	734,211	22.1	816,258	20.6	861,368	18.5
West Virginia	117,754	6.2	114,867	5.7	89,378	4.8	67,342	3.9
North Carolina	981,298	27.5	1,047,353	25.8	1,116,021	24.5	1,126,478	22.2
South Carolina	814,164	42.9	822,077	38.8	829,291	34.8	789,041	30.5
Georgia	1,084,927	34.7	1,062,762	30.9	1,122,596	28.5	1,187,149	25.9
Florida	514,198	27.1	603,101	21.7	880,186	17.8	1,041,651	15.3
East South Central								
Kentucky	214,031	7.5	201,921	6.9	215,949	7.1	230,793	7.2
Tennessee	508,736	17.4	530,603	16.1	586,876	16.5	61,261	15.8
Alabama	983,290	34.7	979,617	32.0	980,271	30.0	903,467	26.2
Mississippi	1,074,578	49.2	986,474	45.3	915,743	42.0	815,770	36.8
West South Central								
Arkansas	482,578	24.8	426,639	22.3	388,787	21.8	352,445	18.3
Louisiana	849,303	35.9	882,428	32.9	1,039,207	31.9	1,086,832	29.8
Oklahoma	168,849	7.2	145,503	6.5	153,084	6.6	171,892	6.7
Texas	924,391	14.4	977,458	12.7	1,187,125	12.4	1,399,005	12.5
Mountain								
Montana	1,120	0.2	1,232	0.2	1,467	0.2	1,995	0.3
Idaho	595	0.1	1,050	0.2	1,502	0.2	2,130	0.3
Wyoming	956	0.4	2,557	0.9	2,183	0.7	2,568	0.8
Colorado	12,176	1.1	20,177	1.5	39,992	2.3	66,411	3.0
New Mexico	4,672	0.9	8,408	1.2	17,063	1.8	19,555	1.9
Arizona	14,993	3.0	25,974	3.5	43,403	3.3	53,344	3.0
Utah	1,235	0.2	2,729	0.4	4,148	0.5	6,617	0.6
Nevada	664	0.6	4,302	2.7	13,484	4.7	27,762	5.7
Pacific								
Washington	7,424	0.4	30,691	1.3	48,738	1.7	71,308	2.1
Oregon	2,565	0.2	11,529	0.8	18,133	1.0	26,308	1.3
California	124,306	1.8	462,172	4.4	883,861	5.6	1,400,143	7.0

The so-called "etiquette of race relations" which governed until recently all contacts between blacks and whites in the South was an elaborate ceremonious code which rendered these interracial contacts as impersonal as possible. For the most part, it was not written into the law. Its purpose and effect were to prevent members of the two castes from knowing each other as people.

As compared to most European countries, the United States is not characterized by a high degree of social importance or ritualism connected with meals. Despite the contrary stereotypes, most observers seem to agree that eating in the South, when only whites are present, is generally even less complicated than in the North. It is only as part of the "etiquette of race relations" that eating became ritualized and took on enormous social significance. In this code, eating together was a sign of an intimate relationship; any whites and blacks who had the temerity to eat together would be seriously condemned anywhere in the South, and if a black man and a white woman were to eat together it would be considered an extremely grave matter. In factory lunchrooms, blacks either waited until all the whites had finished or else used separate rooms.

Apparently, drinking was considered less intimate, partly because it does not take as much time, and partly because the participants need not sit down. (And, of course, blacks might not sit in the presence of a white person unless invited to do so.) However, the weakened taboo against interracial drinking applied only to men; for a white woman in the South to take part in a drinking party in which there were some blacks was considered as bad as if she had eaten with them. Consequently, such breaches of the code were almost unknown.

In the North, a white person's neighbors sometimes objected to his inviting blacks to a party or social gathering in his home; the few breaches of this taboo, however, generally led to no punishment stronger than hostile gossip. In the North, blacks and whites were often found eating together. Many restaurants, however, tried to enforce their own segregation by one or another stratagem, as, for example, overcharging blacks or giving them such bad service that they would not return.

The next most violent reactions, in the South, occurred to violations of the separation of restrooms, toilets, and drinking fountains—a series of relations which involve, like eating, the satisfaction of physiological needs. These separations were legally enforced, and as a result of the civil rights movements eventually declared unconstitutional. In the North such separate facilities simply did not exist.

Also prohibited was the participation of blacks with whites in any activity in which the body is used—and this extends beyond semi-sexual activities, like dancing, to any sport or game involving physical activity. This taboo applied only to adults; black and white children were allowed to play together in the South. In the North there was no general prohibition against blacks taking part in sports and games although individual whites might refuse to play with blacks. Professional sports were another matter. Even in the North, blacks were excluded from most major professional sports until World War II, but the color barrier is now the exception and not the rule.

So far the caste sanctions have consisted of simple prohibitions—essentially, "Negro, thou shalt not." It is not until we come to the rules governing bodily actions and, especially, the rules governing conversation during face-to-face contacts between blacks and whites that the elaborate ritualization involved in the southern "etiquette of race relations" becomes evident.

Conversation was regimented both in form and in content. With very few exceptions, there were no serious discussions between blacks and whites concerning politics, whether local, national, or international, nor about the "news," nor about the problems of their daily lives, such as earning a living or the search for pleasure. The one exception was that some white women used black servants as a source of gossip. The only serious discussions which were allowed concerned shared business interests. A white employer, for example, might give orders to blacks who worked for him, or a polite but formal inquiry might be made by either the white or black person as to the state of the other's health or business. Any conversation beyond this was a breach of the code.

Recognition of black inferiority was embodied in the ritual of face-to-face discussions by the use of distinctions in the forms of address. Blacks were expected always to show respect by using the title "Mr.," "Mrs.," or "Miss" when talking to a white person, while the white person addressed a black by the latter's first name, irrespective of how little acquaintance the two may have, or by the condescending epithet "boy" and its alternatives "uncle," "auntie," "elder," etc. These were used with no regard to the age of the black person being addressed. By using exaggerated titles, even though they were not at all applicable in their literal sense, a white man could show some respect for blacks without contravening the code. Although southern whites knew that blacks found the terms "nigger" and "darkie" insulting, they habitually used these terms in the presence of blacks, thus reinforcing the latter's ritualized degradation. In the 50's, some southern newspapers broke from this pattern far enough to refer to black veterans as "Mr.," "Mrs.," or "Miss."

Blacks were expected to never refer to a delicate subject directly when speaking to whites, and were expected to never, on any account, in speaking of any subject contradict a white.

It is clear that this etiquette was designed to demonstrate that blacks are inferior *and* that they recognize it in the sense that they are willing to act out the ritual. (Of course, there was no real alternative.) The other consequence of the code was to prevent any effective communication between blacks and whites. Southern whites liked to perpetuate the myth that they "knew" their blacks, yet the etiquette they had forced upon them prevented the latter from knowing anything except the details of this very ritual. The white southerner was in the position of a playwright who, upon seeing his own play, feels he knows the actors because he knows the lines they speak on stage. As a matter of fact, most southern whites in their franker moments admitted their feeling that blacks were hiding things from them. In the North, this etiquette of conversation did not exist. Northern whites not only did not expect it, but they were usually unaware that such a code existed. They were embarrassed when a southern black acted out the ritual. It was thus possible for whites and blacks to get to know each other as people in the North when they met socially as equals, but, of course, such contacts were not common.

In the sphere of bodily actions, there were rituals concerning sitting. As mentioned, blacks ordinarily sat down in the presence of a white person in the South only when the white person invited them to do so; frequently, the white person never issued such an invitation and the black person then had to stand throughout the conversation. In public places, blacks sat down without invitation but the seats were usually segregated. In the North, there were no special restrictions on when or where blacks sit. When one found segregation here, it was not based strictly on whether on was black or white; it seemed to be more a question of separating different social or economic classes. Blacks were segregated because they are lower class and poor. Instances of segregation did, of course, arise from the spontaneous acts of individuals; many whites preferred not to sit near blacks and there were times when blacks preferred to sit with or near other blacks. One exception to the lack of restrictions in the North on where blacks may sit was seating in theatres. Many theatres even in the 50's never allowed blacks to enter, and there were others in which blacks were assigned to a separate section. Even in states with Civil Rights laws, many theatres tried to make things so unpleasant for blacks that they will stay away of their own accord. But there were many theatres where no special difficulties were encountered by blacks. Again, blacks occasionally found themselves isolated, not by an action of the theatre management but because individual whites who did not like sitting near blacks moved away.

The ritual in the South proscribing anything but impersonal contacts between blacks and whites extended to the handshake, which is characteristically a gesture of friendliness and human warmth. The gesture generally implies warmth on the basis of equality, and it is therefore significant, but nor surprising, that it was one of the actions ritualized by the "etiquette of race relations." In the first place, as with most signs of personal warmth, the greatest ban was on a white woman and a black man shaking hands; this was almost never done. A white man and a black man might shake hands if the white man offered to do so, while a black man must under no circumstances offer his hand to a white man. In the North, of course, no such ritual was imposed.

In the North there were no special rituals followed when blacks enter a white home, or vice versa. In most parts of the South, a black person might enter the house of a white man only by the rear door. But when a white man enters the house of a black person, his whole code of conduct was such as to show no sign of respect for the occupants. The white man would not knock; he would simply enter the house. He would not take off his hat. He not only would not rise when a black woman comes into the room, but might even insist that the blacks whose home he had entered remain standing while he was there. Actually, there was little reason for a white man to enter a black home. It was more usual for a white man to send for a black person, telephone him, or, at most, drive in his car to the home of the latter and summon him by honking his horn without getting out ot the car.

A breakdown in the social ritual of the South was undoubtedly a prerequisite to any real understanding of whites by blacks, or of blacks by whites. The breaches which occurred are therefore significant. They did occur, at times, throughout the South, and were increasing by 1950, especially in activities which are least intimate and furthest removed from sex. For example, an upper-class black was frequently allowed to escape much of the debasing rituals. It was understood in such cases, by both blacks and whites, that this was granted to him as a privilege and not a right, and that at times he might be required to debase himself in full accordance with the code.

In the North, the elaborate ritual just did not exist. The way in which blacks and whites acted toward each other when they come in contact was governed by no special code of conduct. The northern technique for isolating the two groups consisted in allowing ordinary relationships during what contacts occurred, but minimizing these contacts. The limited number of types of segregation used for this purpose are institutionalized and rendered impersonal. The question of black-white relations is then forgotten insofar as possible by the whites.

Political sanctions

In terms of direct effects, the lack of equal protection of the law is probably the most important of the political sanctions against blacks in the South. This makes possible all sorts of infringements upon their rights, including the use of violence, and makes it difficult, if not impossible, for them to attempt to better their position. The importance of the use of violence in perpetuating the caste situation cannot be overestimated. Throughout the South, it was customary to allow whites to use force or threaten to use force against blacks. It was permissible for a white man to jeopardize the property, freedom of movement, personal security, or even the life of a black by violence. The white man might use force in many different ways—from mild warnings to murder—in order to maintain his control over blacks. These practices, which go back to slavery and to the post-bellum days when the nominally freed blacks were subjugated by force, were made possible by the lax and unequal administration of law and justice in the South. Any white man might attack a black person physically, cheat him of his property, or steal or destroy it without much fear of legal reprisal. Cheating and striking blacks were commonplace occurrences, but the most serious forms of violence were rare enough to cause some stir by 1950.

Obviously, blacks tried to avoid any situation they think might lead to a violent attack on them. Ordinarily a mere command or threat without further violence was all that a white man need use to control blacks when he was angry or did not like what they were doing. The fact that blacks were dependent on whites economically would suffice to make such verbal controls potent, even without the possibility of violence. Nevertheless, southern whites did resort to physical violence against blacks: an accidental insult might set off the insecurity or sadism of some southern whites, and, in many parts of the South, he could with impunity wreak his fury, no matter how unreasonable, upon a victim. For some people such an opportunity is heady wine.

It would be wrong to assume that there were no checks on this violence. Most white southerners were not, and did not want to be, cruel, mean, or even dishonest when they themselves dealt with blacks. But they felt it was none of their business when someone else was cruel or dishonest—after all, such things help keep blacks in their "place." If a black person was viciously beaten or killed, they reassured themselves that "he must have deserved it." If someone cheated or beat his black tenants, "that's his business." The attitude was one of not rocking the boat.

What protection, then, did a southern black have? To all intents and purposes, none. If his white assailants were poor or had particularly unsavory reputations, he might be able to get some protection from his white employer; but only in such cases. He could not do anything on his own. He might try to stand up for himself, but if he did he knew this would only lead to more violent retaliation. A black man who protected himself endangered the rest of the black community, since whites took his self-defense as an affront to the white community and as an invitation to organize a punitive expedition.

The southern concept of law and justice was peculiar to that region. Both the police and the courts were accustomed to ignoring what happened when white people, either as individuals or as organized groups, took the law into their own hands. Often the law-enforcing agencies lent active support to such extralegal activities. The American ideal of an impartial law which governs all groups in the society and is impartially enforced seems never to have taken a strong hold on the South. As Rose observes, it is no wonder that:

> The difference in feelings of personal security between the two regions is most striking to an observer. The Southern Negro seems to suspect a possible danger to himself or to other Negroes whenever a white stranger approaches him. The Northern Negro, in general, appears different in this respect. His self-assurance in behavior often seems preposterous or obstreperous to the Southern white man, who has become accustomed to the submissive and guarded manners of the Southern Negro. (Rose, 1948, p. 173.)

Lynchings, largely a rural southern phenomenon, were condoned by the community in which they occurred. Frequently, they took on the characteristics of a mass orgy. In a lynching, the black victim is helpless, with no power to fight back and no danger to the white population. In this respect it differs from a race riot, which is a northern and urban phenomenon. In a riot, blacks may be outnumbered, but they can and do fight back; both whites and blacks are in danger. Lynchings have decreased markedly to the point where they have all but disappeared in recent years, but other types of violent retaliation remain.

In the South, the police (and other minor officials) saw it as their function to keep blacks in their place. Offenses of whites against blacks were treated lightly, while offenses of blacks against whites were handled severely. The courts were corrupted in favor of whites. The guilt of the black was often assumed on scanty evidence. For the same crime, blacks were given longer sentences than whites. Until recently blacks were rarely appointed to the police, and practically never to jury duty or to any other office connected with the administration of justice. The relative lack of concern of the police and the court with black crimes against blacks is, of course, resented by responsible elements in the black population as giving them no protection while encouraging the dangerous elements. The black in the North receives a roughly equal administration of justice (see Rose and others). Most northerners feel he is entitled to equal justice. What discriminations he feels are, for the most part, the same as are felt by any group of poor and uneducated people. The police in most northern communities are more likely to arrest a black person than a white under suspicious circumstances, and to treat him discourteously or brutally. As in the South, blacks are given longer sentences than whites for the same crime. Police have also been known to take part in race riots. On the other hand, the courts have not shielded the white transgressors afterward in the manner that has become typical of the South. Although civil rights laws, prohibiting various kinds of discrimination, are found in many parts of the North, blacks often find it difficult to get the courts to enforce these laws. But in northern cities there have been black judges, police, court officers, and lawyers, for a long time, and administration of the law is thereby less likely to be one-sided.

In addition to inequality in the *administration* of the law, there are inequalities in the law itself. Many patterns of segregation were embodied in state laws, which were then enforced by the state. Such laws were universal in the South, and relatively scarce in the North. Laws which *prohibit* segregation or discrimination occurred almost exclusively in northern states. State laws concerning intermarriage between blacks and whites are summarized in Table II-2, and those concerning segregation in public schools and segregation in public transportation are shown in Tables II-3 and II-4, as of 1955. All of these laws have since been declared unconstitutional by the Supreme Court.

The lack of concern of southern state governments (administrations, legislatures, and judiciaries) with the needs or rights of blacks was, in general, made possible by the fact that throughout the South they did not have the right to vote. Southerners often explained that blacks can vote in the South,

Table II-2   STATES WITHOUT ANTI-MISCEGENATION LAWS (Murray, Pauli)

Connecticut	New Hampshire
District of Columbia	New Jersey
Illinois	New Mexico
Iowa	Ohio
Kansas	Pennsylvania
Maine	Rhode Island
Massachusetts	Vermont
Michigan	Washington
Minnesota	Wisconsin
Nevada	*California

*Law without criminal penalty declared unconstitutional by state supreme court in 1948.

Table II-3   SEGREGATION IN PUBLIC SCHOOLS (Ashmore)

Segregation Required	Segregation Permitted in Various Degrees	Segregation Prohibited	No Legislation
Alabama	Arizona	Colorado	California
Arkansas	Wyoming	Connecticut	Maine
Delaware	Kansas	Idaho	Montana
District of Columbia	New Mexico	Illinois	Nebraska
Florida		Indiana	Nevada
Georgia		Iowa	New Hampshire
Kentucky		Massachusetts	North Dakota
Louisiana		Michigan	Oregon
Maryland		Minnesota	South Dakota
Mississippi		New Jersey	Utah
Missouri		New York	Vermont
North Carolina		Ohio	
Oklahoma		Pennsylvania	
South Carolina		Rhode Island	
Tennessee		Washington	
Texas		Wisconsin	
Virginia			
West Virginia			

Table II-4   SEGREGATION IN PUBLIC TRANSPORTATION (Murray, Pauli)

	Railroads	Buses	Streetcars	Waiting Rooms
Alabama	*	*		*
Arkansas	*	*	*	*
Florida	*	*	*	*
Georgia	*	*		
Kentucky	*			
Louisiana	*	*	*	*
Maryland	*		*	
Mississippi	*	*	*	*
North Carolina	*	*	*	*
Oklahoma	*	*	*	*
South Carolina	*	*	*	*
Tennessee	*		*	
Texas	*	*	*	*
Virginia	*	*	*	*

"but that they do not care to" (Rose, 1949, p. 160). It is true that no
southern state had a law forbidding blacks to vote; that would be a violation
of the federal Constitution. But the white primary (the one-party system
making the primary the only election that matters), the poll tax, property,
and educational and "character" requirements for voting were so used as to
eliminate blacks from the polls. In addition to these pseudo-legal procedures,

techniques which are blatantly illegal, ranging from intimidation to trickery, were used to keep blacks from exercising the right to vote. The threat of violence could be, and was, used to dissuade them from voting. If the threat alone was not sufficient, acts of terrorization would be carried out. Less crude were the "tricks" which were played on blacks to keep them from voting. "Didn't you know there are no registration cards?" "You are in the wrong place." "It looks like your name was forgotten when they made up the voting lists."

The defenses against blacks stultified the whole process of politics in the South. Southern politics were notorious for their lack of issues; for, if there were a controversy, one of the sides might be tempted to vote with blacks. There was, for all practical purposes, one party. The North had a Republican government during the Civil War, and the South has never forgotten this. Partly because the one-party system and the lack of issues resulted in apathy of the voters, and partly because the restrictions, such as the poll tax, which were used to exclude blacks, also excluded part of the white population, voting was light even among whites. Political corruption, as Myrdal points out, was even more prevalent than in the North.

Southern politicians were returned to office again and again because of the lack of effective opposition within their states. This had important repercussions on the national scene. Inasmuch as committee chairmanships in both the House of Representatives and the Senate are awarded on the basis of seniority, southern Democrats tend to receive more than their share of committee chairmanships whenever Democrats are in control of Congress. This, plus the unlimited debate rule of the Senate, allowed the South to effectively block any alleviation of the situation of blacks by the legislative branch of the government. One of the important consequences of the continuing northward migration of blacks was that the migrants became enfranchised by moving into areas where they were allowed to vote. Not only were state and city authorities responsive to the needs of blacks in the North, but federal authorities were also influenced by the northern black vote. The South by itself cannot elect a president. Further, blacks in the North are concentrated within large urban areas in states which are keystones (because of their large number of electoral votes) in a presidential election. Federal agencies are therefore likely to treat blacks nearly equitably. Even in the South, where local administrators often prevent blacks from getting their fair share of federal benefits, they receive a larger share of the federal benefits due them than they do of state benefits.

During World War II, one of the significant presidential actions (in response to the "March-on-Washington" organized by A. P. Randolph of the Brotherhood of Sleeping Car Porters) was the barring of discrimination in employment on war contracts. Although this order has since lapsed, the gains in employment which it made possible are of considerable importance in the present economic status of blacks.

The integration of the armed services, which was put into effect during the Korean War, represents a major step by the federal administration toward reducing social separation and discrimination: nearly every American male, whether North or South, black or white, spent some time in the armed forces.

The federal judiciary system has shown a marked change over the years in terms of its treatment of the black. The nadir of the legal status of blacks was reached in 1857 when Chief Justice Taney of the Supreme Court announced in a decision that "a Negro has no rights which a white man need respect." The famous Plessy vs. Ferguson decision (1895) established the "separate but equal" doctrine which has since formed the legal basis for segregation. (In fact, "separate but equal" has rarely meant equal, even in terms of physical facilities.) In more recent times the Supreme Court has repeatedly upheld the rights of blacks. The white primary was declared illegal in 1944. After a series of decisions which limited segregation in transportation and higher education on the basis of inequality of facilities, the Supreme Court finally reversed the Plessy vs. Ferguson decision and held that separate facilities, *ipso facto*, were not equal, and consequently segregation in the public schools was unconstitutional. There is, however, a large gap between the decisions and their enforcement.

Economic sanctions

The simple fact is that blacks suffer acute economic distress. The economic level of most blacks is totally incompatible with any modern concept of a minimum standard of living. Getting and holding a job is more of a problem for blacks than for whites and it is a problem that is faced earlier in life. This is true for all sections of the country. Nevertheless, the income of blacks is lower in the rural South than in the urban South, and lower in the urban South than in the urban North, both absolutely and relative to white earnings.

With respect to agriculture, blacks are usually in the lower rungs of farm workers. Blacks are sharecroppers rather than independent farmers. The political and social discriminations of the past have allowed plantation owners a free hand in administering "justice" paternalistically in dealing with black tenants and sharecroppers. It is not surprising that advantage has been taken of blacks. There is very little recourse from the economic bargain that a white plantation owner cares to enforce against his black sharecroppers; they will get their due only as long as they enjoy the good will of the owner. Attempts to stand up for one's rights are largely fruitless, if not dangerous. The southern black tenant farmer has been made to understand that being black is all the excuse he needs for not being able to take care of himself, and that he will be rewarded more for accepting a low position without complaint than attempting to better his position. The best security he can attain is to become attached to some white person of high standing in the community.

With respect to nonagricultural employment, blacks have been largely restricted to unskilled labor, especially to jobs which are low-paid, dangerous, dirty, involve heavy physical labor, or imply low social status. When working conditions improve in an industry, this may lead to the displacement of blacks by whites rather than to improvement in the working conditions of blacks.

One of the factors keeping blacks out of better jobs is that they are often prevented from receiving the necessary training. For example, the segregated schools of the South, in most places, have been inadequate by northern standards even for whites; for blacks, they have often been hopeless. In the North, because of housing segregation, blacks are concentrated in slum areas where schools are apt to be inferior. Even well-meaning advisors in northern schools are apt to advise blacks to prepare for those jobs which will be open to them, i.e., lower-paying, less desirable jobs.

Because of their lower economic security, blacks are more likely to be forced to leave school in order to take a job. Further, awareness of the difficulties involved in getting a job often dissuades them from getting appropriate training. As one black interviewed by Kardiner and Ovesey described it:

> I never had a chance to go to school so I could never accomplish what I wanted. But suppose I do finish school. How'll I get a job being colored? I keep thinking all the time: Is that true that I won't even get a chance? I keep trying to tell myself it ain't true, but all the time there's a doubt. . . . I try to study, I try to read, but I just don't seem to be able to do it. Maybe it's just lazy. I just don't feel like doing anything at all. Regardless of what you do, you can't get anywhere. You work and you go to school and you work and you go to school and you're still in the same place. . . . You work eight hours a day and all you get is twenty-five dollars a week. You can't live—you can only exist. So what's the use? . . . There's no use trying—you just can't. There just ain't no use. (Kardiner and Ovesey, pp. 85-86.)

On the other hand, even where blacks have received appropriate training, it is often difficult for them to find a job even now. Many industries, North and South, until recently did not hire blacks, and even in industries that did not discriminate, they were apt to be hired only by certain firms, or only in the less attractive jobs.

Unions have affected the economic welfare of blacks differently, depending upon whether the union did or did not practice discrimination. (The
merged AFL-CIO officially opposes discrimination.) In the South, unioniza-
tion has often foundered upon race relations attitudes. If the union is segregated, blacks are available as strikebreakers; if integrated, the white supremacy issue can be used to discourage whites from joining the union. Further,
according to Myrdal, the corruptibility and the responsiveness to special interests of southern state governments and courts (which owe their continuance
largely to the pseudo-legal sanctions against blacks) have been utilized to
combat labor unions.

Black-owned businesses are negligible, since whites will not extend
credit to blacks. A better opportunity for increased status is afforded by the
professions, but even here the difficulties in obtaining training and in securing
a position and/or clientele afterward are so great that these occupations, too,
represent but a very small group of blacks.

Because of these economic restrictions, most blacks are concentrated in
the lower socio-economic class. However, the opportunities for employment
are much better for women than for men; black women can get better paid
jobs, and longer lasting ones, than black men.

Unemployment is common among blacks as compared with other
groups in the United States. Although this is true in the North and South, the
sections differ in that the black in the North is more likely to receive the
unemployment benefits to which he is entitled.

Still another area of economic discrimination is housing. Most housing
available to blacks in the South and the North is inadequate. Not only are
blacks restricted to the substandard housing available to other low-income
groups but, in addition, caste restrictions on the neighborhoods in which they
may live intensify the problem of overcrowding. Moreover, blacks must pay
far more than the true value of the inadequate housing which is available.
Black migration to urban areas accentuates this problem since the residential
areas available do not increase anywhere near as rapidly as the population.
The rural South, in general, has poor housing, and the black population, as
might be expected, is limited to the poorest of what is available in that area.

Class structure

By observing whom we treat as social equals—that is, by observing
whom we invite to our homes, who invites us to their homes, and with whom
we interact socially—regularities are revealed in the ways in which Americans
deal with each other. Friendly interactions occur most frequently between

people on the same level, so that people in the United States can be separated into classes according to social status. The boundaries between social classes are not as rigid as those between castes; people can, and in the United States frequently do, move up or down in the class hierarchy. Nevertheless, there is a regular pattern. Our social class is reflected not only in who our friends are, what we do for a living, what income we receive, what education we have, and what section of the city we live in, but also in such things as sexual behavior, how we raise our children, and our set of values, that is, our ideas about what is important. Sociologists generally distinguish three broad classes, described, appropriately enough, as upper, middle, and lower. The large majority of blacks are in the lower class, and share the characteristics of other lower class people. Many "black characteristics" are merely those of lower class people in general (as compared with those of the middle class): being poorer, less educated, "loose" sexually, and more interested in present pleasures than in long term goals.

It is the caste sanctions which prevent blacks from rising from the lower class. As might be expected, the percentage of middle and upper class blacks is greater in the North than in the South.

The criteria for class distinctions are very much the same among blacks as among whites, with the additional determinant of color. Kardiner and Ovesey (p. 72) list as criteria used by blacks: (1) Occupation and steadiness of job, (2) Education, (3) Family organization, (4) Housing, furnishings, and appurtenances, (5) Relationship to the white world, (6) Characteristic recreations and amusements, and (7) Skin color. Skin color, which (along with pre-Civil War status of the family) was once the major determinant of status among blacks, has steadily decreased in importance, while education and stability of the family have increased in importance as criteria of class status.

Family structure

In isolated rural areas of the South, sexual activity tends to start early, and marriage is more casual (of a common law type) than in the rest of American society. Bearing an illegitimate child is not considered a great crime. Although the pattern of sexuality is somewhat looser than in the rest of the American culture, there are restrictions: one man at a time, etc. This behavior does not lead to a great deal of guilt until it comes into conflict with the values of the dominant American culture, as it does in areas which are less isolated. As we go from rural to urban areas and from South to North, the pattern slowly fuses over to the more usual American patterns of behavior.

Illegitimate children are not, in general, treated with the same harshness among black society that they are in white society. In rural areas, relatives and even unrelated people will look after children who have no one else to care for them.

Much has been written about the mother-dominated family among blacks. Its prevalence may be attributed partly to a carry-over from slavery (where the mother-child bond was allowed to develop, while the father-child bond was discouraged), but much more important is the prevalence of illegitimacy and desertion among American blacks, either of which necessarily leads to a family headed by the mother. In the rural South, the mother-dominated family may take the form of a more or less stable extended matriarchal family. In southern cities the mother-dominated family which prevails has more of the character of a disorganized family structure. And in northern cities the mother-dominated family and loose sexuality, although frequent, is simply a pathological and disorganized form of the general American family structure.

The high desertion rate (which leads to the mother-dominated family) can be traced back to economic sanctions, whereby black women are able to get better jobs and hold them longer than black men. But blacks share with whites the notions about the proper roles for a husband and wife, namely, that the husband is the "breadwinner." Economically, however, the black man cannot fulfill the role of provider as both he and his wife understand it. His economic dependence on her tends to make him a weak figure. Her disappointment in him and his own frustration at his wife's having to support the family are likely to build to the point where he finds the situation intolerable and deserts.

While real disorganization is most frequent in northern cities (among lower class blacks), middle class families in the white pattern emerge there, too, frequently. In rural areas of the South after the Emancipation, the black family, following its own pattern, was able to achieve a fair degree of stability. But the stream of migrants of both sexes to the towns and cities (and to the turpentine and lumber camps) continually undermined the stability both in the communities from which they had come and in the communities to which they came. Thus, a large proportion of disorganized families have for a long time characterized the black communities of southern towns and cities. In northern cities the mass migration of blacks during and after the First World War drastically increased the number of disorganized families. Nevertheless, as time went by and blacks acquired education and economic security, black families in these cities have become increasingly stable; a middle class family life has developed, and many blacks are adopting this way of life.

Migrations from the South to the North have continued, however, and have increased during and after World War II. Disorganization of the family, therefore, continues to be one of the most serious of the social problems facing blacks. Lack of a stable family life means a lack of continuity, of tradition, of "roots" for the individual. Life is fragmented, casual, and precarious, and only the immediate problem of how to live from day to day seems of any consequence.

Somewhere between one-third to one-fourth of black families have no man at the head of the family. Since the discipline and authority of a father are missing in the lives of the children, the process, usual in our culture, of little boys learning to grow into men by identifying with their fathers as strong figures is forestalled. Even the mother, who heads the family, is forced to neglect the children since she must earn their living.

What does growing up in such an environment do to a child? Nearly every aspect of the black adaptation to life bears the imprint of the warp imparted in childhood. Growing up in a family with strong traditions and consistent parental discipline teaches a child to have strong goals for himself; lacking this experience, many black children grow up aimless and unambitious. The public schools provide formal instruction and attempt to instill positive goals, but the gap left by the lack of training and tradition within the family is too great to be filled by the school. Indeed, education seems to some black children to be unrelated to any meaningful part of their environment, and especially to their home experiences. They become totally uninterested in education, and the school, consequently, may be unable to reach them. Moreover, the fact that there are not likely to be many jobs, especially good jobs, open to them encourages the black youth never to waiver from the pattern of avoiding ambition and long-term goals.

If children cannot learn their standards of behavior at home or in school, where do they learn them? In the streets. They are the only standards which are presented to them consistently and which seem obviously related to their way of life. Since disorganized families tend to be concentrated in the least desirable sections of any city, the codes of conduct that are offered to the child by the street corner gang are likely to be at best socially disapproved, and at worst blatantly antisocial.

Thus the social and economic pressures in the community fuse with the disorganization within the family to create a marked sense of irresponsibility in such black youth. It is not surprising that many of the criminals and juvenile delinquents of our cities spring from such disrupted backgrounds.

Child rearing practices

There is not a great deal of data on how blacks differ from whites in the way that they raise their children.

Dai stresses the preponderance of lower class families with, consequently, lower class mores, broken homes, dominance of maternal authority, preoccupation with skin color and other racial features, and extraordinary emphasis on social status.

Kardiner and Ovesey (pp. 38-76) stress the absence of paternal care, the tendency for the mother, because of the necessity to work, to turn into a "loveless tyrant." They also stress the inconsistent discipline and lack of affectionate background to be found in the lower class, as well as the absence of "affectionate relatedness" between the parents. In addition, they point out the accentuated hostility and rivalry among brothers and sisters. They report that sex training is Victorian, although it may not be enforced by beatings as are other sorts of training in the lower class. Sexual behavior among lower class blacks, as among lower class whites, is anything but Victorian, especially among males.

Davis and Havighurst, in comparing blacks and whites in Chicago with respect to how they raise their children, found that almost all aspects of child rearing could be subsumed under class differences and that, in general, there were few differences between blacks and whites of the same economic class (but Chicago is the North). The major differences between blacks and whites of comparable social and economic status were:

1. More permissiveness in oral training (weaning, breast feeding, etc.).
2. More strictness in toilet training.
3. Girls are given more responsibility earlier, and also middle class girls are not allowed to play across the street or go to the movies alone until later (which may be due to the neighborhoods they live in).

The developing situation in the North—summary (as of 1958)

American social institutions relating to blacks are in a process of change.

In the North, complete political equality, at least in theory, has been granted to blacks from the time of the Civil War. Equality before the law and in its administration has been fully granted in the North, and public facilities and services are, in general, available on an equal basis. However, the treatment received by the impoverished and the uneducated is seldom truly equal, and blacks are no better treated than other such groups.

Racial prejudice and discrimination in the North sharply increased with the mass migration of southern blacks of low socio-economic status and education which began during World War I and continued thereafter. The shortage of housing for blacks in the North became acute. But this same migration increased the concentration of blacks in a few big cities to the point where they began to wield real political power, especially on issues which directly concerned them. There are Civil Rights laws in at least eighteen states to protect blacks against the impact of prejudice. Since the cities in which blacks are concentrated are crucial in presidential elections, the federal government has also become increasingly responsive to the needs of blacks.

In the cities of the North, the number of blacks who are following a middle class way of life has been steadily increasing as they acquire more education. Middle class blacks have the same ideas about what are the proper ways to live, and have the same aspirations for themselves as do middle class whites, but these aspirations conflict with the existing pattern of discrimination. The fear of engendering or justifying social discrimination leads the middle class black to impose upon himself standards of personal conduct and morality which are even less tolerant of unconventionality or deviant behavior than the corresponding standards of middle class whites. These are the blacks who pushed the fight for civil rights, and it is as a result of their efforts, as well as of the increased effectiveness of organizations such as the NAACP and the Urban League, that civil rights laws, where they exist, are becoming more effectively enforced. However, neither the attempt to circumvent discrimination for themselves by adhering to a rigid code of conduct, nor the attempt to abolish discrimination for all blacks (including themselves), by continuously pushing the fight for civil rights, is ever more than partially successful; it is no wonder, then, that the feelings of middle class blacks toward whites are often characterized by cynicism and, in some cases, outright hatred.

The biggest problems for the northern black of any class are getting a decent house and a decent job. Whether or not there is a general housing shortage in the United States, blacks always suffer from an acute lack of living facilities. In every large northern city, black homes are only found in certain areas, not by any choice, but because they are excluded from the rest of the city. These areas have been grossly overcrowded and run-down for a long time; considering the heavy increase in northern black populations, the new residential areas which are made available to them are few indeed. It is again the middle class blacks who most resent this lack since their standards require decent housing and they are able and willing to pay for it.

Blacks have been, and remain, at a considerable disadvantage as compared with whites in getting or holding jobs, especially in getting and holding any position above the level of unskilled laborer. During times of unemployment, a disproportionately large number of biacks remain without jobs. With the shrinkage of unemployment during the Second World War, the absolute and relative economic status of blacks showed tremendous gains. The prosperity following the Second World War enabled blacks to retain much of these gains. There were, however, some losses, partly because of discriminatory hiring and firing policies but also because blacks, in general, had less seniority than whites in industries that had to cut back personnel once the war was over. Nevertheless, during World War II, blacks had been able to enter new industries, rise to skilled jobs, and join unions, although they still remained at a disadvantage as compared to whites. Further, some states and cities passed FEPC laws, assuring protection of equitable treatment by employers. Moreover, in most cases where blacks joined unions, the latter protected their black members from discriminatory firing. Clearly, the black population has made many gains in the field of employment and still encounters a vast amount of discrimination; it is by no means clear how solid these gains are.

The developing situation in the South—summary (as of 1958)

The forcible suppression of blacks in the post-bellum South reached its lowest ebb in 1900. The development of industry in the South, the growth of cities, the gradual improvement of education for both whites and blacks, and the pressure of disapproving public opinion from other parts of the country (as improved communications made the sections of the country more interdependent) have since led to a steady rise in the status of blacks.

The so-called "etiquette of race relations" which continually demonstrates the inferiority of all blacks, no matter how distinguished, to all whites, no matter how degenerate, is progressively, albeit slowly, breaking down. There has been a gradual movement among whites to take account of differences in education, class, or ability among blacks, and to treat them differently according to these characteristics. The "no social equality" theory is not quite so rigidly held as before. "Separate but equal" is still the legal doctrine of the South, but occasional voices of southern liberals can now be heard arguing that the Jim Crow apparatus be made equal as well as separate.

Even white conservatives have advocated improving black facilities in order to lessen the pressures from blacks and from the North for the abolition of Jim Crow.

Whatever improvement may be occurring in the "equality" aspect of segregation, the "separateness" is becoming more severe. This is not true of the actual physical segregation (which, indeed, is slowly diminishing) but of the mental isolation between the two castes. Southern whites and blacks are becoming even more estranged from each other than before, both as a result of exclusionist policies on the parts of whites, and of reactively bitter race pride and sullen resentment on the part of blacks. Some future decreases in physical segregation, as, for example, in the school system, may eventually reverse this trend.

Equality before the law is accorded blacks nowhere in the South. Despite the clearly worded intent of the Constitution, the South has continued to deny voting privileges to blacks. Public services of every sort which have been made available to blacks have been grossly unequal as compared with those afforded whites. However, there has been steady but slow improvement. Public services are gradually moving in the direction of becoming equal, and so, too, is the administration of justice. The restrictions that have denied political power to blacks have also effectively excluded the mass of southern whites. In the South, real issues have been kept out of politics, but maintaining such a political structure has become increasingly difficult.

At the beginning of the Second World War, the status of blacks was slowly improving in these respects, but it was worsening in the sphere of employment. The burden of the difficulties encountered by agriculture in the South was laid with disproportionate weight upon the shoulders of the black tenant farmer. For blacks displaced from farms, there was no alternate source of livelihood capable of taking up the economic slack. The expanding industries of the South did not offer much in the way of jobs for blacks. Even the unions failed to materially advance the position of blacks. Black businesses had not been particularly successful, and the gains realized in the professions had little significance in the total employment picture. The Second World War drastically affected the status of blacks. The conscience of white Americans was stirred by the fact that the enemy proclaimed a racist ideology, against which in sharp contrast stood the democratic ideology—the goal we were fighting for. The inconsistency of the southern tradition with the American creed thus became more apparent. The tremendous need for manpower, the federal FEPC, and the policies of national labor unions served to create a solid economic advance for blacks.

The use of black police has become increasingly common in the South, an important step toward providing fair and equal justice. Gradual extension of the right to vote may have far-reaching effects. The whole texture of southern politics, and even of national politics, may be expected to be radically altered with the passage of time, as blacks gain the right to vote. For the first time since Reconstruction, Congress passed a bill enlarging the legal status of blacks when such a bill was submitted by the President. Although the Civil Rights bill in its final form was limited to the right to vote (and somewhat weakened in its enforcement provisions), it is significant both of the lessened power and lessened intransigence of the South's spokesmen, and of the increased importance which members of both Houses of Congress and of both parties outside the South attached to the problem of black rights, that any such bill could have been passed. In the long run, one can expect an integration of the South politically with the rest of the country, a larger proportion of both poor whites and blacks voting, and the growth of the two-party system. The gains in legal status have resulted in organized extra-legal attempts to intimidate blacks lest they attempt to make use of their newly won status.

The southern white felt threatened by the increasing independence of the blacks consequent upon their improved economic position after the Second World War. The activity of black protest organizations, black demands for more equality, and the increasingly apparent hostility of southern blacks augmented the whites' feelings of insecurity. These feelings led them to resist the progress of blacks and, consequently, the latter have made losses as well as gains in the South. Black veterans have at times been denied their GI rights; "white supremacy" has been raised increasingly in political campaigns; and bombings of the homes of black leaders have become more frequent. When violence is employed, however, it now usually has a surreptitious character which contrasts sharply with the mass-orgy type of lynching characteristic of an earlier era. Despite this pressure, southern blacks are beginning to show themselves increasingly willing and able to work together for their common goals. A striking example is the Ghandi-like passive resistance with which the blacks of Montgomery, Alabama, carried out, despite harassment, a boycott against segregation on busses in that city.

One of the most significant legal battles in the history of black-white relations in the United States has centered on the educational system. The campaign of the NAACP to win equal facilities for blacks resulted eventually in the series of Supreme Court decisions requiring educational facilities, if separate, to be truly equal. The decisions spurred improvements in black school systems in order to avoid undermining the continuance of segregation. The crowning blow to the legal status of the Jim Crow laws was dealt by the Supreme Court decision in the school segregation cases that separate facilities are, *ipso facto*, not equal. The decision eliminated the legal basis of segregation, and opened a way for change in the practice of segregation.

Desegregation has begun in Washington, D. C., most of Maryland, including Baltimore, most of West Virginia, most of Missouri, including St. Louis and Kansas City, more than half the school districts in Kentucky, including those in Louisville and Frankfort, most of Oklahoma, including Oklahoma City and Tulsa, a considerable portion of Delaware, including Wilmington, and some of Texas.

In Alabama, Florida, Georgia, Louisiana, Mississippi, North Carolina, and South Carolina there have been no instances of desegregation in the schools. It is a sign of the changing times that, in these seven "hard core" states, resistance takes the form of legislation: declarations by the state legislatures that the Supreme Court decision was "null and void" and asserting the "right" of "Interposition" (of the state over the federal government) which had not been claimed since pre-Civil War days; "pupil assignment" laws giving local school boards unlimited power to place a pupil as they see fit (often not explicitly mentioning race as a factor); laws withholding state funds from any integrated school; laws providing for the abolition of public schools rather than integrate (generally with the intention of substituting "private" segregated schools, with the state paying the tuition); laws aimed at hampering the NAACP, etc. Existing laws, too, are administered so as to maintain the system of segregation and economic sanctions invoked against those advocating integration. Even in the "hard core" states the educational opportunities of blacks are improving, since these states are pushing ahead with "equalization" programs intended to relieve the pressure for integration by providing adequate segregated schools for blacks.

Notable by its absence in these Deep South states is the use of violence. Although there have been some rioting and surreptitious bombings of the houses of black leaders, or of schools, in areas where desegregation was actually being initiated, the fight against segregation in these seven states has been pushed largely by other means. Indeed, throughout the South, violence as a way of life is becoming less and less acceptable.

When rioting occurred in Clinton, Tenn., because of desegregation, Governor Clement used the National Guard to quiet the disturbance. Similarly, a year later, when the disturbances over desegregation in Nashville culminated in the dynamiting of a school, state and local authorities put an immediate end to all disorders connected with the desegregation. It was not that these southern officials wanted to push integration, but simply that they would not tolerate violence and the destruction of property in defiance of law and order.

In Little Rock, Arkansas, the upheavals took a particularly dramatic form. The city authorities, in complying with the Supreme Court decision, proposed a plan for a very gradual integration of the public schools, one which the NAACP disputed in court was too slow to be considered compliance with the law. When a federal court ruled in favor of the city's proposed plan, city authorities began to prepare for its inception. A handful of black high school students were assigned (at their own request) to a white school. On the first day of school, however, the governor of the state intervened by calling out the National Guard to prevent the black children from entering the white high school. Although the National Guard units were there ostensibly to prevent violence, they permitted crowds of whites to gather and did nothing when they physically assaulted blacks. Eventually, a federal court issued an injunction ordering the Governor and the commanding officer of the state's National Guard units to desist from interference with the carrying out of the court's orders (that is, the beginning of desegregation). When the National Guard units were withdrawn, the crowds continued to gather. City authorities withdrew the black children from the school for fear that the mobs could not be controlled. Finally, President Eisenhower, with obvious reluctance, sent federal troops to restore order and federalized the Arkansas National Guard (which was now used as part of the force stationed in Little Rock to ensure peaceful compliance with the law).

The split in thinking between North and South was clearly demonstrated in this episode. The majority of southerners did not realize the shock with which most northerners reacted to the pictures and stories of black children being kept out of the schools by National Guardsmen and the pictures of blacks being attacked or chased, with these same Guardsmen standing by. Nor did they realize the tremendous loss of international prestige which we suffered as a result of these episodes. On the other hand, President Eisenhower's use of troops to enforce the law was greeted with immediate cries of southern protest and horror, especially from southern politicians. The northern reaction, in general, was one of approval—it was regrettable that such action by the President was necessary, but it was far better than allowing the principle of rule by law to be overthrown by force.

Even the reaction in the South can be overestimated. Although the majority of white southerners did not like the President's action, the results of Gallup polls taken on the subject of approval of the Supreme Court decision on integration revealed some interesting trends. In every poll on the subject since the decision was handed down, the majority of southern whites disapproved of the decision and the majority of northern whites approved. But the percentage of southern whites who approved the decision reached its lowest ebb after the Governor of Arkansas used the National Guard to prevent integration, and the percentage jumped upward after the President's actions.

Observers have noted an increased pressure toward conformity of expression, if not of thought, among southern whites since the Supreme Court decision. Southerners report with dismay their feeling that it is increasingly difficult to express any opinion except one that is extremely pro-segregationist, and that anyone expressing doubts about the system of segregation may find himself the object of social or economic reprisals. Nonetheless, Rose's (1949, pp. 316-317) summary of the outlook for the future still seems apt:

The truth is that the South is at present under terrific pressure to change her ways, and, since her ways are bound up in all respects with the Negro problem, her attitudes towards the Negro are undergoing drastic changes. The pressures include the South's own needs for increased industrialization and economic efficiency, for more and better education, for incorporation into the rest of the nation both economically and culturally rather than remaining a backward region, and the general American need for vitalizing democracy, both at home and abroad, and for increasing security of her citizens. Therefore, in so far and as quickly as the South succeeds in bringing her standards up to the rest of the nation's, to that extent will she succeed in solving the Negro problem in terms of the American Creed. . . .

It is much easier now to make the South change than it used to be. For one thing, leading Southerners themselves now publicly state that the South ought to change. As Federal Judge J. Waties Waring of Charleston, S.C., said in his 1947 decision outlawing the white primary, "It is time for South Carolina to rejoin the Union. It is time to fall in step with the other States and to adopt the American way of conducting elections." For another thing, the popular theory behind race prejudice is breaking down. In the South three generations ago, white people had for their defense a consistent and respectable theory, endorsed by the church and all the sciences, printed in learned books and periodicals, and expounded by the South's great statesmen in the Capitol in Washington. The Negro was regarded as a completely different species of mankind: undeveloped, "childlike," amoral, and much less endowed with intellectual capacities than the white man; he was meant by the Creator to be a servant forever; if kept in his "place" he was tolerable, and there he was also happy; "social equality" was unthinkable as it implied intermarriage which would destroy the white race and Anglo-Saxon civilization. Most of this theory remained until a couple of decades ago. But now it is almost destroyed for upper-class and educated people. Its maintenance among lower-class and uneducated people meets increasing difficulties. It is significant that today even the white man who defends discrimination frequently describes his motive as "prejudice" and says that it is "irrational." The popular beliefs rationalizing caste in America are no longer intellectually respectable. This makes the prejudiced white man nearly as pathetic as his Negro victim. It also makes his attitude more susceptible to change.

Chapter III

THE PSYCHOLOGY OF THE BLACK

Some of the characteristics of blacks in the United States have become apparent in the description of the social institutions affecting them. They are characteristics that are readily evident to any impartial observer who cares to watch blacks and ask direct questions about their experiences and feelings. There are, however, aspects of the mind which are just as important but not so readily apparent, even to an acute observer. Even a trait such as intelligence cannot always be assessed from everyday behavior; a seriously maladjusted person may show no sign of high intelligence in any of his everyday activities, and yet possess a high intelligence, which can be revealed only in a specialized test situation. After the maladjustments of such persons have been treated with psychotherapy, they frequently begin to function in their daily lives on a level commensurate with their tested intelligence. Thus, someone with high intelligence, and a neurotic maladjustment specifically interfering with his use of it, will behave in the same way in many situations as does a person of low intelligence; psychologically speaking, however, they are radically different. The psychologist must be concerned with both the readily observable and the not-so-readily observable.

Before undertaking a new investigation, one ordinarily begins by reviewing what others have found. It would therefore be appropriate to review what is known about the differences in personality between people who differ in the degree to which caste sanctions are enforced against them. Perhaps the best comparison for our purpose would be that between northern and southern blacks. Unfortunately, there has been little work on the psychological differences between northern and southern blacks with the exception of studies on intelligence. On that characteristic, the evidence is clear-cut: on the average, northern blacks score higher on intelligence tests than do southern blacks.

For ideas on what further differences there may be, we can turn to the literature on black-white differences if we make the assumption that the differences between blacks and whites are the result of social institutions and not of innate factors. If this assumption is not justified, our only loss is that the ideas we have so gathered will not work out. If the assumption is justified, then we will find that northern blacks differ from southern blacks in the same ways whites differ from blacks.

Most of the research, however, on black-white differences, especially the early work, was intent on finding differences that were primarily innate. Sometimes this was prompted by a desire to justify differential treatment by proving that blacks were born inferior; on the other hand, it is reasonable to state, as did Franz Boas, that "it does not seem probable that the minds of races which show variations in physical structure should act in exactly the same way." Yet, surveying the evidence, one can only agree with the conclusion of Huxley and Haddon: "It is not without significance that such an enormous mass of investigation has failed to demonstrate what so many were eager to prove." (Both cited by Myrdal, p. 146.)

Klineberg ends his excellent review of the research up to the early 1940's on black-white personality differences with:

The differences between Negro and white personality as reflected in tests and experiments seem not to be marked. There is an inconsistency in the findings, and significant differences are rare. This is undoubtedly due in part to the nature of the tests, probably also to the fact that a substantial similarity in cultural backgrounds results in a corresponding similarity in the responses to the tests. We can only repeat that the conclusions obtained through the use of tests cannot be more valid than the test used and that completely satisfactory research in this field will have to wait until psychologists have devised more adequate measures for the study of personality. (Klineberg, Part III, p. 138.)

In the light of this conclusion, we shall make no attempt to survey the literature, but before describing the results of our own study of black-white differences (Chapter VI) we will review one research study which is unique in its thoroughness, depth, and breadth, namely Kardiner and Ovesey's study of 25 black subjects by means of psychoanalytic interviews, Rorschach tests, and Thematic Apperception Tests. The three sources of materials in that study were analyzed independently, and the results then integrated. Moreover, the findings of most other investigators tend to be implied by some aspect of their complex conclusions (cf. Clark [1964], Grier & Cobbs [1968]).

Because of the depth and thoroughness of their study, the number of people studied was necessarily small (each person received twenty to a hundred one-hour psychoanalytic interviews); consequently, Kardiner and Ovesey describe their research as a pilot study, that is, a preliminary study which is aimed at getting ideas rather than putting these ideas to a definitive test.

Their study has been criticized in terms of the small number of cases and the lack of consideration of sampling. All their subjects were living in Harlem at the time of the study. More than half were patients who had come for psychotherapy and who would therefore be expected to have serious problems whether or not the caste sanctions had any effects. Nevertheless, Kardiner and Ovesey did get to understand their subjects thoroughly, the conclusions of their three different techniques of measurement were strikingly concordant, and they placed their findings within a meaningful causal nexus of theory—relating them to the social institutions whose effects we intend to study. Our own study serves as a larger scale test of, at least, some of their findings. It is important to note that only if our findings confirm their conclusions would we accept their conclusions as generally valid.

One consideration which should be kept in mind in evaluating their results is that, although their black sample was drawn entirely from a northern city, nearly half of the sample, like the majority of blacks living in the North, had spent an appreciable part of their early lives in the South. Kardiner and Ovesey's conclusions on the basis of the psychoanalytic interviews (pp. 301-317) about the psychological functioning of blacks in 1950 may be summarized as follows:

The direct effects of discrimination on blacks are low self-esteem and anger at the way they are treated. Both of these lead to fear which may be manifested in self-abnegation, caution, and apologetic behavior. Low self-esteem may be reflected in unrealistically high aspirations. It may also be manifested by apathy, hedonism, living for the moment, or turning to a life of crime. The anxiety-provoking feeling of being angry leads the black to act ingratiating but removed, hesitant, and mistrustful, and to focus on what is manifest and simple: he is afraid of looking into anything too closely. The anger is denied and there may result a cover of good humor and affability, as well as irritability. This denial of hostility also leads to passivity and resigned acceptance, to not meeting problems head on. There is a general diminution and constriction of emotional life as a result of this denial of aggression. Suppressed rage may be manifested, therefore, as fear, submission, irritability, explosive discharges, ingratiation for purposes of exploitation, or even denied altogether and expressed as laughter. Suppressed anger, as is well known, is often redirected toward someone other than the original instigator of the anger, and when the black directs his displaced rage against someone he loves, he does not express it but instead becomes depressed. The most common of these psychological mechanisms, according to Kardiner and Ovesey, are low self-esteem and depression.

The indirect effects (through family structure, etc.) of the caste sanctions are discussed separately by social class. In the lower class, the frustrations experienced continuously in childhood lead to the development of an adult personality which includes no confidence in other human beings and which is, consequently, eternally vigilant and distrustful of others. This distrust defends such a person against repeated traumatic disappointments; but to maintain this protection, the assumption on which he operates must be that the world is hostile. Only a low degree of emotional relatedness to other people is safe in such a world. There also develops a wish to be like a white man, or to be a white man, which necessarily leads to emotional tension.

There is little or no evidence of rigid toilet training in childhood among lower class blacks, especially in those from the South. (This finding contrasts sharply with that of Davis and Havighurst.) Sex training is Victorian, but little trouble is taken to implement it. Sexual guilt in these blacks is not due to the parents' threats (as with whites), but to a confusion of socio-sexual roles: the dominant social and economic role played by the woman and the dependent role played by the man are psychologically inconsistent with their appropriate sexual roles, as defined in this culture. Contrary to the stereotype, Kardiner and Ovesey found that the sexual drive of adult blacks is relatively weak. A strong conscience is lacking, but, nevertheless, there is a strong fear of detection. Great vigilance is maintained by the black lest his anger and antisocial impulses break through. This, as he sees it, is his greatest danger.

The lower-class black engages in various sorts of compensatory behavior: flashy dressing, denial of black attributes, narcosis (alcohol, etc.), vindictive and vituperative gossip and disparagement, gambling, and explosive spending. He tends to live from day to day because of an inability to plan.

In the middle and upper class, there is some improvement in emotionality, but nearly all of that is canceled out by the pressure for status (which again limits the emotional life of blacks). They drive themselves harder, and refuse the compensatory activities of the lower class. They are vulnerable to depressed self-esteem, and have a harder time with the control of anger. This in turn has a constricting effect on all their emotions. The self-hatred of this group is projected outward and felt as a hatred of both whites and blacks lower than themselves. Guilt over their hatred of other blacks, plus a fear of retaliation, leads to a "success phobia." They also tend to overshoot the mark of conformity to white ideals (e.g., sex and toilet training). Their feelings of worthlessness may take the form of an unconscious identification of self with feces, and this leads to meticulousness as a reaction formation. The confusion of socio-sexual roles is not the factor that it is in the lower class, but the overconformity to white sex mores leads to frigidity and sex guilt anyway. Marriages are more stable, but the value of conventionality is high; marriages are not happier. Their emotional life seems improved, but it is largely on the formal side; they are in fact extremely cramped, constricted, and unspontaneous.

They are unable to abandon themselves to any activity because of dissatisfaction with themselves, nor are they able to relate effectively to other people because of self-hatred and their consequent mistrust of other blacks. Spontaneity seems to imply getting hurt by retaliation, and they choose the lesser evil. Further, lest what they see hurt them, or instigate them to act in such a way as to provoke retaliation, they prefer not to see things as they are, nor to probe too deeply into anything. Apathy and resignation are characteristic feelings in this group of people. Their psychodynamic problems are thus very much the same as those of lower-class blacks, although for slightly different reasons.

Goldfarb, independently, did a "blind" Rorschach analysis (that is, an analysis of the Rorschach tests without knowing the life histories, symptomatology, or any of the material from the psychoanalytic interviews) on the same subjects and concluded:

...a summary of ratings of intellectual status on the basis of Rorschach Test results indicates that all the subjects are assayed as average or better. However, 92% of the group give evidence of reduced efficiency and incomplete utilization of potential capacity.

Profound anxiety is hypothesized in all the records. Life is viewed as dangerous, hostile, and assaultive. They feel small and inferior; and they have a persistent fear of mutilation and destruction.

Another universal trait in this group is a sweeping, pushing, impelling hostility or aggressive inclination. Equally conspicuous in all the subjects is their inability to give free rein to their assertive and aggressive drives and destructive impulses. These impulses are a source of conflict and disability; and they are not accepted complacently. The subjects are tense and strained and they sit uncertainly on the lid of a turbulent and explosively simmering cauldron of hostility. They expend great energy in containing and controlling aggression. Yet always, it remains a problem to them.

Their defenses against their intolerable urge to hurt include denial or rejection of the impulse and the assumption of a cool, reserved exterior. Of importance is the defensive adaptation of ingratiating compliance observed in all of the subjects. They tend to be passive, submissive, and resigned to their dangers and insecurities. Although they typically present the external features of social conformability, it is interpreted that they are all characteristically distrustful and suspicious. They tend to be isolated and in poor rapport with other humans.

In the individual test interpretations, a compelling keen desire for status is interpreted in 54% of the group. This wish manifests itself in such qualities as intellectual pretentiousness, cultural and aesthetic striving, wordiness, and the investment of great value in outward show and decoration. Verbal expression, too, is often highly valued though words may be used stiffly and awkwardly. While aspirations are elevated, potentialities are not well-fulfilled. Indeed the majority are prone to turn from difficult accomplishment and to be more comfortable with the simple and uncomplicated activity and life experience.

Finally, in 46% of the cases (7 of 13 males, 4 of 11 females), sexual maladjustment is conspicuous. This expressed itself in sexual conflict and uncertainty with regard to sexual integrity. In this group with manifest sexual problems, the men appear particularly confused with regard to their sexual role and they are perplexed and doubtful of their masculinity. (Kardiner and Ovesey, pp. 325-326.)

The consistency of these two separate analyses of two separate sets of data on the same subjects is striking. Kardiner and Ovesey add a number of relevant considerations in their final synthesis (pp. 331-335):

The failure of the black subjects to use their potential intelligence effectively is accounted for by their inner conflicts which make them unable to focus their attention or react spontaneously. The continuous struggle against expressing hostility, and the energy consumed in maintaining a fearful vigilance for any possible sign of hostility from others, are also invoked to account for the discrepancy between potential and effective intelligence. Of course, this lowered effective intelligence gets in the way of any efforts by a black person to achieve whatever goals he sets for himself, and thus reinforces the effects of the social barriers to success.

Kardiner and Ovesey report that both the aspiration of blacks and their drive to achieve are often high, but that the social barriers are so formidable that they are tempted to accept, in place of their real aims, symbolic substitutes that have, all too often, little to do with what they originally wanted. Thus, in the face of the near impossibility of moving up in the social ladder, a black may replace his original goal of higher status with a substitute goal of flamboyance. Even where the original goal is maintained and the original motivation is still strong, a black person may, because of his circumstances, feel satisfied to achieve a small fraction of his original aims. The authors, further, point to the high frequency with which blacks see mutilation in the Rorschach inkblots as indicating that the subjects felt that they were being disintegrated by forces which they could not resist, that the challenges of the outside world were overwhelming as compared with their own resources. This helpless feeling of being disintegrated by the onslaughts of the outer world is furthered by the fact that the defenses of blacks are so rigid that they cannot allow themselves the luxury of ordinary rage even when in pain. Kardiner and Ovesey suggest that anger in the blacks they studied must be denied, impersonalized, treated with aloofness, intellectualized, watered down, covered with attitudes of "everything's wonderful," or turned into wish-fulfillments.

The frequency of flexor responses on the Rorschach is interpreted as indicating a submissive attitude to which, they suggest, blacks resign themselves in order to escape having to be aggressive.

The authors see anger in blacks as being expressed only when it is displaced, as in competitive sports, where they suggest that this same aggression, displaced from its original instigators, accounts for the apparent proficiency of blacks. They even go so far as to suggest that blacks express not joy, but hatred, in dancing, and that their "hedonistic abandon" in singing or dancing represents a denial mechanism and not any feeling of well-being, joy, or happiness. (These conclusions deserve a degree of skepticism.)

In the psychoanalytic interviews, the middle and upper classes seemed to show a healthier emotional life than did the lower class, but in the Rorschachs there was no such improvement. In considering this discrepancy, Kardiner and Ovesey accept the Rorschach findings as being the "correct" ones. In the lower class there is little pressure to conform to middle class white standards, and the problems are played out more openly. For the middle and upper class black, it is important to conform to the accepted white ideal, and a great deal of control and attention is directed toward this end; it is necessary to appear to have a good middle class way of life. Although their way of life does present greater possibilities for an effective adaptation, and although they seem to act as if such a better adaptation were taking place, their problems in handling aggression, and especially their self-hatred, make impossible any real improvement. They appear on the surface to be better adjusted emotionally, but their inner life really is not any freer, and this, Kardiner and Ovesey believe, is why the lack of improvement comes clearest on the Rorschach.

The Thematic Apperception Test, or TAT, analyses produced substantially the same findings as the Rorschach. Several points, however, emerged with particular clearness. One of these was the increased use, among blacks, of the defense mechanism of denial. Another was the emotional equation: anger+control=no emotion at all. Lastly, the psychodynamic constellation underlying the sexual difficulties of the black subjects is traced out in lucid detail. The so-called "sexual" problems of these subjects seem to be the result largely of confused social roles. As stated earlier, the black woman looks to the man to play the same role in the family as any other man in the United States, namely, provider and head of the family. But the economic situation of the black woman is better than that of the black man, and he is unable to play this role. In the TAT's the hostility engendered in the black woman by the failure of her man to play the male role emerged clearly. He is resented because of failure to provide for his family, and is seen as irresponsible, exploitative, and dangerous. The black man, faced with the same situation, reacts by seeing women as masculine and authoritative. The TAT's revealed that he does not trust women, and, although dependent on them, he resents his dependency and may hate them for displacing him from his proper role.

The authors sum up their findings as follows:

> The major features of the Negro personality emerge from each (analysis, Rorschach, TAT) with remarkable consistency. These include the fear of relatedness, suspicion, mistrust, the enormous problem of control of aggression, the denial mechanism, and the tendency to dissipate the tension of a provocative situation by reducing it to something simpler or entirely different. All these maneuvers are in the interest of not meeting reality head on. (Kardiner and Ovesey, p. 337.)

The North and the South

Is there any reason to expect that these reported differences between whites and blacks will be the same as the differences between northern and southern blacks? Is it not possible that (1) these differences may be due to heredity, or (2) as has been suggested frequently by southern whites, the southern black lives under a consistent code of conduct which both he and the whites obey, and the caste sanctions only become a problem for the northern black who does not know what to expect, or (3) the difficulties involved in being a black in the United States, either North or South, are so great that the improvement in the situation in the North may be too slight in comparison with the remaining problems to have much effect on personality?

All of these are possible. But to the first objection one may point out that the hypotheses have arisen within a dynamic, environmentalist framework of theory and are consistent with what is already known about psychodynamics, whereas there is no known genetic basis demonstrable for most of these characteristics. If, in fact, northern and southern blacks are differentiated on the *same* traits as are whites and blacks, this will argue strongly for the environmental causation, since it is clear that the special restrictions on blacks are most heavy in the South, whereas there is no evidence that northern blacks possess "white-like" genes. (That argument, which has been maintained with respect to intelligence, will be reviewed below.) Further, if these are the results of environmental pressures, then the differences between northern and southern blacks should stand out at least as clearly in a pilot study comparison of northern whites and southern blacks as in a pilot study comparison of northern and southern blacks, though the latter are the populations upon which the differences will be tested. In the research reported later, both types of pilot studies were carried out to find characteristics that might differentiate northern from southern blacks, and the characteristics located were tested on additional samples.

To the second objection, namely, that southern blacks are not disturbed by caste sanctions, Frazier's comment (1957, p. 674) is apt:

Negroes who compose the lower caste do not accept the discriminations. . . . Race relations in the South represent an accommodation of external adjustment which always involves a latent conflict.

To the third objection, that the difference between North and South is trivial, one can cite Malzberg's data on psychosis rates in New York State. Blacks have much higher psychosis rates than whites, but this increase is due entirely to high rates among migrants: blacks born in New York State have the same psychosis rates as do whites. (The rates are, in fact, slightly lower, probably due to the differential age distribution.)

This increase is most striking for alcoholic and syphilitic psychosis (the black-white ratios are greater than 3.5 to 1), obviously due to social disorganization and lack of education. The functional psychosis, dementia praecox, and manic-depressive disorders, which are more directly related to emotional stress are also increased in relative frequency. (Black-white ratios are 2.0 and 1.5 to 1, respectively.) Thus, either southern blacks, or migrants, or both, are more prone to mental disease. Unfortunately, mental disease statistics from southern states are so inadequate that it is impossible to determine with any degree of accuracy the psychosis rates among non-migrant southern blacks. (The comparison between migrant and non-migrant northern blacks on psychosis rates has changed in the 60's, because of the changes in the North.)

It has been possible, however, to compare southern blacks living in the South with northern blacks with respect to one aspect of mental functioning —the one characteristic which has been extensively studied in relation to black-white differences, namely, "intelligence." The differences between northern and southern blacks are, in fact, in the same direction as the differences between whites and blacks. Insofar as the research reported later in this book comes up with positive results, the effect of even the degree of improvement which occurs in the North as compared with the South will have been demonstrated.

The intelligence controversy

It is worthwhile to review briefly what is known about black-white differences in intelligence. (Klineberg, Part II.) The consistent findings in a number of studies that, on the average, whites do better than blacks on intelligence tests were seized upon as evidence of an innate inferiority of blacks. (Although Binet, the founder of intelligence testing, had pointed out that intelligence tests were affected by environment, his successors seem to have forgotten this.) Doubt was cast upon this conclusion by the fact that northern blacks differed from southern blacks in the direction of white-black differences. In fact, the average score of blacks from some northern states on army intelligence tests were higher than the average score of whites from some southern states. But a new hypothesis was devised, that of selective migration—whereby it was "obviously" the more intelligent blacks who came North—so that innate differences could still be maintained as the true basis for the difference between whites and blacks as well as the differences between northern and southern blacks. Meanwhile, evidence accumulated for the effect of environment on tested intelligence. Further, the intelligence of blacks in the North was found to vary consistently with the number of years they lived in the North, while no consistent relationship was found between degree of white characteristics and intelligence among blacks.

The most decisive blow to the selective migration theory was dealt by Klineberg's study of the school records of 562 black migrants to the North from three different cities in the South. He compared their school record with the records of their classmates who did not migrate and found no significant difference.

In short, one can conclude that whites and blacks, and northern and southern blacks, do differ in average intelligence as measured, that intelligence tests are affected by environment, that the environments involved do differ in respects known to be related to intelligence test scores. One cannot conclude that there is *no* difference due to hereditary factors between the groups, but only that there has been no *demonstrated* hereditary difference, whereas there has been demonstrated an environmentally based difference of considerable magnitude.

These issues are raised anew in each generation. Most recently, Jensen and Shockley have received considerable publicity for their espousal of inmate intellectual inferiority of blacks, but their evidence and logic is essentially the same as that already discredited a generation ago (Morris).

Characteristics of the migrants

What are the characteristics of the black migrant? We have already seen that he is neither more nor less intelligent than the non-migrant. What, then, determined whether or not he migrated? Probably the most important determinant was whether or not he had any relatives or friends in the North. The most important motive for migrating is economic—to get a job. Migrants are more apt to be people without vested interests or close ties to the community. Migrants are more likely to be male than female, and single than married. They are likely to be in the 20 to 44 age range. Economically, they cannot be so well off that they have much property in their home town or so poor that they cannot afford transportation; the harsh vagrancy laws of the South tend to discourage poor blacks from attempting to travel unless, of course, they believe they can evade the law. Moreover, the law courts may act on behalf of plantation owners to prevent sharecroppers from leaving and, during World War II, war manpower regulations permitted southern farmers to hold farm laborers on the land as being necessary to the war effort.

The determinants of who will migrate seem to be diverse. There is no evidence that any particular type of individual is being selected, aside from the factors already mentioned. (Frazier [1949], pp. 180-182, 194; Klineberg, Part II, p. 39; Myrdal, pp. 195, 233-234; Rose [1944], pp. 65-66, 80.)

The problem

For those who would deal with any aspect of the Negro question, a more penetrating analysis than is commonly found among scholars today, concerning the Negro's actual problem, the sub-structure of emotional tensions, and the types of character formation resulting therefrom, must be obtained before constructive work of real import can be done in this field. (Cayton, p. 388.)

It is to this problem that we address ourselves.

Chapter IV

THE PICTURE ARRANGEMENT TEST

In view of Klineberg's conclusion, cited in the preceding chapter, that "completely satisfactory research in this field will have to wait until psychologists have devised more adequate measures for the study of personality," it is not surprising that the studies on which this book is based arose out of the development of a new technique for measuring personality, the Tomkins-Horn Picture Arrangement Test, or PAT. Prior to the development of the PAT, the methods of assessing personality which were generally considered most satisfactory were techniques like those employed by Kardiner and Ovesey: psychoanalytic interviews, Rorschach, Thematic Apperception Test (TAT). These tests consist of highly ambiguous situations to which one can respond in an endless number of ways. Whatever way someone reacts must then be interpreted by a highly trained specialist. The fact that a specialist must spend hours administering and interpreting the test for each individual obviously places a drastic limit on the number and geographical dispersion of people included in a study. The dilemma is obvious: either one abandons these techniques for something simpler and faster (in which case the relevant variables are not adequately measured) or the choice of subjects is so limited that even an enormous amount of work can produce, at best, only a "pilot study."

The PAT makes use of the same processes as those involved in the longer tests, but the services of highly trained specialists are obviated by eliminating the subjectivity of the interpretations. The interpretations of the possible responses are built into the scoring manual so that the test can be scored adequately by any reasonably intelligent clerk (with or without the aid of IBM machines), and can be administered in a short period of time by relatively untrained interviewers. There is, of course, some loss of information as compared with the longer techniques, but this loss is not so serious as to overshadow its advantages. (The main disadvantage of the PAT is that there are many aspects of personality which it does not attempt to measure; only a little over 150 characteristics are measured by the test.) Just what the difficulties were in developing such a technique, and how they were solved, will become clearer if we first consider what is meant by "personality," and what is involved in its measurement.

The measurement of personality

"Personality" has many definitions. As used by psychologists, it includes all aspects of a human being's behavior and thought. The definition generally accepted by psychologists is that of Allport (1937, p. 48): "the dynamic organization within the individual of those psychophysical systems that determine his unique adjustments to his environment." In other words, all of the subject matter of psychology becomes the concern of the student of personality. The sole distinguishing criterion is that the individual human being is taken as the unit of conceptualization. As a result, certain aspects of behavior which receive insufficient attention elsewhere become stressed: the organization and interrelation of characteristics within the functioning individual, motivation, unconscious processes, fantasy, defense mechanisms, psychopathology, etc.

The measurement of personality becomes, consequently, the attempt to measure some few out of the infinite number of dimensions which may be invoked to describe and predict human behavior. Each of these dimensions represents a way of thinking about behavior; our present theories of personality are not yet so adequate that we have found the concepts which most adequately predict and describe human behavior with the fewest dimensions. For many years to come, we shall simply have to try various "bets" as to which concepts will be most useful, and see which of them pay off.

Once we have decided on the concepts we wish to use, there remains the problem of measurement, of devising situations that are best suited for assigning values to individuals with respect to these concepts. To take a physical example, a ruler, a tape measure, an automobile mileage indicator, and triangulation are used to measure length; which of these techniques is best depends on the object whose length we wish to measure. Measurement, as used here, does not require any specified number of possible values. For some concepts, such as length, there may be an infinite number of possible values; for others there may be as few as two. For example, a gauge which separates pipes into two categories—those more than six feet long and those less than six feet long—is still "measuring" length.

Logically, one would begin by deciding what concepts one is interested in, and then devise situations that would best measure them. Historically, however, the concepts used in the study of personality have generally arisen from the technique of measurement.

Some of the most fruitful techniques in the history of psychology have been the techniques of the psychoanalyst: free association and the closely related techniques of dream interpretation and observation of transference reactions. With these techniques data were obtained which made possible the constructs of classical Freudian and later psychoanalytic theories. These theories in turn provided the foundation for almost all our present-day theories of personality.

The technique of free association consists in asking the patient to speak his thoughts aloud without reservation. He is to continue without further prompting from the analyst, and he is to scrupulously avoid holding back anything on the grounds that it is "bad," foolish, unimportant, or irrelevant.

In a sense, free association is a prototype of most so-called projective techniques of measurement. A situation is used which may be structured in an infinite number of ways. The difference between individual reactions in this situation can be attributed to the difference between people in characteristics that they carry around with them in other situations. The situation is arranged so as to allow for reconstruction of what it is in that particular person which causes his responses to differ from those of other people. Although the technique has led to the development of Freudian notions, it can be employed equally profitably by investigators using alternative theoretical frameworks.

Such "projective" tests might better have been called "structuring" tests; while some of them make use of the psychological mechanism of projection (whereby an individual attributes his own feelings, motivations, characteristics, etc., to other people), many of them do not. All these tests make use of incompletely structured situations which the individual structures, thereby revealing himself.

The most popular of the projective tests has been the Rorschach (Rorschach; Beck; Klopfer and Kelley), whereby the subject is asked what he "sees" when looking at a set of inkblots. The responses are easily conceptualized in terms of what part of the inkblot is used, what determined this particular response, and the quality of the response (how closely what the subject "sees" fits the stimulus, how frequently other people see the same thing, how well organized a picture it is, etc.). This led to a set of concepts for characterizing personality which differed somewhat from the psychoanalytic variables. For instance, Rorschach's concept *Erlebnistypus* (experience type) is concerned with the degree to which one's experiences are determined by stimulation from outside as opposed to inner determinants. It is possible, however, to translate a description in these terms into a description in terms of psychoanalytic theory. It is even possible to analyze the Rorschach in terms of content instead of the above "formal" qualities and to arrive at the psychoanalytic variables more directly. The latter analysis is usually performed as a supplement rather than a substitute for the "formal" analysis.

The next most-used projective technique is the Thematic Apperception Test (Murray et al.) in which the subject tells stories based on pictures. There are many variants of this (CAT, Blackie Test, Four-Picture Test). The original TAT consists of a standardized set of 20 plates, 19 pictures, and one blank card, with alternative pictures on some plates for male and female or for adults and children. The subject is given one picture at a time and asked to tell a story about it. There are many ways of analyzing these protocols; they are as flexible as free association in this respect.

Murray and his co-workers developed a special vocabulary, the *need, press, thema* terminology, in their attempts to find maximally useful concepts for the analysis of this type of protocol. Their basic variables are needs (a person's internal motivational states) and presses (aspects of the environment which have a facilitating or obstructing effect on an individual). Their basic unit of analysis is the thema: a sequence of activity consisting of the interaction of one or more presses with one or more needs and the subsequent resolution. The stories are analyzed in terms of recurring themas. Tomkins (1947) presented one of the most comprehensive and detailed rationales for the analysis of TAT protocols, a rationale based on searching for the constancies which the subject imposes under differing circumstances (i.e., in stories told to different pictures). He considered in detail the problem of assessing the psychological level at which tendencies within a given person operate and the relative strength of opposing tendencies. The one major omission is any consideration of the stimulus value of individual pictures; they are simply treated as a roughly random sample of all possible situations. Although Tomkins does not restrict his analysis to the use of the particular needs and presses postulated by Murray, he does make use of the thema as his unit of analysis in the sense that the variables he uses may all be seen as abstracted sequences of activities, which are postulated to occur again and again in the psychological life of the subject. An analysis such as that outlined by Tomkins is extremely painstaking, time-consuming, and laborious. It is not surprising that more cursory and, consequently, more superficial procedures are often employed, which waste a good deal of the information in the protocol; thus the TAT as generally used falls far short of its theoretical potentialities.

But there is a more basic and general problem in the analysis of TAT protocols than the limitation of time. Psychometricians refer to the problem as scorer reliability (Gulliksen, pp. 211-214). Given the same protocols, different scorers, especially if their experience is limited, will not come up with identical interpretations. Clearly, they cannot all be right. The inability of the scorers to agree with each other places an upper limit on the validity of their inferences. This upper limit is, in some cases, quite low. The unreliability derives from the subjective nature of the inferences about what is going on in the person tested as well as from the differences in the theory, training, and experience of the scorers.

There is one major type of disagreement in interpretation which must not be confused with unreliability. From the infinite number of possible personality characteristics, two investigators may choose to score different variables. The interpretations, if correct, will then be different but compatible. It is probable that it is more the human inability to conceptualize than the lack of richness of the protocol which limits the number of aspects of a human being about which it is possible to gather information from the TAT.

The obvious way to reduce scorer unreliability is to develop objectively scored projective techniques, ideally, such that can be machine-scored, or, the next best thing, that offer scoring categories which are so explicit that they can be scored reliably by any clerk with training. Both lines of development have been attempted with various projective tests, including the TAT. But there is danger of eliminating what may be the specific source of the power of projective techniques when the subjective element is eliminated from the scoring. To go back to our prototype, free association, it has been an accepted dictum of psychoanalytic technique that a proper use of free association requires that the analyst make use of his own unconscious as well as conscious processes in arriving at his interpretation. The practitioners who have had the most experience with free association feel that the best inferences are drawn from the data when the interpreter makes use of processes whose nature he cannot verbalize, let alone objectify. (The *results* of such processes can, of course, be objectively verified. We can test the validity of an inference, whether or not we can describe the process by which that inference was drawn.)

Nevertheless, the idea of an objectively scored projective technique is enormously appealing. One of the efforts to develop such a technique has resulted in the Tomkins-Horn Picture Arrangement Test, or PAT. Whereas the TAT attempts to gather material about all aspects of personality, the PAT includes stimuli which deal with only a limited set of variables. In place of the more ambiguous single picture which is the stimulus for the TAT, the PAT substitutes a set of three line-drawings which are far more clear-cut in focusing upon a particular situation. In place of the lengthy story which the subject is asked to tell or write in the TAT, he indicates his resolution of the stimulus situation by placing the three pictures in order (which may be scored perfectly objectively) and by writing only a one-line description of each picture.

But what distinguishes the PAT from other attempts to develop an objectively scored projective test, and accounts for its unusual effectiveness, is not the nature of the stimulus materials so much as the rationale on which it is based. Its rationale is essentially the same as that of the TAT, but there are a few modifications to allow for objective scoring. This modified rationale (Tomkins, 1955) brought the solution to the problem within reach. Since then Tomkins and Miner have undertaken the work necessary to the development of the PAT as a workable, useful, objectively scored projective test. It is the resulting measuring technique which is employed in the research reported in this book.

The rationale of the PAT

The philosophical assumption that mental processes are rigidly determined, though essentially untestable, has been widely accepted by personality psychologists. Whether or not it is "true," it has proved to be a valuable working assumption insofar as it has led to the investigation of the determinants of phenomena which, at first glance, seemed undetermined. Most notable is, of course, Freud's research into the determinants of errors, dreams, and pathological symptoms. But the assumption of rigid "psychic determinism," which led Freud to such brilliant discoveries, has led other personality psychologists astray, and has done so in the field of projective testing. For, implicitly, a conclusion has been drawn whose defective logic is obvious when explicitly stated: if all behavior is rigidly determined, then any behavior may be used to discover the determinants. Clearly, whether or not any event, psychological or physical, is determined does not depend on any observer's ability to unravel the determinants. The task for projective testers is not to devise situations in which there are differences between individuals, but to devise situations in which the differences in behavior are such as to readily reveal the differences in underlying determinants. Not all behavior in the test situation is of this sort.

Further, not all determinants of behavior are of interest to the user of projective tests; for insofar as it is a *test*, the technique is designed to reveal determinants which are not the same for all individuals. If, for example, breathing is universal, then it is valueless to be able to say from a test protocol that any particular subject breathes.

Information about universal determinants is useful to the investigator only if he can conceptualize individuals for whom it would not hold. Even then he must be careful about his techniques of investigation. No one would seriously consider as evidence of the existence of a love for one's mother or a hatred for one's father the fact that such themes will occur in stories written by subjects who have been explicitly instructed to tell a story in which a boy is in love with his mother and hates his father. The situation is too structured; the subject can do very little other than give such a story. We would be much more willing to infer that a person had these feelings if, in an apparently unstructured situation (e.g., where he apparently had an infinite number of alternative possibilities), he told a story about a little boy who loved his mother and hated his father, as, for example, in a free association session or in response to the blank card on the TAT.

What do we mean by a structured or an unstructured situation? We mean either that, in the opinion of the investigator, the situation is or is not structured, or that, empirically, most people do or do not manifest the same behavior in that situation. If we wish to investigate a phenomenon that may be universal, we have no alternative but to use the first criterion, despite its pitfalls. Since the psychological world of every individual (including psychological investigators) contains certainties which may be certainties for no other person (Kilpatrick), the use of such a criterion is hazardous. Even free association is structured by the attitudes of the analyst, the expectations of the patient, and even the patient's bodily position (e.g., lying down predisposes to the production of passive and child-like material). The second alternative avoids this difficulty, but its use precludes any investigation of universal processes (except, of course, for qualitative and quantitative variations among individuals).

Fortunately, universal determinants are not of importance to the user of a diagnostic *test*. Here free association has proved a false guide to the construction of projective tests, for, as generally used, free association is not a diagnostic but a therapeutic instrument. The psychoanalyst is interested in reconstructing those determinants of the patient's behavior and thought that are strongest; most of these are not unique to any one patient. The analyst is interested in discovering them in such a fashion that the patient will be able to gain a sense of conviction about them which is based on the patient's ability to adapt to reality, and not merely on suggestion (i.e., transference). All of this is irrelevant to the diagnostician who wishes to know the things which differentiate one person from another; hence he may safely use the responses given by a standard reference population to determine the degree and nature of the structuredness of a situation.

It has been pointed out that only an extremely unstructured situation is appropriate for investigating universal determinants. If the same were true of individual differences, there could be no solution to the problem of devising an objectively scored projective test; such a technique requires that the possible alternative structures be built into the instrument, so that the number of alternatives must be finite and relatively small, and the situation, to that extent, structured.

Another possibility remains, however. Just as it is very rare that any situation is completely unstructured in the sense that the response of every subject is different from that of any other subject (recognizing that which is called the "same" or "different" depends upon the ability of the observer to discriminate and categorize and not upon the uniqueness of the response as experienced by the subject), so it is equally rare that any situation is completely structured in the sense that every subject gives the same response.

Let us again consider the case of instructing people to tell a story about a little boy who loves his mother and hates his father. If one thousand male subjects of normal intelligence, hearing, and vision had these instructions read to them as well as printed on the sheets on which the stories were to be written, we can well imagine that almost all subjects would write stories which included all the elements mentioned in the instructions. If all but one of the subjects did this, we could say that the situation was highly structured, and describe the nature of the structure by describing these themes. We could say practically nothing about the 999 subjects. But with respect to the remaining subject who, let us say, has told a story about a little boy who hates his mother and hates his father, we may reasonably infer that some strong inner determiner of behavior must have been activated for him to avoid the structure which seems, according to the behavior of the others, so strongly determined. From what is known about the way the human mind operates, it would be inferred that the person tends to avoid the feeling of love toward his mother, and possibly, the feeling of love in general, because such an emotion seems to him to be, in some way, dangerous. We thus see that more or less highly structured situations may be used projectively to make inferences about the important determiners of behavior for those individuals who avoid the strong structures.

Therefore, it is possible to use an objectively scored technique if one is willing to throw away, without interpretation, the responses given most frequently. This is the procedure that was adopted with the PAT. It seems wasteful, since one makes statements about only a small percentage of people from their response to any particular plate (set of three drawings). Of course, by using twenty-five plates, the percentage of the population giving a rare response on some plate becomes much larger. But we can go further than this by considering the pattern of responses across a number of plates. Inasmuch as there are six possible responses (sequences of the three pictures) to any plate, the total number of different configurations possible across the twenty-five plates is 6^{25}, or 284×10^{17}, most of which would be rare indeed in any given population. For practical purposes it is, of course, unfeasible to consider each of these 284×10^{17} configurations in advance and build in their interpretation. Then, too, whatever the potential interpretability of the configurations, there exists no human being with the psychological understanding necessary to interpret all of them.

The practical solution to the problem which was decided upon by Tomkins and Miner is as follows. Inasmuch as very few individual responses allow of an unambiguous assignment of a single underlying determinant as operating in all subjects who give that response, Tomkins and Miner constructed scales, each of which consisted of all responses across the twenty-five cards which had a specified personality characteristic as one of the possible determinants.

For example, if a subject had an extremely strong urge to work, he would, when given a choice between arranging three pictures so that the hero ends up working or arranging them in such a way that the hero ends up not working, tend to choose arrangements in which the hero ends up working. Conversely, someone with an equally strong urge not to work would tend to give the opposite ending. Of the twenty-five plates, fourteen include at least one picture of the hero working and at least one picture of him not working, so that it is possible to have the hero end up either working or not working. Two of these plates are 7 and 18. If we follow Tomkins and Miner's practice of denoting by O the picture in each set of three which has the circle next to it, by V the picture in each set which has the triangle next to it, and by L the picture in each set which has the rectangle next to it, we can denote arrangements of the pictures by sequences of the letters: LVO, OVL, etc. Then, arrangements VLO, OLV, LVO, and LOV on plate 7 would be included in the high work motivation scale, while arrangements VOL and OVL would be included in the low work motivation scale. Similarly, on plate 18, responses OLV and LOV would be included in the high work motivation scale, and responses VOL, VLO, OVL and LVO would be included in the low work motivation scale.

The test material has been so constructed that the underlying determinants which operate to produce the same response on one plate will operate to produce different responses on other plates. If the subject gives enough responses which have the same underlying determinant, we can presume that one (and not any of the alternative determinants) to be the determinant operating within him. The question of how many responses were enough was resolved by choosing a degree of rarity—5 cases in 100. A cutting point was established for each scale so that as close as possible to, but less than, this

7

18

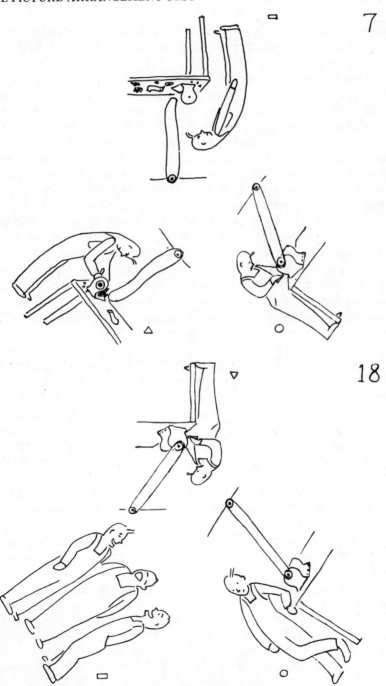

percentage of the reference population was beyond it. Each scale is scored as a dichotomy, that is, whether or not the person taking the test is beyond the cutting point.

To go back to the example of high and low work motivation, the cutting points for those two scales were found to be nine and eleven, respectively. Thus, in order to be scored as having high work motivation an individual must give an arrangement in which the hero ends working in at least nine out of the fourteen plates where it is possible for the hero to end either way; to be scored on the low work motivation scale he must give arrangements in which the hero ends not working in at least eleven out of the fourteen plates. Of course, more than nine out of ten people are scored as being extreme on neither scale.

The scales, as defined so far, do not take into account the differing rarities of the individual responses. Although some weighting scheme might have been evolved based on rarity, Tomkins and Miner chose to take account of rarities by separating the responses on each scale into three groups: populars, semi-populars, and rares. The original scale was termed the "a" variant, and the populars, semi-populars, and rares were termed the "b," "c," and "d" variants. Two more variants were devised for each scale by combining the "b" and "c" variants, populars and semi-populars, and by combining the "c" and "d" scales, the semi-populars and rares. These were termed the "e" and "f" variants. In the same manner as for the "a" variant, a cutting point was established for each of the other variants. It is obvious that it takes many more responses to pass the cutting point on the "b" variant than on the "d" variant, and the use of equally rare cutting points confers a degree of comparability between variants. Not all variants exist or can be scored; no variant is scored which has less than two responses or on which the most extreme number of responses is given by more than five percent of the reference population.

In the studies on which this book is based, only the "a," "d," and "f" variants were scored. An individual was considered extreme on a variable if he was extreme on any one variant of that variable.

The use of an empirically defined degree of rarity (that is, the frequency observed in an experimental population) to determine the cutting points raised the problem of what is an appropriate reference population. Tomkins and Miner decided that the "normal" population of the United States over the age of ten years would be appropriate. They arranged for the test to be administered to a nationwide Gallup sample. In addition to the PAT itself, the age, sex, vocabulary I.Q., education, geographical location, rural-urban residence, marital status, race, religion, occupation, social class identification, and the occupation of the head of the family were recorded for each subject.

Examination of the results revealed that the only variables which seemed to make a great deal of difference were age, education, and vocabulary I.Q. Consequently, Tomkins and Miner determined separate frequency distributions and cutting points on each scale for each of eight subgroups by age, each of six subgroups by education, and each of five subgroups by I.Q. They suggest a rough procedure for combining the three variables in scoring individual protocols. (The cutting point for each of the subgroups is, for most scales, very close to the overall norms. Instead of using separate norms, the protocols in this study were scored using the cutting points determined by the overall norms; the variables of age, education, and I.Q. were taken into account by a regression procedure. This was done in order to facilitate the use of machines in processing the data.) Thus, Tomkins and Miner's empirical reference population is that portion of the "normal" population of the United States which is of the same age, education, and I.Q. as the subject.

In addition to the scales, one aspect of the write-ins is scored. On certain plates, certain descriptions are regularly given by most normal subjects. The absence of such a description is taken to indicate a denial. For example, on plate 4, two of the three pictures are seen by most normals as dealing with a fierce physical fight. When a subject makes no mention of any fighting, aggression, or even bad feeling in either picture, this is scored as a "denial of physical aggression."

The descriptions of plates 4, 13, 16, 21, and 25 are scored by categorizing them into those which describe the threatening content of the pictures, those which deny it, and those which mute it. Muting is an in-between category which indicates that although the stimulus is not distorted, its significance is in some way "softened." For example, if a person recognizes plate 4 as a fight, but says it is an exhibition rather than a real fight, his response would be scored as muting. In this study, however, only the percentage of denials has been considered, and the subjects who mute have been classed with those who do not deny.

The scoring keys for plates 4 (physical aggression) and 16 (physical injury) are given in the Tomkins and Miner manual. Denials on plate 21 are scored on essentially the same basis as denials on plate 16, and no new scoring key is required.

Scoring keys for denials of aggressive press (plate 13) and for denials of symbolic aggression (plate 13 and plate 25) have not been published heretofore; therefore, a brief list of typical responses which would be scored as no denial, denial, and muting on those plates follows.

The testing materials

The PAT consists of twenty-five plates, each of which consists of a set of three relatively simple line drawings. The twenty-five plates are arranged into a booklet with one plate on each page, preceded by printed instructions and an illustrative example.

Each of these sets of three pictures is arranged on the page in the form of a circle, so that it is necessary to turn the page around in order to get them right side up. The circle arrangement is intended to suggest that any order of the three pictures is equally good.

In each set the pictures are identified by a symbol below them: a triangle (△), circle (○), or rectangle (□). In order to avoid any association of a particular symbol with a particular place on the page, the symbols were assigned randomly throughout the plates, so that the picture in any given position on the page is equally likely to have below it any one of the three symbols.

At the bottom of each page are three lines. The subject writes on the top line the symbol of the picture he places first, and on the remaining lines the other two symbols corresponding to their position in his story; he tells his story by writing a one-line description of each picture after the appropriate symbol.

SYMBOLIC AGGRESSION (Plates 13 and 25)

No Denial	Denial	Muting
The worker is angry at the boss	Injured in eye	He is not satisfied, he still is not, he is more satisfied
He apparently becomes angry and sticks his finger up to his nose	Dream of being boss	
	Worried about calling repairman	He is disgusted here
Worker sasses behind his his back by a gesture	He is tired out thinking what he had to do	Here is where the boss gave him a cussing
He thumbs nose at foreman	He is examining his nose	I ought to quit this lousy job
He was mad	He is crying; he's giving up	Gets burned up and quits
Tired working and mad at somebody	He is spying over something	His thoughts are unpleasant
Thinks what he would like to tell his boss	He blows his nose	He is thinking about the boss telling him off
Making face	He is studying about the job	Can't make up his mind whether to work or go home
Hands up yelling at someone	He is standing with his hands up	
I am going to stick until the boss quits	The man makes a salute and goes to work on a machine gun	

SYMBOLIC AGGRESSION (Plates 13 and 25) (Contd.)

No Denial	Denial	Muting
Because he cannot do it he blames foreman	Is thinking his appreciation of foreman's help	
Man feels he has been unjustly criticized	He done hurt his hand	
He has his back turned	I don't know whether he is preaching or praying; here I believe he is praying	
Throwing a face to boss		
He is expressing what he thinks of the boss	Man in deep study	
He dislikes it	He is wiping his face	
He's seeing another man he don't like	Friend is looking at man	
	Thank the Lord, I made it	
	Hands in his pocket and worried about something	
	Thinks of home	
	He thinks boss man is right and is not angry	

PRESS AGGRESSION (Plate 13)

No Denial	Denial	Muting
Foreman telling he's doing something wrong	Boss gives him lecture on safety first	Boss changes work plans
Employer scolding	Boss is giving him helpful criticism	Standing there, boss tells him he has to work, works.
Boss is mad at him	They are talking about something	Working, boss comes along, man gives up, can't satisfy him
The boss is getting in this man's hair	Foreman gives him good advice	He is just dreaming they are having an argument
Boss tells him he's fired	Asking advice from partner	They are discussing a problem
Boss is bawling him out	Asking advice from boss	
Foreman gives him heck	The boss comes and helps him again	
Boss gives him the devil	One comes where the other is working and talks to him, he told him to go to work, he finished and leaving	
Boss told him he made a mistake		
Boss is hot under the collar	He is talking to him concerning machine	
Boss gives him a piece of his mind	This man is giving him a job	
One is the boss and he is telling the other off	The mechanic telling him everything OK	

The instructions which are printed in the test booklet read as follows:

This is an experiment to see how well you can arrange pictures so as to tell a story that makes sense.

Each page contains a set of three pictures. Each of the three pictures has a mark at the bottom of the picture; one is marked Δ, another is marked □, and another is marked O.

Your job is to put one of these marks on each of the three lines at the bottom of the page in the order which makes the best sense. Following each mark write one sentence which tells the story.

You will have to turn the booklet around to see the different pictures.

Now turn the page and you will find a sample showing just what you are to do.

Study the sample and then turn to the next page with the set of pictures numbered 1. Fold the booklet so that you have just this set of pictures in front of you and write down your answer using the three marks and a short sentence following each. After you have finished with 1, turn the booklet over and go on with the set numbered 2, and so on for the rest of the experiment. There are twenty-five sets of pictures in this experiment.

Be sure you understand just what you are to do.

Now turn the page and go on with the experiment.

In addition to the PAT booklet itself, the testing materials consist of a vocabulary scale and background questionnaire. The vocabulary scale used was the Thorndike-Gallup Vocabulary Test, a twenty-item multiple-choice vocabulary test devised for public opinion studies. The background questionnaire varies from sample to sample, but it must include the subject's age and education for the PAT protocol to be interpretable. The other variables included in the questionnaire will depend on the purposes for which the data are being collected.

Administration of the PAT

The PAT may be administered individually or in groups. The administrator need not be a highly trained specialist, and the total administration may take as little as half an hour of the subject's time. The test is not timed, and the subject should be given as much time as he needs. (In the case of psychotics this has sometimes meant as much as ten hours stretched over a period of two weeks.)

As stated above, the rationale devised by Tomkins (1955) required that precise normative data on the normal population be available. Consequently, Tomkins and Miner undertook the procurement of a nationwide representative sample of the normal population of the United States.

The gathering of this Gallup standardization sample made possible the studies in this book. For the first time projective test protocols of normal subjects, blacks and whites, of all ages and backgrounds, and from all sections of the country, were readily available. The first part of the research was carried out entirely with cases drawn from the Gallup data.

Tomkins and Miner have described their procedure in a good deal of detail; they describe the administration of the PAT as follows:

The normal sample was collected by the interviewers of Public Opinion Surveys, Inc., of Princeton, New Jersey.... Interviewers were assigned selected areas or clusters of blocks and were required to work within the boundaries of such areas, where they chose respondents on the basis of quota assignments by sex and age.... [The original sample was deficient in certain categories and 396 additional respondents were interviewed so as to fill out the deficiencies.].... In all, 1,896 completed protocols were obtained from which a representative sample of 1,500 cases was selected. The survey included 329 sampling areas in 228 localities (cities, towns, and counties). In each sampling area from five to seven interviews were assigned.

The standard interview consisted of the PAT, a 20-word multiple-choice vocabulary test, and a group of cross-section questions. The time required to complete these varied from 45 minutes to 2½ hours per respondent. In a few cases the interviewer was unable to get responses to all 25 PAT plates on the first call and had to return at a later date to complete the interview. Only complete protocols were accepted for the final analysis.

The interviewer introduced himself as follows:

"I'm an interviewer for the Gallup Poll. We're making a nation-wide survey for a group of leading psychologists on a picture-arrangement experiment. Is there a table inside where we can go over this together?"

After being seated the interviewer opened the test booklet to the sample page and gave the following instructions:

"This is an experiment to see how well you can arrange pictures so as to tell a story that makes sense. Each of the three pictures has a mark, or symbol, at the bottom. One is marked with a triangle, like that one (pointing to the triangle at the bottom of the picture on the sample page with that symbol), another is marked with a circle, like that one (pointing to the circle at the bottom of the picture on the sample page with that symbol), and the other is marked with a rectangle, like that one (pointing to the rectangle at the bottom of the picture on the sample page with that symbol). For each page, give me the symbol of the drawing which should come first, then the symbol of the drawing which should come second, and then the symbol of the drawing which would come last. Then, tell me the story for that page, using one sentence for each drawing. You don't have to write anything.... I'll take care of that."

In a few cases (0.9 percent) the respondents insisted on writing down their own responses. The interviewers were instructed to take down the responses verbatim and not to assist the subjects in any way in interpreting the pictures. The only exception was in the case of illiterate subjects where it was necessary to read the very limited amount of written material included in the pictures. Occasionally a respondent would use the same symbol arrangement for a number of plates or adopt a position preference, such as always going from top to lower left to lower right. In such cases it was explained that the arrangement which makes the best sense may vary from plate to plate, and the subject was requested to start again. Occasionally these records slipped by the interviewers but every case of symbol and position preference was removed from the final sample. These preferences were most frequently found to occur throughout a whole record. However, they also appeared in portions of the test, usually at the beginning. Thus a subject might start out with a position or symbol preference and then after a number of plates change over to responding in terms of actual stimulus content. Occasionally these preferences were started in the middle of the record. All records with seven or more consecutive arrangements of this type were subjected to a special check; and unless the arrangements involved were largely those which had been found with a high frequency on the total sample, they were eliminated from any further analysis.

The vocabulary test . . . was introduced next as follows:

"We're trying to find out how familiar these words are to people. Will you please look at this card and give me the number of the word that seems closest to each word in capital letters."

Again, responses were recorded on an answer sheet. In the case of illiterate subjects the test was given orally. If the respondent obviously had difficulty in using the English language, due to a lack of exposure to it, and spoke some other language fluently, no intelligence score was computed. All subjects were urged to guess if they did not know a word. If a test was not completed, a correction for not guessing was added to the total score according to the number of words skipped. Utilizing a chance expectancy, we added nothing if two or less words were left out, one for three through seven, two for eight through 12, three for 13 through 17, and four for 18 or more. In 92.7 per cent of the protocols no correction of any kind was necessary.

The interview was terminated with a series of cross-section questions consisting of the last grade completed in school, occupation, occupation of the head of the family, marital status, religious preference, age, race, sex, rural-urban residence, and subjective class identification.

In conjunction with Tomkins and Miner, I had gathered additional data on high school students from various parts of the country to check on the adequacy of the norms for that group. It was possible, therefore, to choose two northern and two southern communities from those in which high school students had been tested; ninth-grade black students in the selected communities were used as the final samples for the studies in this book.

The high school samples had been gathered by group administrations, generally carried out by the local school authorities.

The directions given to the subjects and to the administrators varied slightly from place to place. A typical set of directions read as follows:

TO THE ADMINISTRATOR

Inside the front cover of each PAT booklet, there are a set for background questions and a vocabulary test, each on a separate sheet. Each set of materials bears an identifying number just in case the subject forgets to write his name on one of them.

The background questionnaire has been rewritten so as to be more suitable for high school students. Question 6 (social class identification) may be difficult for them; it is not worth taking too much time with, get them simply to put down their best guess.[1] The background questions which it is essential to get fairly accurately are questions 1 (grade), 4 (age), 7 (city and state of residence), and 9 (city and state of birth).[2]

The vocabulary form, unfortunately, has some wrong directions written on it. (They are directions for oral administration.) However, it has been our experience that children will ignore these and follow the instructions which are given to them by the administrator.[3] They should be told to circle the correct answer and the example at the top of the page may be demonstrated to them. They should be instructed to guess if they do not know the answer.

With respect to the PAT itself, it should be emphasized that they may turn the booklet around as much as they please, and that they are not to skip any of the pages. They should be told they are *not* to use the same

---

[1] This sentence was eliminated, along with the question to which it refers, in localities where the school authorities objected to asking about social class.

[2] When questions were eliminated, the numbering was, of course, changed appropriately.

[3] These instructions read:

"Please look first at the word in capital letters on each line. Then look at the other words in smaller type on the same line and tell me which ONE of these words comes closest in meaning to the one in capital letters.

EXAMPLE

The correct answer in this example is number 4, since the word "animal" comes closer to "beast" than any of the other words.

IMPORTANT: Do only one line at a time, and please take each line in order. Call off the word you are referring to first, and then the number of the word on the same line that you think comes closest to it."

For later samples the directions printed on the vocabulary test were changed by eliminating the last sentence, and changing "and tell me which" to "and put a circle around the". For these samples, the first part of this paragraph of the instructions to the administrator was eliminated, and the remainder suitably rewritten.

order of symbols (e.g., △○□, or ○□△) on every card, and they should also be told that they are *not* to give the same order of positions (e.g., lower left-hand picture, then lower right-hand picture, then upper picture) for all pages. We have found that a considerable proportion of high school students will do one of these two things unless they are specifically instructed not to.

The order of the administration is not crucial, although it is a good idea to give the PAT while the subject is still fresh. It is essential to get as many complete sets of materials as possible (incomplete sets are of very little real use to us). The PAT should be administered at one sitting, but the vocabulary test may be completed at a different time if necessary. The order of administration we recommend is background data first (inasmuch as this might require special instructions or the answering of questions), then the PAT, then the vocabulary scale. A set of instructions follows. It is intended as a model; you should feel free to alter the wording as you see fit.

INSTRUCTIONS

"Does everyone have a pencil?

"You are going to be passed out a booklet like this (holding one up). When you get it, write your name on the outside at the top (pointing to the top of the page)."

(Pass out booklets.)

"Now inside the first page of the booklet you will find two sheets of paper like this (takes them out). Take them out and write your name at the top of each sheet.

"Put away this sheet (the vocabulary test) and take the sheet that says "background questions" at the top (holding up that sheet). Put your name at the top and fill out the rest of the sheet. Today's date is _____. Write your grade on line 1. (Give directions slowly enough so that the students can keep up with you.) Write the kind of work your father does on line 2, and the kind of work your mother does on line 3. If your mother does not hold a job, write "housewife" on line 3. Write your age on line 4. Put a checkmark next to your religion. If it is not Protestant, Catholic, or Jewish, check Other and write in what it is.[4] Put a check mark next to your social class. If you do not know what your social class is, just make your best guess. It is not worth puzzling over. Just make your best guess.[5] Fill in the city and state where you live on line 7. Fill in the city and state where you were born on line 8. Now put a check mark next to White or Colored[6] and either Boy or Girl. If you live on a farm,

[4] These two sentences, as well as the question to which they refer, were eliminated in areas where the school authorities objected to asking about religion.

[5] These four sentences, as well as the question to which they refer, were eliminated in localities where the school authorities objected to asking about social class.

[6] In areas where the schools were segregated, this was changed to "Now put a check mark next to White (or Colored, depending on the school)." In localities where the school authorities objected to asking this question, it was deleted.

check Yes on line 10, otherwise check No.[7] When you finish turn to the booklet and read the instructions inside the first page.

(When everyone has finished the face sheet:)

"This is going to be an experiment to see how well you can arrange pictures to tell a story that makes sense. Each page has 3 pictures on it. You will have to turn the book around to see all of the pictures. The idea is to put them in order so that they tell a story that makes the best sense and to write down in a couple of sentences just what the story is. You can turn the book any way you like. Each picture has a symbol on it—a circle (draw them on the board, perhaps), a triangle, or a box. You are to put the symbol of the picture which goes first on the first line, the symbol of the picture which goes second on the second line, and the symbol of the picture which goes third on the third line. Then next to each symbol write a sentence which tells what is going on. For example, on this first page (holding up picture of the miner) this one goes first, this one goes second, and this one goes last (point to the appropriate pictures), so we put a triangle on the first line, a circle on the second line, and a box on the third line. Then next to the triangle we write, 'This is a man going down to the mine to work,' next to the circle we write, 'He is going down the elevator of the mine shaft,' and next to the box we write, 'He has finished his day's work and is going up the shaft.' Do the same kind of thing on every page. Look at only one page at a time and do not skip any pages. Remember, the idea is to find the order that makes the best sense. Do not use the same order of symbols on every page since the right order will be different on different pages. On some pages the triangle will be first, on others the box will be first, and on others the circle will be first. Do not always give the picture in any position on the page in the same order, because the right order will be different on different pages. Sometimes the first picture will be here, sometimes here, and sometimes here (pointing to them), and the second picture may be any one of the other two, so do not give the same positions all the time. Now turn the page and go ahead. Just put them in order and give a line after each symbol telling what is going on. You can turn the book around as much as you like. Do not skip any pages."

(When they seem to have finished the PAT, tell them to turn to the vocabulary test.)

"Now take up this sheet. It is a vocabulary test. After each word on the left, you will find five other words. Circle the one that is most like the one on the left. For example, at the top of the sheet you will see the word 'beast' at the left, and after it the words 'afraid, words, large, animal, bird'; put a circle around the word 'animal' since that comes closest to the word 'beast' of any of the words there. If you do not know the meaning of a word, guess, since a guess is more likely to be right than wrong. Your first guess is as good as any. Do not puzzle over them. Nobody is expected to

---

[7] In all the communities tested, it was possible to categorize the rural-urban residence dimension from the name of the city or town and the question concerning farm residence. In cities where none of the children could possibly be living on a farm, this sentence (and the corresponding question) was deleted.

know them all. if you don't know, guess. Do not leave any lines blank. When you have finished everything, put the other two sheets inside your booklet and hand the booklet in. Then you may leave."

The use of projective tests of personality with black subjects.

One question which may be raised is the one of whether projective tests of personality, such as the PAT, may be interpreted in the same way with black subjects as with white subjects. Will they interpret the pictures on the test as depicting whites or blacks, and does not this affect their reactions? In particular, if they interpret the pictures as showing white people, may they not respond in terms of some stereotype of what whites are like rather than identifying in any way with the hero of the pictures? This is complicated in the PAT by the fact that the pictures are simple line drawings on white paper, and hence the "skin" of the people depicted is white. Luckily, we do not have to speculate. Evidence on this question is available.

In studying another projective test of personality, the Sentence Completion Test, Hanfmann and Getzels found that white subjects were likely to be certain, when asked, that their responses referred to whites and not to blacks. But black subjects were not likely to be able to tell; they described their responses as applying to "people" in general. Of course, the Sentence Completion Test does not use pictures; it is therefore noteworthy that when Cook studied identification on the TAT, which does use pictures, by using alternative sets of pictures, one set depicting whites and the other set depicting blacks, he found that there was some difference in the results when examining white subjects, but none when examining blacks.

More recently, "blind" predictions from the TAT's of black psychiatric patients of their current functioning and of the length of their hospital stay in the six months following the evaluation were found to be highly accurate (Karon & O'Grady). Similarly accurate predictions were also made from Rorschach protocols (Karon & O'Grady; Long & Karon).

Chapter V

DESIGN OF AN EXPERIMENT

"What does it mean to be black?" was no longer an unsolvable problem. The data were available. To discover the differences in personality structure which result from the caste sanctions enforced against blacks, apparently all one would need to do would be to compare the responses to the PAT of two groups of people, one living under severe caste sanctions and one living under milder sanctions, as, for example, blacks and whites, or southern blacks and northern blacks, and see if there were any differences.

Unfortunately, it is not that simple to arrive at conclusions with any degree of assuredness. The development of the PAT solved one of the major problems holding back research in this area: the need for an appropriate measuring instrument. But there was an equally great stumbling block on which research had foundered in the problem of how to gather and analyze the data in such a way as to maximize the certainty of one's findings. These problems belong to the field of statistics, which, to many people, means something mysterious, confusing, or misleading having to do with numbers. The true flavor of the field is imparted by R. A. Fisher's statement that "there is something rather horrifying in . . . the doctrine that reasoning, properly speaking, cannot be applied to empirical data to lead to inferences valid in the real world" (p. 6). Statistics is simply part of the process of reasoning.

It is not the logic of this reasoning process, but the mathematical language in which it is expressed, that bothers those of us who are not mathematicians, since mathematics is, for the non-mathematician, a foreign language as incomprehensible as Greek, Latin, or Sanskrit. For the most part, the problems involved in this study, and the solutions that were devised for them, can be discussed in ordinary English. This chapter represents such a presentation.

Of course, there are good reasons why statisticians ordinarily use mathematical language, namely, its precision and lack of ambiguity. The description of the details of some of the procedures does require the use of technical and/or mathematical expressions, and these details are therefore presented in the last sections of this chapter so that those who have sufficient training in statistics may judge for themselves the adequacy of the techniques. These sections are headed by an asterisk (*) and may be skipped by those without such training, since the general argument will already have been presented.

One way to discuss the statistical problems is to consider the following questions:

1. Which groups should be compared?
2. Are the differences between blacks and whites hereditary?
3. Are there any differences between northern and southern blacks?
4. Are the differences due to chance?
5. Are there any other explanations for the differences?
6. What are the specific natures of the differences?

Which groups should be compared?

The problem is to determine the effects upon the human personality of the caste sanctions, the social pressures enforced against blacks, by comparing a group of people living under more severe caste sanctions with a group of people living under less severe caste sanctions. The obvious groups to compare would be a sample of blacks, against whom these sanctions are enforced, and a sample of whites, who live outside the caste sanctions. But any differences which might be found could then be attributed to heredity; there is nothing in the comparison to rule out that possibility. In fact, the bulk of the early research comparing blacks and whites was undertaken with the hope that hereditary characteristics would be revealed.

If, however, northern and southern blacks are compared, the differences may not be as striking, but the argument that the findings may be due to innate differences between blacks and whites can no longer be applied. Thus, a study of the effect of the caste sanctions should focus upon the differences between northern and southern blacks, and the differences between blacks and whites are irrelevant unless we can rule out the possibility that they were born different.

Are the differences between blacks and whites hereditary?

The question of whether blacks and whites inherit, in a biological sense, different personalities is of interest in its own right. The early research comparing blacks and whites assumed that the differences were, in fact, hereditary; more recently social scientists have grown skeptical of this assumption and tend to assume that any differences are the result of social pressures. In part, this reflects a general increase in skepticism about the evidence for genetic bases for most personality characteristics. In part, it is a generalization from the studies on "intelligence" where a socially based difference in intelligence test scores has, on the average, been found between blacks and whites, while no evidence has been found for a difference in the genetic determinants of intelligence. But, outside the area of intelligence, whether the differences are attributable to heredity or to environmental pressures remains a question that can never be decided by comparing blacks and whites.

At first, this seemed unfortunate, since both black and white subjects were available in the Gallup sample, and if the assumption were warranted that the differences in personality were due to the caste sanctions, the effects of these sanctions might be more clearly revealed by comparing blacks with whites than by comparing two groups of blacks. After all, northern blacks encounter the caste sanctions to some degree, though less than southern blacks, but whites encounter them not at all.

This consideration leads to a way of testing the assumption itself. If, on the one hand, the effects of the caste sanctions account for the differences in the personalities of blacks and whites as well as for the differences between northern and southern blacks, then whites will differ from blacks on the same characteristics that differentiate northern from southern blacks. If, on the other hand, there are hereditary differences in personality between whites and blacks, the differences will be found on characteristics which are *not* the same as those which differentiate northern from southern blacks. Thus, if we include in the research a comparison of a group of whites with a group of blacks, as well as a comparison of a group of northern blacks with a group of southern blacks, we will be in a position to test the assumption. But, again, we can conclude that the differences between blacks and whites represent the effects of the caste sanctions, only if the differences are also found in the comparisons between northern and southern blacks.

Are there any differences between northern and southern blacks?

If we compare a group of northern blacks with a group of southern blacks on some personality trait, it is an elementary statistical fact that we will almost always find a difference. Indeed, if we compare any two groups of people on almost any characteristic, such as height, weight, what they had for dinner, or how they feel about their parents, we will almost always find a difference. This is true even if we divide a group of people at random (for example, by tossing a coin) into two smaller groups which we then compare.

Are these differences real? Unquestionably, if we talk only about the five, ten, 50, or 10,000 people we actually observe. But if we wish to make statements which apply to anyone other than the people we actually observe, then the differences may or may not be real. And almost never are we interested in making statements which apply only to the people we actually observe.

To use an example, suppose we wanted to know which of two baseball teams was the better, and all we knew was the outcome of a single game. Most of us would hesitate to say that the winning team would prove to be better over the whole season, especially if the score had been close. We could definitely say which had been the better team in that game, but we would know that, even if their records over the whole season were identical, one of the teams must win any particular game. Furthermore, even the worst team in the league usually wins at least one game from the league leaders. If we were forced to guess which team would have the better record over the whole season, on the basis of the only game we knew anything about, we would pick the winner of that game but would not have much faith in our guess.

Similarly, if we compare a sample of southern blacks with a sample of northern blacks, we would guess that any differences we find between the samples might also occur between the populations from which the samples were drawn, but we would not have much faith in that guess, unless we can exclude the possibility that the difference was due to chance. (The word "sample" is used to refer to the people we actually observe, and the word "population" is used to refer to the larger group of people we are interested in.)

Are the differences due to chance?

Thus, the question has changed from "Is there any difference between northern and southern blacks?" (there almost always will be) to "Is there any difference between the samples we observe which is greater than that which would arise by chance?" This question is what is referred to by statisticians as testing the significance of the difference, and the significance level obtained is simply the probability that a difference as large or larger than the difference observed between the samples would arise by chance, that is, when the populations from which the samples are drawn did not differ at all. It is usual to choose some arbitrarily low probability, say five percent, and consider only differences which reach that level of significance as not due to chance.

To return to our example from baseball, although ordinarily we would not put much faith in our guess at the relative standing of two teams over the whole season, knowing only who won a single game, we would not feel at all uncertain if the score were sufficiently one-sided, say 25-0. We would feel that a score this overwhelming could only indicate a considerable difference in ability between the two teams. A statistician would agree with our increased faith in the difference between the teams, pointing out that a score as overwhelming as (or more overwhelming than) 25-0 has an extremely low probability of occurring if there is no difference between the teams, and therefore the difference is statistically significant. There is far less than one game in a hundred whose score is this one-sided, even when there is a considerable difference in ability between the teams, and such one-sided scores would be even rarer if the teams were matched in ability. Therefore, the difference between the teams is clearly well beyond the one percent level of significance.

The question of what significance level an observed difference must reach before we are willing to consider the difference as not due to chance is, of course, somewhat arbitrary. If we accept only extremely improbable events as significant, we decrease the risk of accepting a chance difference as real and increase our risk of overlooking real differences. Similarly, the larger the probability that we are willing to accept as the significance level, the greater our risk of accepting a chance difference as real, but the smaller the risk of overlooking real differences. In many fields, the one percent and five percent levels (i.e., one chance in 100 and five chances in 100 of occurring by chance) have proved to be convenient.

More convincing, however, both to the naive observer and to the trained statistician, than the fact that the difference reached any given significance level in a single experiment would be the finding that, when the experiment was repeated, the same results recurred. Similarly, we would be even more convinced that one team was better than the other if we knew that it had consistently won a series of games than if we knew it had won a single game by an overwhelming score.

When a statistician is "more convinced," he can generally translate this into his mathematical language of probability; there are techniques for "combining independent tests of significance" in order to obtain a level of significance for a whole series of experiments. For our purposes, it is sufficient to note that if we test a theory twice, and in each experiment the difference between the samples is as the theory predicts, then the *probability* of both experiments reaching a given level of significance, e.g., five percent, is considerably beyond that significance level. For example, when two independent experiments are both beyond the five percent level, that is, the results of each experiment have less than one chance in 20 of occurring by chance, then the probability of both occurring by chance is less than one chance in 400. Similarly, if each experiment separately had reached beyond the one percent level of significance, that is, if the results had less than one chance in 100 of occurring by chance, then the probability of two experiments *both* reaching beyond this level is less than one chance in 10,000.

These probability levels are not, however, the ones that would be obtained from any of the appropriate techniques for "combining independent tests of significance." The reason for this can be shown in an example. If one experiment had fallen just short of significance, e.g., reached the six percent level, and the probability of the results of the other experiment was sufficiently small, say, one chance in a hundred, we would ordinarily want to consider this result as being at least as meaningful a departure from chance as having both experiments just reach the five percent level. The techniques for combining independent tests should, and do, include in the final significance level the probabilities for all results we would consider as being as meaningful departures from chance as the results we obtained. The exact significance level of each experiment is used in the mathematical formulas. One appropriate technique for combining the results of two independent experiments yields as the significance level for two experiments which both just reached the five percent level, one chance in two hundred; for two experiments which both just reached the one percent level, one chance in 5,000. The important point is that these probabilities are still a great deal smaller than the significance level for each experiment separately.

In order to rule out the possibility that chance accounted for the findings of the research reported in this book, not only were the significance levels of each of the findings evaluated, but no less than three completely independent experiments were carried out, in each of which a sample of southern blacks was compared with a sample of northern blacks.

Here we may recall Klineberg's statement (Part III, p. 138) concerning research on black-white differences: "There is inconsistency in the findings and significant differences are rare." The study reported in this book was designed so that upon its completion we would know both the significance and the consistency of the findings. Any findings that met both of these criteria would merit serious attention.

If, of a series of experiments, all are significant, the set of experiments taken together are overwhelmingly significant. If some, but not all, are statistically significant, evaluation of the results is not as simple or straightforward, and some mathematical technique for "combining" significances will generally be necessary in order to draw any conclusions. Some understanding of the effect of repeating an experiment over and over can be gained from the following examples.

First, to return to baseball, if two teams were evenly matched in ability, the chance of either one winning would be one-half. If, therefore, we did not know the score, but knew which team had won a single game, we could not be at all sure that this was the better team. But if we knew that one team had won six games out of a series of six, we would ordinarily not hesitate to conclude that it was in fact the better team. However, if we knew that it had won six games, but had played a series of twelve and lost the other six, this would mean something entirely different, namely, there was no evidence of this team being superior.

Similarly, if we perform a single experiment and it reaches the one percent level, we would conclude that the results are extremely unlikely to be due to chance. If we perform 100 experiments, all of which are beyond the one percent level, we would consider the possibility that the results were due to chance as infinitesimal. If, however, only one experiment out of 100 had reached the one percent level, this would be precisely what we would expect, on the average, by chance, and we could not rule out the possibility that chance factors alone accounted for our results.

We are not faced in this book with the problem of evaluating the results of asking the same question in 100 experiments; but we are faced with the closely related problem of what happens when you ask 100 different questions in a single experiment. Just as, when we carry out 100 experiments, and find that one of them reaches the one percent level of significance, we cannot from this exclude the possibility that chance accounted for the results, so if in a single experiment comparing two groups, we ask 100 questions and find that for one of them the difference between the groups reaches the one percent level, we cannot on this basis alone exclude the possibility that chance accounts for the difference.

Of course, if we had asked only one question, then the probability level obtained would stand as appropriate. Moreover, if, when we had asked 100 questions and found one significant, someone were to ask us, "If there is a real difference between the populations on one of these questions, which question is it most likely to be?" we would choose the one that had been significant as the best guess. But we could not be sure that there were any real differences at all.

The problem of asking many questions must be dealt with in this study because personality is not a single characteristic but consists of many traits. Indeed, as mentioned in the preceding chapter, there are probably an infinite number of possible dimensions of personality, any one of which may differentiate northern from southern blacks. The PAT, the measuring instrument used in this study, includes over 150 of these characteristics, and it would be unreasonable to expect the caste sanctions to affect all of them. Undoubtedly, most personality characteristics are not appreciably affected; the problem is how to pick out those few which do relate to this kind of social pressure.

The usual technique for dealing with this kind of problem is to run two experiments, the first of which is called a "pilot study." In the pilot study, the differences between the samples on all of the questions in which one might possibly be interested are investigated in order to get ideas. Then, on the basis of the findings of the first study, those questions are selected which seemed to show the greatest differences. These questions can then be tested on new samples. Since there are only a few questions in the second experiment, the problem of asking so many questions that there are bound to be some which are significant becomes less troublesome.

For example, an investigator may believe that out of 100 questions he might ask, there are some, but certainly not all, which will differentiate his groups. Unknown to him, there is only one question which does distinguish the populations from which his samples were drawn. When he asks all 100 questions, he might find that two questions were significant at the one percent level. Although this is slightly more than the one question at this significance level which, on the average, would occur in such an experiment by chance, it is not sufficiently greater than one to exclude the possibility that the findings are the result of chance. If, however, he runs a new experiment testing only these two questions, and now finds that one of them still reaches beyond the one percent level, he might reasonably feel that he had a real basis for believing that what he now observed was not due to chance.

Since the purpose of a pilot study is to get ideas, or hypotheses, which will be tested later, it is appropriate to use, if one wishes, a much lower significance level than that which one would accept in the final research. Thus, in place of the conventional five percent and one percent levels of significance, the twenty percent level of significance was used in the pilot studies in this book. By using this significance level, even "hints" in the data would be picked up, thereby decreasing the chance of missing any real difference. Of course, the danger of finding differences due to chance was increased, but since all the findings of the pilot study were to be tested again rigorously in the final research, using the more conventional levels of significance, this was no problem.

Even the use of a pilot study, however, does not solve all the problems that arise when we ask many questions. Let us go back to the example of the experimenter who, on the basis of his pilot study, selects two questions out of 100, and then tests them in a new experiment and finds that one of them is beyond the one percent level. At that point the experimenter felt that he had a real basis for believing that chance did not account for his finding, but that no specific probability was given for the finding that one question was significant beyond the one percent level when two questions were tested. The reason is that no rigorous answer can be given unless the items are independent or the degree of dependency is known. (For a statistician, two questions are independent of each other only if, when one knows the answer to one of them, one is in no way in a better position to guess the answer to the other than if one did not know the answer to the first question.)

If the questions were independent of each other, the probability by chance that, when only two questions are tested, neither one will be significant beyond the one percent level is slightly more than .98. Therefore, if one of them is found to be significant at the one percent level, this finding has itself reached the two percent level. But this statement of probability holds only when the two questions are completely independent of each other, which they are not likely to be. None of the techniques for "combining independent tests of significance" are appropriate if there are any questions which are not entirely independent of each other.

To take an example of what happens when questions are not independent of each other, suppose that, among other questions, two groups of people are asked their height and weight, and both of these questions are found to significantly differentiate the two groups. It would be a mistake to consider that we had found two independent tests which reached beyond our level of significance. For, if the people in one group tend to be taller than the people in another, *even if the difference in height is due to chance* (as when people are assigned to the two groups by flipping a coin), then they are almost certain to be heavier.

This question of the relationship of one question to another will not make much difference in the interpretation of our results when we test only a couple of questions. But even after completing the pilot study, we may find ourselves with five, ten, or twenty questions we are interested in testing. And in that case the question of the degree of interdependence may drastically affect how sure we can be that chance did not give rise to our findings.

As in most research comparing two groups on many characteristics, the characteristics measured by the PAT are not completely independent of each other, but vary in their relationship to each other from some which are independent, to others which are positively related, and to still others which are negatively related. Insofar as the caste sanctions might be expected to affect more than one personality characteristic, it was necessary to allow for the eventuality that a number of characteristics would be revealed in the pilot study. In evaluating the results of the later experiments a technique was needed which would take into account the interdependencies, and assess the significance level of the differences between the samples on all of these characteristics taken together. Only if this overall test were statistically significant could we reasonably conclude, on the basis of the data, that there were any differences in personality characteristics between northern and southern blacks.

The technique used to appropriately combine all of the variables for an overall test was a simple one. It will be recalled that the characteristics measured by the PAT are not continuous variables but dichotomous attributes which either do or do not characterize a person. ("Height" is a continuous variable, while "blue eyes" is a dichotomous attribute.) The characteristics which, in the pilot study, seemed to be related to the caste sanctions would be combined by weighting them equally. Each person would be given a score of +1 for every characteristic he had which in the pilot study had seemed to be more frequent among people who lived under more severe caste sanctions, and a score of −1 for every characteristic he had which in the pilot study had seemed less frequent among people who lived under more severe sanctions. These +1's and −1's could then be added up for each person to give him a score which reflected the overall effect of all the variables simultaneously. This score, which will be referred to as the discriminant score, obviously must be higher on the average in any group in which these characteristics are more common than in a group in which these characteristics are less common. Thus, it is only necessary to show that the average discrimination score increased significantly with increased caste sanctions in order to show that overall the differences in personality characteristics are significant.

This technique is simple, easy to compute, and readily lends itself to the further statistical procedures that are necessary to exclude the possibility that there are reasonable alternatives to the differences in caste sanctions as explanations for the differences in personality. The chief disadvantage of the technique is that it is conservative, in the sense that there exists more complicated procedures which are more sensitive; in comparing samples from populations which do differ, the more complicated procedures would generally yield more extreme levels of significance. Nonetheless, it seemed reasonable to expect that if the caste sanctions had an effect on personality, the effect should be striking enough so that even the simple procedure would suffice.

Are there any other explanations for the differences?

The usual practice in investigating group differences is to compare a sample from each population in order to locate characteristics on which these samples differ, and then gather new samples, each drawn from the same population as one of the original samples, and test whether the same characteristics differentiate the new samples. In this usual procedure of cross-validation, the samples used to locate differences and those used to test these differences deviate from each other only by sampling error. It is unnecessary to relate one's findings to any explicit theoretical framework beyond the observations themselves; one can merely state that one has found something and then has found it again when the experiment was repeated.

In our experiment we can do better than this. If the differences between blacks and whites are due to the caste sanctions, then the two most widely separated groups would be a sample of southern blacks, who live under severe caste sanctions, and a sample of whites. The differences in personality due to the caste sanctions might be expected to stand out more clearly if we compare these groups than if we compare two groups of blacks. The pilot study, therefore, consisted of just such a comparison of whites with southern blacks. Of course, the validation samples, that is, the samples of people who were compared for the purpose of testing rigorously whether the characteristics which differentiate whites from southern blacks were due to the caste sanctions, had to be a sample of northern blacks and a sample of southern blacks, if we were to be able to exclude the possibility that hereditary differences between blacks and whites explained the findings.

Thus, in the present study, differences found in one situation, a comparison of whites with southern blacks, are tested in a different situation, a comparison of northern and southern blacks. The samples used to locate differences and the samples used for testing them differ by far more than sampling error; the only connection between the two situations is a theory which says they are related. Only with a theoretical structure which allows for generalization beyond the circumstances of the original experiment can such a research design be employed. Insofar as theoretical formulations play a greater role when such a design is employed, the theoretical implications of the results will tend to be more convincing than the results of a simple replication.

Of course, it is not true that all whites live outside the caste sanctions. The southern white is constantly concerned with the caste sanctions, and sociologists have suggested that he is as strongly affected by them as is the southern black. Although the effects of the caste sanctions upon southern whites would make a fascinating study in its own right, it is deferred to the Appendix to investigate this problem. Our concern here is to ensure that the effects of the caste sanctions on the personality structures of southern whites, the caste enjoying the upper status, do not mislead us in investigating the effects upon blacks, the caste assigned the lower status. It was therefore clear that southern whites should be eliminated from the white sample used in the pilot study, so that the white sample would consist entirely of whites whose lives are essentially untouched by these social pressures. It will be recalled that, while the southern white actively maintains the caste system, the northern white tries to avoid the black and the race relations problem, and is, in general, successful in these efforts. The northern white lives neither as the upper nor the lower caste in a caste situation; he lives outside the caste situation, and is therefore an ideal choice for one of the samples in the pilot study. (These statements obviously refer to the North and South of the 1950's.)

Let us suppose, however, that the assumption that the differences between blacks and whites are due to the caste sanctions is not warranted. In that case, characteristics located in the pilot study will not differentiate northern from southern blacks. Since we are interested in the effects of the caste sanctions, whether or not they account for the differences between blacks and whites, the research should include some way of studying these effects even if the assumption about black-white differences is not confirmed.

One way of doing this is to compare the samples used to validate the findings of the black-white pilot study, that is, the northern black sample and the second southern black sample, on all the characteristics measured by PAT, and use this comparison as a second pilot study. The characteristics which then seem to differentiate the two samples can be combined into a second discriminant score. We may now gather two new samples, one of northern and one of southern blacks. If the differences between blacks and whites are not due to the caste sanctions, the discriminant score determined from the black-white pilot study will again not differentiate the samples, while the discriminant score on the basis of the comparison of northern versus southern blacks will differentiate the samples.

On the other hand, if the assumption is warranted that black-white differences are due to caste sanctions, the discriminant score located in the black-white comparison will not only differentiate the first pair of black samples significantly, but it will also differentiate the second pair of black samples. In fact, it should differentiate the second pair of black samples at least as well, and probably better, than the discriminant score determined from the first comparison of northern and southern blacks, even though the comparison on which the discriminant scores are tested is of northern and southern blacks.

At this point, a critical observer might object: "You still cannot convince me that the differences you find will be due to the effects of the way blacks are treated as blacks. You may have been ingenious in testing the assumption that the differences between blacks and whites are innate, and, if they are not innate, using these differences to reveal the effects of the caste sanctions. You have provided another way of studying the effects of the caste sanctions if you find that black-white differences are innate. You have described the differences between a sample and a population, the problem of excluding chance variation as an explanation for the differences, and the way in which the problem is complicated when you compare groups on many characteristics instead of just one. I agree that ignoring these things accounts for many of the inadequacies of previous research. But there are problems you have not discussed which, as far as I can see, make your entire research worthless.

"You have told us that Tomkins and Miner found that the age, education, and intelligence of a person affect the way he responds to the PAT and must be taken into account before interpreting anyone's responses. But you know that southern blacks, northern blacks, and northern whites differ from each other, on the average, in the amount of education they have received, with southern blacks having the least education and northern whites having the most. How do I know that the differences you find are not simply the difference between educated and uneducated people, and have nothing to do with caste?

"Furthermore, when you discussed the intelligence controversy, you convinced us that the caste sanctions affect intelligence as measured by intelligence tests. Although I realize that there are people of very high and very low intelligence in all three groups, and that the differences among the people within any one of these groups is many times greater than the differences between the groups, nevertheless, on the average, the three groups come out in the same order on intelligence tests that they do on amount of education. How do I know that any differences you find are not simply the differences between more and less intelligent people, and again have nothing to do with the caste sanctions?

"Even when it comes to something like how old they are, the three groups are not the same. For example, people of certain ages occur less frequently among southern blacks and more frequently among northern blacks than they do among northern whites because of the heavy migration from South to North. How do I know that whatever you find is not simply the effect of the difference in ages?

"Even the ratio of the number of men to the number of women is not the same in all three groups, since black men are more likely to move North than are women. Surely you are not going to palm off the difference between men and women as being due to the caste sanctions.

"And while eliminating southern whites from the sample of people unaffected by the caste sanctions may have been necessary, don't you realize that all of the comparisons are now between a northern group, either white or black, and a group of southern blacks, so that any differences between the North and South might account for your findings? It is not enough to say that in the long run most of these differences are tied in with the caste sanctions—that is true, but the differences may affect personality in their own right. The South is less industrialized, and less heavily populated, and a larger share of the people in the South live in rural areas than do people in the North. This is particularly true when you consider northern blacks, since almost all northern blacks live in the big cities. How do I really know that what you will find is not simply that there is a difference between country folks and city folks?"

These are telling criticisms, and it would be a serious flaw in the design of the investigation if we could find no way to allow the observations to answer the question of whether such objections are justified.

Fortunately, there are much wider differences in these extraneous background characteristics among the people within each sample than there are between samples. We can therefore investigate the relationship between the discriminant score, which represents all the differences we are investigating, and each of these background characteristics *within* the samples; and only if we find some such relationship can we take seriously the possibility that the background variables account for the findings.

The age and sex of every person in the Gallup sample was known, as well as the extent of his education. We also knew where he lived, so that we could easily determine how rural (or urban) a community it was. The population density of the general area in which he lived could easily be determined, using the state as a unit of area broader in scope than the local community. The degree of industrialization could be determined from the percentage of the population employed in manufacturing industries, all of which information was readily available from the census. Finally, the "intelligence" of each person could be determined from his score on the Thorndike-Gallup Vocabulary Test, since a surprisingly close relationship has been found consistently between scores on well-constructed short tests of vocabulary and scores on the best full scale intelligence tests we now have (cf. Wechsler, p. 101; Miner).

We could examine the relationship of each of these background characteristics to the discriminant score. Only if the relationship was statistically significant need we be concerned with it. It was not likely that every one of these characteristics would be appreciably related to the discriminant score, but neither was it likely that none of them would be related. The effects of those background characteristics which were related would have to be taken into account in some fashion.

One way to do this would be to match the samples on the relevant background variables. Another, and better, way would be to determine their effect from the differences within the samples and to compute statistical corrections for the discriminant score on the basis of the effects of these background characteristics within the samples. The corrected discriminant scores would then not reflect the effects of the differences between the samples on the background factors, and any differences remaining could not be explained away on any such basis.

"Very well," our critic might reply, "but you have outsmarted yourself. Let me give you an example. The reason there is a difference between the groups in the amount of education is because preventing blacks from getting an education is part of the caste sanctions. Now, blacks who are most successful at getting an education may be most successful at circumventing other caste sanctions. If this were the case, you would find a high correlation between education and the discriminant score, even if education, in itself, had no effect on personality. When you corrected for this, you would be eliminating precisely what you wish to study, namely, the effects of the caste sanctions."

Again, the point is well taken. It is the effects of education *per se,* the differences between educated and uneducated people wherever they occur, that we wish to take into account, and not any interaction with the caste sanctions, such as that in the example of education. This type of interaction between a background characteristic and the effects of the caste sanctions might occur in any of the black samples. But there is one sample in which it cannot occur, the northern whites. These people live outside the sanctions, and the effects of the background characteristics may be determined from this sample without fear of mistaking the effect of its relation to the caste sanctions for the effect of the background factor itself. Moreover, the people in the northern white sample vary widely on all of these background characteristics, and it is by far the largest sample in the whole research, which bodes well for the sensitivity of the tests of significance for the background factors, and for the accuracy of the corrections which were determined for those that were significant.

Let us anticipate some of the findings. When the discriminant score was determined from the personality characteristics which seemed to differentiate northern whites from southern blacks in the pilot study, the relationship between this discriminant score and the background factors was examined, and the significance of each relationship within the northern white sample was tested.

Of the background factors, only age, education, and vocabulary intelligence proved to be significantly related to the discriminant score. Sex, rural-urban residence, population density of the general area, and degree of industrialization of the general area showed no appreciable relationship with the personality characteristics represented by the discriminant score. It will be noted that the three variables which had to be taken into account, according to our findings, were the same three variables which Tomkins and Miner indicate must be taken into account before interpreting the PAT.

The appropriate corrections for age, education, and vocabulary could now be determined from the relationship of each of these variables to the discriminant score within the sample of northern whites. The corrections for age were determined first. When the discriminant scores had been corrected for the effects of age, it was found that the relationship of education and of vocabulary to the corrected discriminant score had decreased. Both relationships now fell just short of the five percent level of significance; the relationships were so close to significance, however, that further corrections seemed warranted. Therefore, the corrections were computed for age and vocabulary simultaneously (since there is a correlation between age and vocabulary, it is necessary to recompute the correction for age). A new corrected discriminant score was now computed for each individual.

The relationship between education and this new corrected discriminant score, which had been adjusted for the effects of age and of vocabulary, was now examined within the sample of northern whites. The relationship was no longer appreciable; the correlation was nearly zero and did not approach statistical significance. Therefore, no further correction was necessary. Any differences we might find between the groups on these final corrected discriminant scores clearly could not represent the effects of the background variables.

"Well," our critic might interject, "that seems to take care of my objections. But, you know, I wonder whether I was entirely right. After all, if people with low intelligence have special problems no matter where they are, and if one of the effects of the caste sanctions is to lower intelligence, then these problems really are part of the effects of the caste sanctions, and you shouldn't have eliminated them by correcting for intelligence."

Luckily, this is one of those rare occasions on which you can have your cake and eat it too. For each experiment, the sets of results will be presented for the uncorrected discriminant scores, for the discriminant scores corrected only for the effects of age, and for the discriminant scores corrected for both age and vocabulary. You can choose whichever you feel is most meaningful, although Tomkins and Miner's rationale for the PAT would indicate the last are the most appropriate ones to consider. Since the corrections turned out to be relatively small, the conclusions one can draw would turn out to be the same, irrespective of which of these scores one chooses to consider.

"Something still bothers me. This business of correcting the discriminant score is pretty complicated. When you determine corrections from one sample to be used with other groups of people, how do I know that this is the right correction for the other groups? If the correction you would compute from the other groups is different from the one you are using, you shrug it away as an 'interaction' with the caste sanctions, but aren't there other reasons why they might differ? I don't know very much about statistics, but it seems to me that I have heard somewhere that such things can happen."

Such problems do arise, and it is reasonable to ask whether, in the absence of any interaction with the caste sanctions, the corrections determined from the sample of northern whites would be the same as those determined from the black samples, or whether the two sets of corrections would still differ, in which case our procedure would become questionable. Furthermore, in view of certain characteristics of the samples, there are good statistical reasons for raising this question. Although a discussion of this is deferred to the starred (*) sections at the end of the chapter, we may note at this point that it was possible to demonstrate that, in the absence of an interaction with the caste sanctions, the corrections determined from the white sample were in fact appropriate for the others.

Our critic, again: "It still seems complicated to me. Wouldn't it have been better, and a lot simpler, if you had matched the samples on the background variables instead of going to all this trouble?"

It would have been simpler. But matching samples on background characteristics is a wasteful procedure, since you have to start with large numbers of people in order to be able to select small groups of people who are matched. Further, it may not be possible to select matched samples, especially if they are to be matched on more than a few characteristics. The research was planned so that no matter how many background characteristics it proved necessary to take into account, the investigation could still be carried out. If we had tried to match samples of black adults, we would find ourselves selecting from northern blacks a sample of the less educated and less intelligent while selecting from southern blacks a sample of the more educated and more intelligent. It would then be questionable how far one might generalize the findings from such a comparison. By using the technique of adjusting the discriminant score, it is possible to compare samples which resemble on all the background characteristics the populations from which they were drawn. The use of adjusted discriminant scores was thus clearly superior to a matched sample experiment for the purpose of testing what we may refer to as the major hypothesis of this research, namely, that caste sanctions have an appreciable effect upon personality as demonstrated by the differences in personality which occur between samples of people living under caste sanctions of differing degrees of severity, and which cannot be accounted for by chance or by the effects of extraneous background characteristics.

Nevertheless, a matched sample experiment was included in the research, and the conclusion which would be drawn from the results of the matched sample experiment was the same as that which was drawn from the experiments which did not employ matched samples. The purpose of including a matched sample experiment was not primarily to test the major hypothesis that there were differences in personality between people living under differing caste sanctions, but to help spell out the nature of the difference.

What are the specific natures of the differences?

So far nothing has been said about the nature of the personality characteristics which differentiate the samples. For confirmation of the theory that the caste sanctions have an effect upon personality it is not necessary to know anything about the meaning of the personality characteristics involved. It is only necessary to locate, either in the comparison of northern whites with southern blacks or in the comparison of northern blacks with southern blacks, some sort of discriminator which reflects personality in some way, and show that it consistently distinguishes northern from southern blacks.

We have gone a step further in the present study. Rather than seeking a best discriminant function in a purely statistical sense, we have confined our interest to a cruder discriminant function, but one composed of theoretically meaningful variables; each component allows us, in the light of present-day psychological theory, to make statements with some surety about the underlying processes to which they refer.

The PAT consists of 25 plates. The response to any one plate is known to reflect personality, but the interpretation of a response to a single plate is ambiguous. If, instead of scoring the PAT using the scales devised by Tomkins and Miner, we had asked the question of what way of combining the responses to all 25 plates into a mathematical function would yield that function most likely to differentiate new samples from the same populations, we would derive a discriminant function that was "best" in a statistical sense. Such a discriminant function would tend to yield more extreme levels of significance than the crude discriminant score that was used in this study. But if the difference between northern and southern blacks were found to be consistently significant, we could only say that the caste sanctions affected personality, without being able to say in what respects.

In this research the responses were first scored by using the scoring procedure outlined by Tomkins and Miner; the resultant scores were added to form our crude discriminant score. Even if the meaning of these scores were not known, we would, as before, be able to conclude that the caste sanctions had an effect on personality if we obtained significant results. But the meaning of these scores is known; each of them has an unambiguous referent which is presented in the Tomkins and Miner manual, and these referents, therefore, are the specific personality characteristics on which the samples differ, if they differ on the discriminant score. It will be recalled that Tomkins and Miner define a scale on the PAT as consisting of all responses (arrangements of the three pictures in any one set) across all 25 plates which reflect the same personality characteristic. For each scale, they give the "cutting point," the number of responses on that scale which a person must give in order to be scored as having that personality characteristic. In scoring a scale all that is retained is whether or not the person is beyond the cutting point, that is, whether or not that personality characteristic describes him. Thus, there is no scale measuring "Strength of conscience," but there is a "Strong conscience" scale, and there might also be a "Weak conscience" scale. People who are beyond the appropriate cutting points are characterized as having a strong or a weak conscience, respectively. Most people, of course, will not be scored on either of these scales, since they are somewhere in the middle.

There are approximately 150 scorable scales on the PAT, and each scale has several variants, each of which must be scored separately. Some procedure was needed to cut down the labor involved in the pilot studies. The obvious thing to do was to use the differences between the samples on individual plate responses, which were easily determined, to select from among the scales those which were most likely to differentiate the samples, and then undertake to score only these scales. The first step in the pilot studies, therefore, was to compare the samples on each of the individual plate responses—a "response" being an arrangement of the three pictures in a set. Since there are six ways in which three pictures may be arranged, there are six possible responses to any one plate (set of three pictures).

The proportion of the northern sample who gave each response was compared with the proportion of the southern sample who gave that response in order to find those responses which were given more frequently in one sample than in the other. The comparison of the proportions was carried out for each of the six responses to each of the 25 plates, making 150 comparisons. The decision as to which individual plate responses seemed to differentiate the samples was made on the basis of a statistical criterion—the difference between the proportions giving that response had to reach the 20 percent level of significance. Since this was a pilot study, the results of which were to be checked in later validations, this "low" level of significance was used in place of the usual five or one percent levels, so that even "hints" in the data could be picked up.

In the original pilot study that compared northern whites with southern blacks, out of the 150 comparisons on individual plate responses, 51 reached the 20 percent level of significance. The problem, then, was how to use these 51 individual plate responses, which seemed to differentiate the samples, so that from among the 158 PAT scales those scales could be selected for scoring which were most likely to distinguish the samples.

There are many alternative procedures that might have been used which would have been equally good. The procedure decided upon is simple, although its description sounds rather complicated. The first step was to examine those scales for which one or more of the 51 differentiating individual responses were included among the responses which compose the scale. The scoring for one variant, the "d" variant, of each scale was then examined, and a scale was selected for further consideration if, among the individual plate responses which compose the "d" variant of that scale, there were a sufficient number of the 51 individual plate responses on which the samples had been found to differ. Since the scales are not all the same length, it was not reasonable to use the same number of responses for all scales as being sufficient to indicate that the scale warranted further attention. Some number was needed which could be used as the basis for selection and which would take into account the differing lengths of the scales. The "cutting points," that is, the minimum number of responses on a scale which an individual would have to give in order to be scored as extreme on that scale, provided a number for each scale which varied with the length of the scale. Arbitrarily, it was decided to use this number as the criterion for selection: if, of the 51 individual plate responses on which the samples differed, there were that many or more which were included in any scale, the scale was selected for further consideration.

Out of the 158 PAT scales, 41 were selected on this basis. Where two or more of these 41 scales were extremely close in meaning, one or more of them were eliminated if they represented a degree of specificity which seemed unnecessary in the present study, or if the relevant information was also contained in other scales which had been selected. Eleven scales were deleted for these reasons. A description of the scales which were selected, as well as those which were deleted, is given in the next chapter.

This was to be the first step in a successive process of elimination (with further steps that would easily weed out bad choices), and the criterion for this step was crude. Certain other scales, which were strongly suggested in the literature, seemed likely to clarify the meaning of the scales which had met the criterion for the first step. They were selected if at least one differentiating response was scored on them, even though there were not enough differentiating responses to meet the arbitrary criterion. Eighteen scales were added on this basis. (These scales, too, are described in the next chapter.)

This is the only point in the pilot study where the selection of variables depended directly upon the judgment of the experimenter. The selection of the final scales from among those which passed this first stage was entirely a mechanical process.

This first stage had reduced the number of PAT scales to be scored from 158 to 48. A second stage of elimination was then carried out. As previously mentioned, the number of responses on a scale given by any subject is ignored in scoring, except for the question of whether or not that number of responses is beyond the cutting point. The scoring consists in determining whether or not the person is "extreme" on each of the scales. Therefore, in making group comparisons, the only meaningful comparison is whether the percentage of "extreme" cases on a scale is the same in both groups or different. But the percentage of "extreme" cases can only be determined by scoring the scale for each person in the two groups, a time-consuming procedure. However, the mean (that is, the average) number of responses of a group on a given scale, which in itself is not a meaningful measure, nevertheless may be expected to reflect any large increase in the number of cases who are "extreme"; the mean number of responses for a group can be easily determined from the number of people who give each individual response without actually scoring the scale for each individual. Therefore, the next step was to use the percentage of each sample who gave each individual response (which had been computed in order to locate the differentiating individual responses) to compute the mean number of responses on the "f" variant (the variant which seemed to be the most discriminating in the group comparisons in the Tomkins and Miner study) of each of the 48 scales for each group. In order to take account of the fact that the scales differ in length (so that a difference of two responses between the means of the groups for a scale of three responses is obviously more impressive than the same difference for a scale of ten responses), the criterion was not the difference between the means (averages) but the ratio. Arbitrarily it was decided to select a scale for further examination if the mean of one of the groups was at least one and a half times the mean of the other. Out of the 48 scales, 20 were selected for scoring.

The "a," "d," and "f" variants of these 20 scales were now scored for each individual. An individual is considered "extreme" on a scale if he is "extreme" on one variant. The groups were compared on the number of "extreme" cases. Of the 20 scales, only seven were found on which the difference in percentage of extreme cases reached the 20 percent level.

The point of using this sequential procedure was to reduce the amount of work involved in scoring the PAT. By using this simple scoring procedure we could eliminate those scales which seemed least likely to significantly differentiate the samples. From the original 158 scales we were able to select 20 that were most promising. These were then scored and treated more rigorously. If we had scored all scales without using such a sequential procedure, the labor of scoring the scales would have been increased eight-fold.

In addition to the scales, Tomkins and Miner define another type of score for the PAT, the "denial" scores, which are not based on the arrangement of the three pictures in a set, but upon the person's description of "what is going on" in the pictures. Scoring procedures have been developed for six types of "denial" on the PAT; these scoring schemes are very reliable, but they require the use of a trained scorer. As with any scoring which must be done by human beings, and cannot be done by machines, the scoring of "denials" is a drawn-out process if the number of tests being scored is at all large. A reduction in the labor of scoring was achieved by reducing the white sample before scoring the scales and the "denials." The original northern white sample consisted of 459 cases drawn randomly from the appropriate areas in the representative Gallup sample. Since the individual plate responses are easily tallied, the percentage giving each of the six possible responses for each plate was determined using this sample. The sample was then reduced to about a third by choosing 148 cases randomly from the 459. These 148 cases were the northern white sample which were individually scored on the scales and on the "denials," and which were used in the later analyses. Since the number of cases in the southern black sample with which this sample was compared was 51, scoring the full white sample of 459 would have meant roughly two and a half times as much work in the pilot study for a small increase in sensitivity. (The standard error of the difference between samples would have decreased only approximately nine percent.)

Special care was taken to eliminate the possibility that the hand scoring might in any way be prejudiced toward yielding positive findings. Although extremely objective bases for scoring "denials" have been developed, the following additional precautions were taken. Four samples were scored at a time: two northern and two southern. The test protocols (the booklets containing the responses of the subjects) from the four samples were combined into one group, using a table of random numbers to ensure that they were randomly arranged. The scorer then went through the stack, scoring one type of "denial" for all subjects, without knowing whose protocol he was scoring and reading only the response to the one plate on which that type of "denial" could occur. Thus there was no way for the scorer to know whether he was scoring the protocol of a northern or a southern subject. When he had scored all cases, the booklets were shuffled and then he began again, scoring all cases on a second type of "denial." This was repeated until all the "denial" scores had been completed. Since there were eight samples involved in all of the studies reported in this book, the scoring of "denials" was carried out in two batches: the four Gallup samples and the four high school samples.

Previously recorded lists of code numbers allowed the samples to be reassembled; there was nothing on the test protocol other than the code number which would allow one to recognize the sample from which the subject had come, and there was nothing about the code number which would indicate the sample without reference to the previously recorded lists.

When the two samples in the first pilot study were reassembled and the "denial" scores tallied, four of the six "denial" scores were found to differentiate the northern whites from the southern blacks beyond the 20 percent level of significance. These, plus the seven scales, made eleven hypotheses to test in the later research. These eleven variables were combined into a crude discriminant function. As mentioned earlier, it is only appropriate to consider any of these as truly differentiating the samples if in the validations (and not merely in the pilot study) this discriminant score, which represents the effects of the eleven personality characteristics taken together, was found to differentiate the samples. If the validation samples were found to differ, if they were found to differ even after the background variables had been taken into account, and if after such an adjustment the differences were still large enough to reach the generally accepted levels of significance, then, and only then, would it be appropriate to examine the personality characteristics themselves—to discover which of them were most responsible for the discriminating power of the discriminant score, that is, which were most effective in distinguishing the samples.

In comparing the groups on each personality characteristic by itself, the technique of using statistical corrections to adjust for the effects of the background variables runs afoul of the problem of "additivity" in the sense that it is not clear that an adjustment determined from one sample would be appropriate for another. It was not possible to settle this problem, as was done for the discriminant score, by any direct examination of the data. The problem is raised by the fact that the PAT scores have only two possible values—like "blue eyes," they either characterize a person or do not characterize him. A group of people can be described by the percentage of the group who have that characteristic. Data which are reported in percentages are frequently transformed into other numbers which retain the information but are more convenient for some statistical purpose. If the corrections determined from one sample for the percentages were appropriate for the other samples, then the corrections determined from one sample for the transformed percentages could not also be appropriate for the other samples; if the corrections determined for the transformed percentages were appropriate for the other samples, this could not be the case for the untransformed percentages. It is by no means clear in which form the "additivity" assumption would hold.

By including in the research one comparison between a northern black sample and a southern black sample in which the samples were matched on the relevant background variables, we could compare the proportions directly, without resorting to statistical corrections, thus circumventing the whole problem of the "additivity" of the corrections. By happy accident, however, the corrections for the background variables proved to be relatively small. We could therefore compare the percentages without correcting even for some of the unmatched samples, and not be too badly in error.

Selection of the samples

Many criteria might be used to decide whether a state was northern or southern in its treatment of blacks; for the purposes of this research three simple, clear-cut, and objective criteria were used to classify a state:

laws with respect to miscegenation (intermarriage between the castes), laws with respect to school segregation, and laws with respect to segregation in public transportation.

A northern state, for the purposes of this study, was a state which (as of 1955) had no valid law forbidding intermarriage between the two castes, which had either a law expressly forbidding segregation in schools or no legislation on school segregation (presumably because it was not necessary), and which had no law requiring segregation in any form of public transportation. There were 18 such states: California, Connecticut, Iowa, Illinois, Maine, Massachusetts, Minnesota, Michigan, New Hampshire, New York, New Jersey, Nevada, Ohio, Pennsylvania, Rhode Island, Vermont, Washington, and Wisconsin.

A southern state, for the purposes of this study, was defined as a state which (as of 1955) had a law with a criminal penalty forbidding intermarriage between blacks and whites, which had a law requiring segregated schools, and which had a law requiring segregation in some form of public transportation. There were 14 such states: Alabama, Arkansas, Florida, Georgia, Kentucky, Louisiana, Mississippi, Maryland, Oklahoma, South Carolina, North Carolina, Tennessee, Texas, and Virginia.

The nationwide Gallup sample which had been gathered in 1954 consisted of 1,896 individuals, each of whom had been administered the PAT, the Thorndike-Gallup Intelligence Scale (a 20-item vocabulary test), and a questionnaire about background data. From this sample, a representative cross-section of the population of the United States between the ages of 10 and 70 was assembled, numbering 1,500 cases. This included 148 blacks. There were another 36 blacks in the extra 396 cases, which brought the total black sample to 184 cases, which were widely differentiated in terms of all the background variables. Of these, 70 were residing in states which have been defined as northern and 103 in states which have been defined as southern. There were only 11 cases from the remaining 16 states.

Of the 18 northern states, only nine were represented by blacks in the Gallup sample: Massachusetts, 1; New York, 21; New Jersey, 13; Pennsylvania, 7; Ohio, 10; Illinois, 11; Iowa, 1; Washington, 1; and California, 5.

Of the southern states all were represented by blacks in the Gallup sample as follows: Maryland, 5; Virginia, 12; North Carolina, 5; Kentucky, 1; Tennessee, 9; Oklahoma, 6; Texas, 7; Florida, 5; South Carolina, 9; Georgia, 8; Alabama, 14; Mississippi, 11; Louisiana, 6; and Arkansas, 5. These 103 southern black cases were placed together, and then separated into groups on the basis of age and intelligence simultaneously. The individuals in each group were assigned at random to one of two samples of 51 and 52 cases, respectively. These samples are referred to as SB-1 (southern black sample one) and SB-2 (southern black sample two).

In selecting the northern white sample it was felt that it was reasonable to include not only those states which had been defined as northern above (for the purpose of drawing the black sample) but also those states outside the South which might have one or another law restricting blacks, but in which, because of small black populations, the caste sanctions had virtually no influence on the way of life of the white population. All cases from the 14 states which have been defined above as southern, as well as those from Delaware, Missouri, and West Virginia, were removed from the representative cross-section of the United States. The northern white sample was then taken at random from all remaining white subjects in that nationwide sample.

In addition to the Gallup sample, high school populations from various parts of the country were tested in 1955 in order to increase the accuracy of norms in that age range. From these populations, ninth-grade black students from two communities in the North and two in the South were selected as final validation samples. A rural area of the Deep South characterized by severe caste sanctions was chosen as one of the southern communities, and an urban area where the caste sanctions are relatively benign by southern standards was chosen as the other.

Inasmuch as the effects of the background characteristics would be known from the comparisons using the Gallup samples, it was possible to use in the further studies samples that were restricted in the range of age and education, as these high school samples were, provided the samples were comparable. The matched sample experiment used two of these high school samples.

One advantage of the high school samples over the samples drawn from the Gallup data was that the high school samples could be limited to people who had spent their whole lives in the area in which they were tested, since they were asked their place of birth. This information had not been obtained from the individuals in the Gallup sample, and they were classified as northern or southern solely on the basis of their place of residence. Thus, the findings for the high school samples might be more clear-cut insofar as the sample of northern blacks drawn from the Gallup data, like any representative group of blacks living in the North, included in all probability a large percentage of blacks who had lived part of their lives in the South and migrated to the North.

Review of the experimental procedure

The research was designed to discover the differences in personality structure which result from differences in caste sanctions. To be more precise, an attempt was to be made not only to discover these differences, but to test in an objective and rigorous manner whether these differences could be accounted for by chance, or by the effects of background variables (other than the caste sanctions) such as age, sex, education, vocabulary intelligence, rural-urban residence, degree of industrialization, or population density of the general area. If they could not be so accounted for, then it may reasonably be assumed that the differences are due to the differential effects of caste sanctions.

The more disparate the caste sanctions encountered by the members of two samples being compared, the more clearly should the differences due to the caste sanctions be revealed by the comparison. Therefore, it was decided that one of the samples used in the first pilot study should be drawn from a population living essentially outside the caste situation, namely, from the white population.

Since southern whites are themselves probably greatly affected by the caste sanctions (Myrdal, pp. 643-644), protocols from the states of Delaware, West Virginia, Missouri, and the 14 states which were defined above as southern (for the purpose of drawing the black samples) were deleted from the representative cross-section of the United States which had been assembled from the Gallup data. Then 459 cases were drawn at random from the remaining white cases; later, 148 cases were drawn at random from these. This sample is referred to as sample NW (northern whites).

The initial part of the research consisted of a pilot study of the differences between these northern whites and a sample of southern blacks in order to locate hypotheses, or ideas, which were then to be tested in the comparison of northern and southern blacks. Insofar as the differences between northern whites and southern blacks are due to caste sanctions, northern blacks, who encounter less severe caste sanctions than southern blacks, should differ from southern blacks on the same variables and in the same direction as did the northern whites.

The PAT responses of the white sample, NW, were compared with those of the first southern black sample, SB-1, to locate responses which differentiated the two groups. Arbitrarily, it was decided not to consider any response as differentiating the two samples unless the difference between the samples on that response was beyond the 20 percent level of significance.

In order to demonstrate that these differences were not solely due to the effects of the background variables mentioned above, the following procedure was employed. Each of the interpretable differentiating responses (scales or "denial" scores) which was located by the comparison of NW with SB-1 was to be assigned a weight of +1 or −1, depending upon whether it was given by a higher proportion of SB-1 (in which case, it was assigned a weight of +1), or of NW (in which case it was assigned a weight of −1). In this way a crude discriminant function was to be determined: each individual would now have a score which was the sum of his plus and minus ones. It should be noted that nowhere was the assumption made that this represented a single dimension, or that people who get the same score need be at all alike in personality structure. Next, the regression of this score on age, sex, education, vocabulary intelligence, rural-urban residence, population density of the general area, and degree of industrialization of the general area was examined. The variables that were not significantly related to the discriminant function score within sample NW were to be eliminated, and correction weights determined for the remainder. These regression weights were all determined from NW so as to represent the effects of the background variables as they operate outside the caste situation, without eliminating interaction variance. A corrected discriminant function score was then determined for each individual by applying these corrections to his discriminant function score. To show that any two samples are differentiated on the set of characteristics which make up the discriminant function score beyond chance, even when the differences in background variables are taken into account, it is only necessary to show that the difference between the means (average scores) of the two samples on the corrected discriminant function scores is significant.

The scale was then applied to the 70 cases of northern blacks, referred to as sample NB, from the Gallup data, and the second southern black sample, SB-2. The significance of the relationships located in the pilot study was thus to be validated and its significance assessed by means of a one-tailed test. Since it is explicitly hypothesized that northern blacks should differ from southern blacks in the direction of northern whites, a one-tailed test is appropriate; the term "one-tailed test" refers to the fact that the probability by chance that the difference between the means will be as great or greater than that which actually occurred is obviously twice as great if it does not matter which mean is larger than it is if you can clearly specify in advance which of the two means will be the larger.

The hypothesis that northern blacks should differ from southern blacks in the direction of whites is based on the assumption that the differences in personality structure between blacks and whites are due to social pressures, i.e., to caste sanctions, and that these sanctions affect southern blacks more than northern blacks. If these assumptions are true, the differences between northern and southern blacks should be more easily located by a pilot comparison of whites and blacks than by a pilot comparison of northern and southern blacks, even though the cross-validation samples will consist of northern and southern blacks. If these assumptions are not true, a pilot comparison of northern and southern blacks should be more effective in locating the differentiating variables. To provide a check on these assumptions, such a pilot study was carried out, comparing samples NB and SB-2 in the same way that samples NW and SB-1 had been compared, in order to locate differences between northern and southern blacks not predicted by the NW vs. SN-1 differences. The differences found were to be combined into a second discriminant function score, and correction weights determined as before.

Both discriminant functions were then applied to new validation samples, so as to compare the effectiveness of the two pilot studies. Inasmuch as the effects of the background variables were known, it was possible to use samples which were restricted in value on these variables for cross-validation purposes. The populations chosen were ninth graders.

These final samples had the advantage that they consisted only of individuals born in the area in which they were now residing, while the place of birth was not available for the cases in the original Gallup sample. (According to the census, roughly three-fifths of northern blacks were born in the South.)

Finally, the differences between the samples on each of the separate characteristics which made up the discriminant functions were examined, so that the conclusions from this study might be as specific as possible. To facilitate these comparisons, one northern and one southern ninth-grade sample were included which had been matched on those background variables that had proved to be relevant.

The problem of the incomplete protocols

The PAT is not a timed test; a person should be allowed as much time as he needs in taking this test. This was possible in the Gallup sample since the test was administered to each person separately by Gallup interviewers. It is not possible when the tests are administered to a whole group at one time, as in the case of the high school samples. The amount of time which could be allotted by a school for the purpose of standardizing the test was limited. Therefore it was inevitable that in almost all groups there were some subjects who did not finish the test.

In the early attempts to test high school groups it was found that as much as 70 or 80 percent of the group would hand in protocols (test booklets) which were incomplete or unscoreable. The chief cause leading to unscoreable protocols was found to be position or pattern preferences. The subjects misinterpreted what they were to do, and acted as if there was one solution to all the plates, so that they arranged the three pictures of a plate in the same order for every plate, either by the position of the picture on the plate, or by the symbol which is printed next to the picture and which is used to denote it. This problem was resolved by using instructions (such as those in Chapter IV) which explicitly tell the subjects not to give "pattern" or "position" preferences, and this type of unscoreable protocol became a minor problem. Nonetheless, a certain percentage of almost any group still will hand in unusable protocols. Most of these are incomplete protocols; in order for the PAT to be scored, there must be responses to all twenty-five plates. The percentage of incomplete protocols tends to vary with the time limit: the shorter the time, the more people in the group who do not finish. For most normal adults, the test takes little more than half an hour. Although the time limits varied somewhat from place to place, in each of the high school groups used in the research the minimum time allowance was an hour, with an hour and a half allowed for those who needed the additional time.

The fact that the percentage of unscoreable protocols varies from group to group (largely as a function of the time allowed) raises the problem of what selective factors determine which people finish and which do not, and whether these differences may not account for any differences between the groups, if we compare the scoreable test booklets from two groups in which the percentage of people who do not finish is not the same.

To circumvent this problem, one high school sample in the North and one high school sample from the South were chosen in which the testing conditions had been nearly identical. The judgment that the testing conditions were nearly equivalent was borne out by the fact that the percentages of incomplete and unscoreable protocols were found to be nearly identical in the two groups. Thus, whatever selective factors are involved in producing incomplete protocols, they operated equally upon both groups and could not be invoked to account for any differences between the groups. These are the samples which are referred to as the North City and South Town samples.

In choosing samples for the matched-sample experiment, it was impossible to follow this same procedure of choosing two samples in which the testing conditions and the percentage of incomplete protocols were identical in both groups. Matching is necessarily wasteful, and it is therefore necessary to start with relatively large samples, which meant using samples gathered in relatively large cities. In each case, the samples were gathered by several different administrations, and the time limits had varied somewhat not only between cities but also between administrations in the same city, so as to yield the largest possible number of scoreable protocols in the time available from the school schedules. Of course, the percentage of incomplete protocols also varied from administration to administration.

Will this mislead us in drawing conclusions from the matched sample experiment? To answer this question, let us review what is known about the factors that produce incomplete protocols. The factor that seems to be most important is, as already mentioned, the amount of time allowed. The percentage of incomplete protocols varies directly with the amount of time allowed the subjects.

But what are the characteristics of the people who do not finish? Most normal adults complete the test in about one-half hour. Children seem to require more time than adults. Psychotic patients take the longest time; some never complete the test, others may require as much as ten hours of testing, a few hours at a time, spread over a period of about two weeks. However, it is not at all likely that a psychotic would be able to maintain himself in the schoolroom situation. The other factors which seem to be major determinants of whether or not a person finishes the test are how fast he works and his intelligence.

Insofar as the difference between those who finish and those who do not represents a difference in intelligence, the difference will not affect our findings, since the samples are to be matched on intelligence (as well as on age, education, and sex).

Aside from what we know of the determinants of whether or not someone finishes the test in a specified time, and whether it seems reasonable to believe that the determinants account for our findings, it is possible to check directly whether whatever selective factors are involved are related to the particular personality characteristics under investigation. Two fairly large cities were selected which were appropriate for the matched sample experiment in other respects—one in the North and one in the South. In each city there had been several administrations.

All usable protocols (scoreable protocols from black subjects who were born in the area in which they now lived) in these two samples were scored. The percentages of unscoreable protocols were found to vary from 6 to 76 percent in the administrations in the northern sample and from 29 to 59 percent in the administrations in the southern sample. In order to check on the relationship of the number of incomplete protocols in an administration to the personality characteristics under investigation, the discriminant score was determined for each subject whose protocol was scoreable. The discriminant score was then adjusted for the effects of age and vocabulary. The relationship between this adjusted discriminant score and the percentage of incomplete protocols in the administration was examined and no relationship was found. (Kendall's tau coefficient of correlation, τ_b, was computed separately for each city; in each case the correlation was found to be near zero, .02 for the northern sample and .002 for the southern sample.) Therefore, it did not seem unreasonable to combine samples in which the percentages of incomplete protocols were not identical, if this would help to elucidate the relationship between the individual characteristics and the caste sanctions. (It will be recalled that this problem of the percentage of incomplete protocols does not arise for the Gallup samples, which were individually administered, nor for the North City and South Town high school samples which were matched on testing time and percentage of incomplete protocols. Thus the conclusions about the major hypothesis that the caste sanctions have an appreciable effect upon personality are solidly grounded on samples for which this problem does not arise.) The one administration in these two cities in which more than 60 percent of the protocols were unscoreable was eliminated, and the matched samples were drawn from the remaining data.

*The background variables

In order to be able to test in the cross-validations whether northern and southern blacks were discriminated by the set of variables located in the pilot study (which are neither theoretically nor operationally independent of each other), and to test whether this discrimination may be accounted for by certain background variables, other than the caste sanctions, which differentiate the South from the North, each subject was given a score of +1 on a variable if he was extreme, and a score of zero otherwise. The scores on each of the variables were summed up for each subject to form a crude discriminant score. We were now in a position to ask whether or not the differences between the samples were due to the effect of various background variables which are known to differentiate the South from the North. It had already been found by Tomkins and Miner that the age, intelligence, and education of the respondent affect his PAT responses and must therefore be taken into account before interpretation. Southern blacks are known to differ from northern blacks in these respects. Moreover, the South is a less industrialized area, with less density of population, and a greater portion of the population living in rural areas. We also know that the sex ratios are not identical in the populations studied. The next step, therefore, was to investigate the effects of these background variables upon the discriminant score.

In testing the effects of the background variables, we are interested in eliminating the effects of these background variables as they operate outside the caste situation, but not in eliminating their interaction with the caste sanctions. That is to say, we are not interested in the fact that a black who has received less schooling is likely also to have encountered more severe caste sanctions in other spheres of life and, therefore, may tend to display more of the personality problems which comprise the discriminant function; rather, we are interested in the effect of a lack of schooling *per se* in producing protocols which would be scored higher. Consequently, the effect of the background variables was determined solely from the northern white sample (sample NW).

Because of the non-normality of the discriminant scores, and because of the fact that it was not always clear what transformation of the background variable would produce a most nearly linear relation, non-parametric tests were used to test significance. (The sole exception, age, will be discussed below.)

Kendall's tau was used to test the significance of the relationship for each of the background variables except sex, for which Marshall's two-sample test was employed.

The population density and the degree of industrialization of the general area were determined, using the state as the unit of area. Percentage of the population employed in manufacturing industries was used as the index of degree of industrialization. Figures for population density, degree of industrialization, and rural-urban residence were taken from the 1950 census.

Table V-1 gives the results of the non-parametric tests of the significance of the relationship between the background variables and the discriminant score. Clearly, none of the variables except vocabulary and education even approach significance; these two variables reach the five and one percent levels, respectively. (Raw score was used for the vocabulary score, rather than the age-corrected I.Q.)

Age was the only variable which was not tested non-parametrically, inasmuch as a curvilinear relationship was expected. It was postulated *a priori* that a second-degree equation (a parabola) should approximate the shape of the regression on age, after the age scale had been transformed to logs. (This assumption was based on the notion that, for many psychological functions, the change which occurs in the course of a year seems to be inversely proportional to the age; hence the log scale. Further, it was felt that some psychological functions increase continuously with age, others tend to increase and

Table V-1 SIGNIFICANCE LEVELS OF THE RELATIONSHIPS
BETWEEN THE BACKGROUND VARIABLES
AND THE DISCRIMINANT SCORES

Variable	S/σ_S*	p
Sex	.19	.85
Population density	.21	.83
Degree of industrialization (Percent employed in manufacturing industries)	.46	.65
Rural-urban residence	1.01	.32
Vocabulary	1.98	.05
Education	3.45	.0006

*S and σ_S refer to the quantities defined by Kendall for all variables except sex, in which case these symbols denote the quantities defined by Marshall which are somewhat different.

then level off, and still others increase to a point and then tend to decline in old age. A second-degree equation would be general enough to provide a rough approximation to any of these relationships.) To test this notion the age scale was transformed to a logarithmic scale (to the base 10) and the data grouped on intervals of .1 on the log scale. The mean discriminant score of each array was then computed and plotted. When the plot was completed, it was found that these means did indeed form a remarkably smooth parabola, as shown in Figure V-1.

The linear product-moment correlation of age and discriminant score was found to be .14; the parabolic correlation was .29. If the usual tests of significance were applicable, the latter would be clearly significant beyond the .01 level. However, the sample was decidedly non-normal. But Pitman has shown that, using the randomization criterion in place of normal curve theory, it is possible to generate a distribution-free test of significance for the product-moment correlation coefficient. It turns out that for large samples the resultant distribution of r under the hypothesis of no correlation approximates the distribution generated by normal curve theory. If this result generalizes to the parabolic correlation, we may state that the effect of age is clearly significant.

In order to compare the significance level generated by such a use of the product-moment correlation with that generated by the non-parametric techniques, the product-moment coefficients were computed for education and for vocabulary. These turned out to be $-.28$ and $-.18$, respectively. These are in the general neighborhood of the results of the non-parametric tests. (Education: $r/\sigma_r = -3.4$; $S/\sigma_S = -3.4$; Vocabulary: $r/\sigma_r = -2.2$; $S/\sigma_S = -2.0$.)

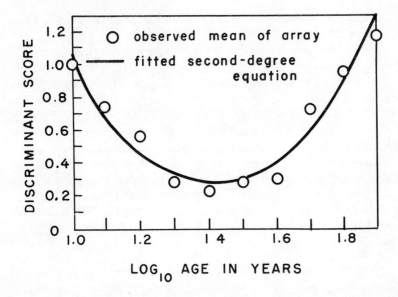

Figure V-1   Regression of discriminant score on age for sample NW

Thus we are left with age, education, and vocabulary, the three variables which previous experimentation had indicated were major factors in the production of PAT patterns.

Adjusting the discriminant score

The next step was to adjust the discriminant scores so as to eliminate the effects of age, education, and vocabulary. It was decided to correct for age first. A parabolic regression equation was computed from sample NW for the regression of the discriminant score upon age. Then an age-corrected discriminant score was computed for each individual by the following formula:

$$D_{i \cdot a} = D_i - b_{da \cdot (a^2)} A_i - b_{d(a^2) \cdot a} A^2_i + C$$

where $D_{i \cdot a}$ is the age-corrected discriminant score for individual i;

D_i is the uncorrected discriminant score for individual i;

A_i is the $\log_{10}$ of the age of individual i in years;

$b_{da \cdot (a^2)}$ is the partial regression coefficient of D on A determined from sample NW;

$b_{d(a^2).a}$ is the partial regression coefficient of D on A^2 determined from sample NW; and

C is an arbitrary constant large enough to eliminate negative scores.

To see if any further corrections were necessary, the product-moment correlations between this age-corrected discriminant score and vocabulary and education were computed for sample NW. It was found that the correlations had decreased but were still appreciable: $-.156$ for education and $-.161$ for vocabulary ($r/\sigma_r = -1.89, -1.95$, respectively).

A new multiple-regression equation was therefore computed, using vocabulary as well as the parabolic relationship with log age as predictors of the original (uncorrected) discriminant scores. On the basis of this equation, corrections were determined for age and vocabulary taken together. A corrected discriminant score was again computed for each individual, this time by the following formula:

$$D_{i.va} = D_i - b_{da.(a^2)v}A_i - b_{d(a^2).va}A^2_i - b_{dv.a(a^2)}V_i + K$$

where $D_{i.va}$ is the discriminant score, corrected for age and vocabulary score, for individual i;

D_i is the uncorrected discriminant score for individual i;

A_i is the $\log_{10}$ of the age of individual i, in years;

V_i is the vocabulary score of individual i;

$b_{da.(a^2)v}$ is the partial regression coefficient of D on A determined from the multiple regression of D on A, A^2, and V in sample NW;

$b_{d(a^2).va}$ is the partial regression coefficient of D on A^2 determined from the multiple regression of D on A, A^2, and V in sample NW;

$b_{dv.a(a^2)}$ is the partial regression coefficient of D on V determined from the multiple regression of D on A, A^2, and V in sample NW; and

K is an arbitrary constant large enough to eliminate negative scores.

The correlation of this new corrected discriminant score with education was computed for sample NW. The product-moment correlation was found to be $-.067$, which is not close to significance ($r/\sigma_r = .82$, p=.42) and it was therefore decided that no further corrections were necessary, i.e., when age and vocabulary are held constant, there is no appreciable effect of education.

At this point, two objections may be raised to the procedure we have employed. One is that we have corrected too much, and the other that we have not corrected enough.

On the one hand, it may be argued that in correcting for the effects of vocabulary, we are over-correcting. For insofar as people with low vocabulary levels tend to have special problems, and insofar as part of the discrimination which is practiced against blacks consists in denying them the education and cultural facilities which lead to increased vocabulary (and intelligence *as measured*), these effects should not be eliminated in studying the effects of the caste sanctions. Although there is some merit to this suggestion, in view of the rationale of the PAT, correcting for vocabulary seems a better procedure than not correcting. Nevertheless, the discriminant scores corrected only for age ($D_{i.a}$), as well as the discriminant scores corrected for both age and vocabulary ($D_{i.va}$), will be reported for each of the validations.

On the other hand, it may be argued that determining the corrections from the NW sample, in order to eliminate the effects of possible interactions of the background variables with the caste sanctions, may lead to an under-determination of the regression coefficients because of a possible statistical dependence of the size of the coefficients upon the mean of the group. In the pilot samples, the variance of the sample was not independent of the mean, the sample with the smaller mean having a considerably smaller variance. If there were a similar dependence of the regression coefficients upon the mean (or upon the variance), and especially if this difference is in the direction of a larger variance being associated with larger regression coefficients, then our procedure is inappropriate and we have under-corrected.

Here we reach a dilemma. We may examine the regression coefficients as determined from sample SB-1 (southern black sample one) to see whether they are the same as those determined from sample NW. If they are not the same, then we can only conclude that there is an interaction with the caste sanctions, or a statistical dependence, or both—and there is no way to distinguish these. If, however, the regression coefficients are the same, we can conclude that there is neither an appreciable interaction nor an appreciable statistical dependence. Further, an interaction effect might be present for one variable and not for the other of the two for which we determined corrections, whereas a statistical dependence would affect all variables.

With this in mind, the first order regression coefficient of the uncorrected discriminant score on vocabulary was computed for sample SB-1 and compared with that determined from sample NW. Interestingly enough, the correlation coefficients varied widely: $-.05$ for sample SB-1 as compared with $-.18$ for sample NW; but the regression coefficients were remarkably close: $-.0466$ for sample SB-1 as compared with $-.0592$ for sample NW. Just how close a fit this is may be appreciated by considering that the standard error of each of these coefficients is .027 for the larger sample NW, and .125 for the smaller sample SB-1. In the light of this finding, we may safely dismiss the possibility of an appreciable statistical dependence of the regression coefficients upon the mean, and proceed to use as correction factors the coefficients determined from sample NW.

Welch's modification of the t-test for samples drawn from populations with unequal variances

Student's t-test, the usual test for the significance of the difference between two means, assumes that the two samples being compared were drawn from populations in which the variances are equal, and therefore cannot be appropriately used in cases where there is reason to believe that the population variances differ.

In the absence of any solid *a priori* reason for assuming that the samples were drawn from populations in which the variances were identical or that they were drawn from populations whose variances were not identical, it is appropriate to examine the sample variances. In the first validation, NB vs. SB-2, the difference between the sample variances was not statistically significant, but it was close to significance ($F_{51,69}=1.46$). In the second validation, North City vs. South Town high schools, the difference in variance was well beyond the one percent level of significance ($F_{36,29}=3.82$). Therefore, a simple conservative procedure, developed by Welch, for testing the significance of the difference between the means of samples drawn from populations whose variances may differ was utilized in all the validations.

Firstly, the sum of squares is not pooled, so that t is defined:

$$t = \frac{\overline{X}_1 - \overrightarrow{X}_2}{\sqrt{\dfrac{s^2_1}{n_1} + \dfrac{s^2_2}{n_2}}}$$

where $\overline{X}_1$ is the mean of sample one;

$\overline{X}_2$ is the mean of sample two;

s^2_1 is the variance estimated from sample one;

s^2_2 is the variance estimated from sample two;

n_1 is the number of cases in sample one; and

n_2 is the number of cases in sample two.

Secondly, the degrees of freedom with which the t-table is entered are adjusted as follows:

$$\frac{1}{f^*} = \frac{A^2_1}{f_1} + \frac{A^2_2}{f_2}$$

where f* is the appropriate number of degrees of freedom;

f_1 is the number of degrees of freedom in sample one;

f_2 is the number of degrees in sample two; and

A_1 and A_2 are defined as follows:

$$A_1 = \frac{\dfrac{s^2_1}{n_1}}{\dfrac{s^2_1}{n_1} + \dfrac{s^2_2}{n_2}}$$

$$A_2 = 1 - A_1$$

Analysis of the matched samples

In the matched sample comparison, each sample was divided into four subdivisions: 14-year-old, low vocabulary; 14-year-old, high vocabulary; 15-year-old, low vocabulary; and 15-year-old, high vocabulary. Each of the four subdivisions of each sample was matched on sex ratio and vocabulary with the corresponding subdivision of the other sample. By weighting each of the four subdivisions of each sample equally, irrespective of the number of cases in that subdivision, the samples would be matched as long as each subdivision was matched with its corresponding subdivision, and it was not necessary that the percentage of each sample falling in a given subdivision be the same for both samples.

For the analysis of the individual variables, the percentage of extreme cases on a given variable was determined separately for each subdivision of each sample. The percentages were then transformed by the well-known arc sine transformation $(\sin^{-1}\sqrt{p})$ and the analysis carried out on the arc sines. The percentage of extreme cases for the total sample was determined by computing the mean of the four arc sines for that sample, and transforming the mean arc sine back into a percentage.

The significance levels were determined by a straightforward analysis of variance on the arc sines. The only difference from standard procedures was the fact that the eight arc sines were based on different numbers of cases so that the appropriate error term is 821 times the average $1/n$, where n is the number of cases in a subdivision.

The total analysis of variance tables for a given variable might be written in the usual fashion:

Source	d.f.
Main Effects:	
North vs. South	1
14 yrs. vs. 15 yrs.	1
High vs. Low Vocabulary	1
Interactions:	
Region x Age	1
Region x Vocabulary	1
Age x Vocabulary	1
Region x Age x Vocabulary	1
Error term	Infinite

However, the only term in the table in which we are interested in the present experiment is the North vs. South main effect. The appropriate term for testing its significance is the error term (821 times the average $1/n$), and it is the result of this F test (the degrees of freedom equal $1,\infty$) which is reported as the significance level for the individual variables in the matched samples experiment.

Chapter VI

THE DIFFERENCES BETWEEN
BLACKS AND WHITES

In this chapter, the initial experiment (the pilot study) comparing blacks and whites will be described, the PAT variables will be listed to indicate the wide range of personality characteristics on which they were compared, and those characteristics will be indicated which were selected at each stage of the successive process of elimination described in the last chapter. The meaning of those characteristics which passed all three stages of elimination, that is, those characteristics on which the samples seemed to differ, will be discussed in detail. Before concluding this chapter, we will consider the discriminant score composed of all the differentiating characteristics taken together, and the effect of correcting for the extraneous background factors.

Description of the samples

The original two samples which were compared for the purpose of generating ideas were taken from the Gallup standardization data.

The southern black sample was chosen entirely from states which (as of 1955) fit the triple criterion of laws prescribing criminal penalties for intermarriage, laws requiring segregation in the schools, and laws requiring segregation in public transportation. The 103 cases of southern blacks available from the Gallup data had been divided randomly into two samples: southern black sample one, or SB-1, numbering 51 cases; and southern black sample two, or SB-2, numbering 52 cases. SB-1 was and for this study.

The northern white sample, or NW, consisted originally of 459 cases drawn at random from the appropriate areas. Comparisons of the frequencies with which particular responses were given to individual plates were based on this sample. Because of the length of time required to score the PAT scales and to score "denials," this sample was reduced randomly to 148 cases which were then individually scored. The statistical analysis was carried out on this reduced sample of 148 cases.

Table VI-1   GEOGRAPHICAL DISTRIBUTION OF CASES

NW (N=148)		SB-1 (N=51)	
Maine	2	Maryland	3
New Hampshire	1	Virginia	6
Vermont	1	North Carolina	3
Massachusetts	5	Kentucky	1
Rhode Island	0	Tennessee	5
Connecticut	1	Oklahoma	2
New York	19	Texas	3
New Jersey	9	Florida	2
Pennsylvania	19	South Carolina	4
Ohio	13	Georgia	3
Michigan	10	Alabama	6
Indiana	5	Mississippi	6
Illinois	9	Louisiana	4
Wisconsin	3	Arkansas	3
Minnesota	4		
Iowa	7		
North Dakota	0		
South Dakota	0		
Nebraska	3		
Kansas	5		
Montana	0		
Arizona	2		
Colorado	2		
Idaho	2		
Wyoming	0		
Utah	2		
Nevada	1		
New Mexico	2		
California	18		
Oregon	0		
Washington	3		

The geographical distribution of the reduced NW sample of 148 cases and of SB-1 is shown in Table VI-1. The distributions of the two samples by age, education, I.Q. (vocabulary), rural-urban residence, and sex are shown in Table VI-2.

Table VI-2 DISTRIBUTIONS OF NW AND OF SB-1 BY BACKGROUND FACTORS

	NW	SB-1
Age		
10-19	20	5
20-29	37	3
30-39	27	4
40-49	15	5
50-59	22	16
60-69	15	9
70-79	11	8
80-89	1	1
Education		
0	0	13
1-6 years	24	20
7-8 years	36	12
High school, incomplete	33	2
High school, complete	33	3
College, incomplete	8	0
College graduate	12	1
Nurses training	0	0
Trade school or beauty school	0	0
Business school or college	2	0
Intelligence (Vocabulary)		
Borderline and defective (Below 80)	9	13
Dull normal (80-90)	30	19
Average (90-110)	70	18
High average (110-120)	21	1
Superior (Above 120)	18	0
Rural-Urban Residence		
Farm	23	21
Non-farm under 2,500	34	12
2,500-10,000	13	4
10,000-24,999	16	7
25,000-49,999	4	0
50,000-99,999	17	2
100,000-499,999	15	3
500,000-and over	26	2
Sex		
Male	71	25
Female	77	26

Procedure

As stated previously, the Tomkins-Horn Picture Arrangement Test can be scored three ways: in terms of individual plate responses, in terms of scales, and in terms of the verbal write-ins. The first is the easiest, but the interpretation of individual plate responses is often ambiguous. The last is quite revealing, but also very time-consuming, subjective, and, except for "denials," of unknown reliability. The scales are objective, reliably scored, and have the interpretation already built into them.

However, even if consideration were confined to one variant of each scale, there would still be approximately 150 scoreable scales on the PAT. In order to avoid the labor of scoring all scales, the sequential procedure described in Chapter V was used.

The two samples were first compared with respect to individual plate responses. Those which differentiated the two groups at the 20 percent level of significance (using the NW sample of 459 cases) were chosen. Using these responses, it was possible to select the scales upon which these responses appear.

It will be recalled that a plate is a set of three pictures, and an individual plate response is an arrangement of the three pictures on a given plate. Since each picture is marked with a symbol, Tomkins and Miner denote a particular response by an arrangement of the three letters, V, L, and O, which are arranged in the same order as the corresponding pictures. (To facilitate typing, V, L, and O are used in place of the symbols △, □, and ○, respectively.) The individual responses which were found to differentiate at the 20 percent level were:

1. More frequent among northern whites:

    2-VOL, 4-VOL, 5-VOL, 6-VLO, 7-OVL, 8-LVO, 9-OLV, 11-LVO, 13-VLO, 14-VOL, 15-VOL, 16-VLO, 17-VOL, 18-VOL, 22-OVL, 23-VOL, 24-VLO.

2. More frequent among southern blacks:

    1-OVL, 2-VLO, 2-OVL, 3-LVO, 4-VLO, 4-OVL, 5-LVO, 5-LOV, 6-OVL, 6-LOV, 7-VOL, 7-VLO, 8-VLO, 9-OVL, 9-LOV, 10-LVO, 10-LOV, 11-OVL, 12-OVL, 13-VOL, 13-OVL, 14-VLO, 14-OVL, 14-LOV, 15-OLV, 16-LOV, 17-OLV, 17-LOV, 18-LOV, 19-LVO, 20-VLO, 21-VOL, 24-LOV, 25-VLO.

These individual plate responses were then used as the basis for the three-stage process of elimination by which the PAT scales that distinguish northern whites from southern blacks were discovered.

Of the 158 PAT scales, all but 41 were eliminated in the first stage. Of these 41 scales, 11 were eliminated either because they represented a degree of specificity which seemed unnecessary, or because the relevant information was contained in other scales which had been selected in this first step. Because of the crudeness of the first step, 18 scales were added which did not quite meet the objective criterion, but which were strongly indicated in the literature, or which might cast light upon the meaning of some of the scales which did meet the criterion, making 48 scales still under consideration.

In the second stage, all but 20 scales were eliminated. (Since this stage utilized the "f" variant of each scale, it should be noted that no "f" variant exists for scales 122, 123, and 180, and that for these scales the "a" variant was used.)

In the last stage of selection, in which these 20 scales were scored for each person, and the difference between the two samples was tested for significance, seven scales were selected.

The list of the PAT scales shows the process of elimination. Those which passed the first stage of elimination are indicated by an asterisk, "*"; those which passed the second stage of elimination are indicated by a double asterisk, "**"; and those which when individually scored reached the 20 percent level of significance are indicated by a triple asterisk, "***". Those which passed the first stage, but were eliminated are indicated by "#"; and those which did not quite pass the first stage, but were added anyway are indicated by parentheses around the *first* asterisk, "(*)". (The numbering begins with 97 since the first 96 PAT scales are special scales which ask only whether or not an individual is typical without specifying any interpretable characteristics.)

The last two scales are not defined in the Tomkins and Miner manual but were devised for this study. Scale 253 consists of sequences in which action by a "father figure" (foreman, doctor), which should be helpful, does not, in fact, help. Scale 254 was devised by separating the sex plate, plate 10, from the other plates which are scored on scale 153 (Freudian super-ego), and scoring only responses dealing with aggression.

I. SOCIAL ORIENTATION

A.   Sociophilia (liking to be with people)

(97)	1.	High General Sociophilia
(98)	a.	Happy Sociophilia
**(99)	b.	Homosexual Sociophilia—Masculine-Masculine
(100)		(1) Homosexual Sociophilia—Friendly Group of Men
(101)		(2) Homosexual Sociophilia—Two Men Together
*(102)	c.	Heterosexual Sociophilia
(103)	d.	Large Group Sociophilia—over four people

(104)   e. Small Group Sociophilia—three or four people
#(105)   f. Sociophilia—Preference for Meeting Eyes of Others
(106)   (1) Sociophilia—Preference for Meeting Eyes of Same Sex Person
                         —Masculine-Masculine
(107)   (2) Sociophilia—Preference for Meeting Eyes of Other Sex Person
(108)   g. Sociophilia—Preference for Physical Contact
(109)   (1) Sociophilia—Preference for Physical Contact with Same Sex
                         Person—Masculine-Masculine
(110)   (2) Sociophilia—Preference for Physical Contact with Other Sex
                         Person
(111)   (3) Sociophilia—Preference for Physical Contact with One Other
                         Person
(*)(112)   (a) Sociophilia—Preference for Physical Contact with One
                              Same Sex Person—Masculine-Masculine
*(113)   (b) Sociophilia—Preference for Physical Contact with One
                              Other Sex Person
(114)   h. Sociophilia in Work Situation
(115)   i. Sociophilia—Work Facilitated by Others
*(116)   j. Sociophilia—Work Initiated but not Sustained by Others

B. Sociophobia (fear of people)

(*)(117)   1. High General Sociophobia
(118)   a. Sociophobia in Work Situation
#(119)   b. Sociophobia—Avoidance of Physical Contact
***(120)   (1) Sociophobia—Avoidance of Physical Contact with Same Sex
                         Person—Masculine-Masculine
**(121)   (2) Sociophobia—Avoidance of Physical Contact with Other Sex
                         Person

C. Aggression

(*)(122)   1. High General Aggressive Need
(*)(123)   2. Low General Aggressive Need
***(124)   3. High General Aggressive Press
(*)*(125)   4. Negativism
(*)(126)   5. High Reactive Short-Lived Aggressive Need
(127)   6. Delayed Expression of Aggression
***(128)   7. High General Aggressive Need; Delayed and Negativistic Aggression

D. Dependence

(129)   1. General Dependence—Support a Necessary Condition of Work or
                    Optimism
(130)   2. General Dependence—Support a Necessary and Sustaining Condition of
                    Work or Optimism
**(131)   3. General Dependence—Support a Necessary but not Sustaining Condition
                    of Work or Optimism
(132)   a. Dependence—Assistance a Necessary Condition of Work and/or
                    Optimism
(133)   b. Dependence—Assistance a Necessary and Sustaining Condition of
                    Work and/or Optimism
(134)   c. Dependence—Assistance a Necessary but not Sustaining Condition of
                    Work and/or Optimism
(135)   d. Dependence—Instruction a Necessary Condition of Work
(136)   e. Dependence—Instruction a Necessary and Sustaining Condition of
                    Work
*(137)   f. Dependence—Praise a Necessary Condition of Work
(138)   g. Dependence—Praise a Necessary and Sustaining Condition of Work

*(139)   4. General Dependence—Continuing Support as End State
#(140)   a. Dependence—Continuing Support as End State—Assistance, Praise, and/or Instruction
(141)   b. Dependence—Continuing Support as End State—Assistance and/or Praise
(142)   c. Dependence—Continuing Support as End State—Dominance and/or Instruction
(143)   d. Dependence—Continuing Support as End State—Instruction
(144)   e. Dependence—Continuing Support as End State—Assistance
(145)   f. Dependence—Continuing Support as End State—Praise
(146)   (1) Dependence—Continuing Support as End State—Praise from Individual
(147)   (2) Dependence—Continuing Support as End State—Praise from Group
**(148)   g. Dependence—Continuing Support as End State—Oral Satisfaction

E. Lability (changeableness)

(149)   1. General Social Restlessness
(150)   a. Social Restlessness—Sociophilic
(151)   b. Social Restlessness—Sociophobic

F. Super-Ego (conscience)

(*)(152)   1. Strong General Super-ego
(*)*(153)   a. Strong Super-ego—Sex Guilt and/or Back to Work after Aggression

II. OPTIMISM-PESSIMISM

A. Optimism

*(154)   1. High General Optimism
(*)(155)   a. High General Self-confidence
(156)   (1) High Self-confidence—Overcome Obstacles and/or Win Approbation from Individual
(157)   (2) High Self-confidence—Overcome Obstacles and/or Win Approbation from Group
(158)   (3) High Self-confidence—Overcome Obstacles
(159)   (4) High Self-confidence—Win Approbation from Individual
(160)   (5) High Self-confidence—Win Approbation from Group
(*)(161)   b. General Happy Mood
(162)   (1) General Happy Mood—Non-work Environment
(163)   (2) General Happy Mood—Work Environment
(164)   (3) General Happy Mood When Alone

B. Pessimism

**(165)   1. High General Pessimism
*(166)   a. Low General Self-confidence
(167)   (1) Low Self-confidence—Failure to Overcome Obstacles
#(168)   (2) Low Self-confidence—Failure to Win Approbation from Group
*(169)   b. General Unhappy Mood
(170)   (1) Unhappy Mood When Alone
*(171)   c. General Hypochondriasis
(172)   (1) Hypochondriasis—Injury Proneness, Pessimism in Hospital and/or Pessimism in Bed
(173)   (2) Hypochondriasis—Injury Proneness and/or Pessimism in Hospital
(174)   (3) Hypochondriasis—Injury Proneness
(175)   (4) Hypochondriasis—Pessimism in Hospital

III. LEVELS

A. *Thinking*

(176)   1. Reflective Problem Solving

B. *Phantasy*

(177)   1. High General Phantasy Life
(178)   a. High Phantasy Life of Passivity and/or Glory
(179)   b. High Phantasy Life of Passivity and/or Hostility
(*)*(180)   c. High Phantasy Life of Hostility and/or Glory
(181)   d. High Phantasy Life Instigated by Work
(182)   2. Phantasy a Necessary Condition for Work
(183)   3. Phantasy Stops Work
(184)   4. Phantasy Produces Passivity Followed by Work
(185)   5. Phantasy Tends to be Acted Out
*(186)   6. Phantasy Leads to Behavior Opposite to Content of Phantasy
*(187)   7. Phantasy and/or Special States (Sleep, Fatigue, Injury, Hypnosis) as
             Escape Mechanisms from Work and/or Activity

C. *Affect*

(188)   1. General Strong Affect
(189)   a. Strong Affect—Happy, Sad, and/or Laughing
(190)   b. Strong Affect—Happy and/or Sad
(191)   c. Strong Affect—Happy, Angry and/or Laughing
(192)   d. Strong Affect—Angry and/or Sad
(193)   e. Strong Affect—Sad Alone and/or Laughing in Group
(194)   f. Strong Affect—Affect Disrupts Physical Work
***(195)   2. General Weak Affect
#(196)   a. Weak Affect—Sad, Happy, and/or Laughing
#(197)   b. Weak Affect—Happy and/or Sad
(198)   c. Weak Affect—Affect not Disruptive of Physical Work
#(199)   3. General Lability of Affect and Restlessness
(*)*(200)   a. General Restlessness—Tendency to Move from One Environment to
             Another
**(201)   b. Lability—Rapid Change of Person and/or Non-social Environment
***(202)   4. General Labile Affect
#(203)   a. Labile Affect—Heterosexual Situations
(204)   b. Labile Affect—Trend to Happy Mood
(*)(205)   c. Labile Affect—Trend to Optimistic Neutrality
#(206)   d. Labile Affect—Trend to Unhappy Mood
(207)   e. Labile Affect—Trend to Pessimistic Neutrality
(208)   5. Non-labile Graded Affect—Tendency to Pessimism
(209)   a. Non-labile Graded Affect—Tendency to Optimism

D. *Overt Behavior*

(210)   1. High Activity Level in Non-work Environment
(211)   a. High Activity Level—Preference for Upright Posture as Opposed to
             Relaxed Posture
*(212)   2. High Activity Level in Work and/or Non-work Environment
(213)   3. General Passivity in Non-work Environment
#(214)   a. Passivity—Tendency to Sit and/or Lean
(215)   b. Passivity—Tendency to Lie Down
(216)   (1) Passivity—Tendency to Lie Down When Alone

IV. WORK ORIENTATION

A. *Strong Work Orientation*

*(217)   1. High General Work and/or Work Interest

*(218)   2. High General Work
(219)   a. High General Work Where Passivity in the Work Situation is Possible
(220)   b. High General Work Where Passivity in the Work Situation is not Possible
(*)(221) 3. High General Work—Preference for Work Environment
(222)   4. High General Work Despite Conflict

B. Weak Work Orientation

**(223) 1. Low General Work
#(224)   2. Low General Work Where Activity in the Work Situation is Possible
(225)   3. Low General Work—Rejection of Work Environment

C. Social Facilitation of Work

**(226)   1. Negative Social Facilitation—Others Stop Work
(*)**(227)   2. Social Facilitation a Necessary but not Sustaining Condition of Work
(228)   3. Temporary Negative Social Facilitation of Work

D. Work Inertia

(229)   1. High Starting Inertia Followed by High Enduring Work—Works After Distraction
(230)   a. High Starting Inertia Followed by High Enduring Work—Works After Passivity
(231)   2. Starting Inertia Followed by Low Endurance in Work—Works After Passivity
(*)**(232)   a. Starting Inertia Followed by Low Endurance in Work—Works After Distraction
(*)(233) 3. Low Work Endurance—Work Interrupted
(*)(234)   a. Extremely Low Work Endurance

E. Super-Ego in Work Environment

(235)   1. Strong Super-ego—Back to Work After Injury, Passivity, Fatigue, Sociophilia and/or Anger
(236)   a. Strong Super-ego—Back to Work After Injury, Passivity, Sociophilia and/or Anger
(237)   b. Strong Super-ego—Back to Work After Injury, Passivity, Fatigue and/or Sociophilia
(238)   c. Strong Super-ego—Back to Work After Passivity, Fatigue, Sociophilia and/or Anger
(239)   d. Strong Super-ego—Back to Work After Injury, Fatigue, Sociophilia and/or Anger
(240)   e. Strong Super-ego—Back to Work After Injury, Passivity, Fatigue and/or Anger
(241)   f. Strong Super-ego—Back to Work After Passivity and/or Sociophilia
(242)   g. Strong Super-ego—Back to Work After Passivity and/or Anger
(243)   h. Strong Super-ego—Back to Work After Passivity and/or Fatigue
(244)   i. Strong Super-ego—Back to Work After Injury and/or Passivity
(245)   j. Strong Super-ego—Back to Work After Sociophilia and/or Anger
(246)   k. Strong Super-ego—Back to Work After Fatigue and/or Sociophilia
(247)   l. Strong Super-ego—Back to Work After Injury and/or Sociophilia
(248)   m. Strong Super-ego—Back to Work After Fatigue and/or Anger
(249)   n. Strong Super-ego—Back to Work After Fatigue and/or Injury
(250)   o. Strong Super-ego—Back to Work After Anger and/or Injury
(251)   p. Strong Super-ego—Back to Work After Injury
(252)   q. Strong Super-ego—Back to Work After Passivity

V. ADDITIONAL SCALES

*(253)   A. Mistrust of Fathers Figures

**(254)   B. Guilt After Aggression

Scoring denials

The verbal descriptions were scored only for "denials." Denials were scored on the following plates:

Plate 4:   Denial of physical aggression
Plate 13:   Denial of aggressive press
Plate 13:   Denial of symbolic aggression
Plate 16:   Denial of physical injury with serious consequences
Plate 21:   Denial of physical injury without serious consequences
Plate 25:   Denial of symbolic aggression

Plate 16 is identical with plate 21 except for one picture, the one usually given as representing the result of the injury. In plate 16, this is a picture of a man in a hospital bed, while in plate 21 this is a picture of a man still at work being taken care of by a doctor. Plates 13 and 25, too, are identical except for one picture. On both plates, one of the pictures portrays a man working, and another shows the same man standing near his machine "thumbing" his nose and thinking of the boss. The remaining picture on plate 13 depicts the boss "bawling out" the hero, while on plate 25 this is replaced by a picture showing the hero standing near the machine, so that the hero is the only person depicted in any picture on plate 25.

Results

The difference between the two samples in the percentage of cases who were extreme reached the 20 percent level of significance for only seven scales out of the twenty which were scored. In addition, four out of the six denial scores reached this level of significance. (The significance of the difference in percentage was tested graphically by means of binomial probability paper—Mosteller and Tukey.) On each of these characteristics the percentage of extreme cases was greater in the black sample than in the northern white sample. These eleven characteristics, the number of extreme cases in each sample, and the significance of the differences in percentage are shown in Table VI-3.

These represent the hypotheses, or ideas about the differences between blacks and whites, located in the pilot study, which were to be tested in the later parts of this research. They are here rearranged according

Table VI-3 RESULTS OF THE PILOT STUDY,
SAMPLES NW (N=148) AND SB-1 (N=51)

Differentiating variable		Number of extreme cases		
		NW	SB-1	p<
Plate 25:	Denial of symbolic aggression	18	27	.002
Plate 13:	Denial of aggressive press	15	21	.002
Plate 13:	Denial of symbolic aggression	24	24	.002
Scale 120:	Sociophobia—avoidance of physical contact with same-sex person—masculine-masculine	2	8	.002
Plate 4:	Denial of physical aggression	5	8	.02
Scale 128:	High general aggressive need—delayed and negativistic aggression	5	8	.02
Scale 202:	General labile affect	5	6	.10
Scale 124:	High general aggressive press	4	5	.10
Scale 195:	General weak affect	4	5	.10
Scale 227:	Social facilitation a necessary but not sustaining condition for work	3	4	.20
Scale 232:	Starting inertia followed by low endurance in work—works after distraction	0	2	.20

THE AREA OF AGGRESSION

to the area of personality functioning, so as to consider their possible meaning.

The area of aggression

According to many observers (e.g., Cayton, Dai, Powdermaker, as well as Kardiner and Ovesey), the core problem of the American black is his handling of aggression. Six of our eleven differentiating characteristics are related to this problem.

Scale 124: High general aggressive press. The first hypothesis located in the pilot study is that a black is more likely to feel that people are angry at him, and are going out of their way to "make trouble" for him; this is what is referred to as aggressive "press." It is not simply a statement of the objective situation. It is a statement about the internalized expectation about other people which an individual carries around with him. This expectation is manifested on the PAT by sequences which end with the hero being aggressed against; therefore, responses VOL and OVL

13

19

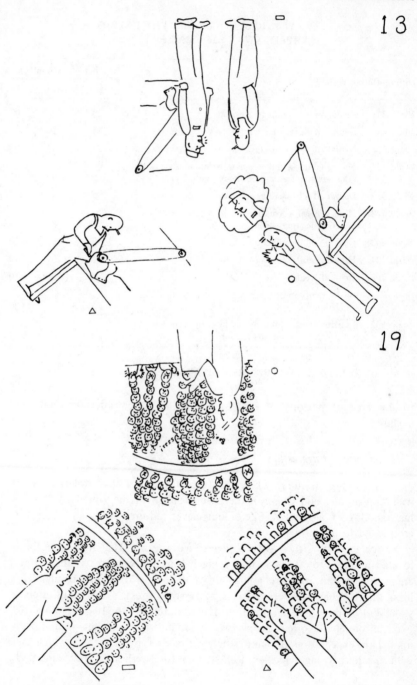

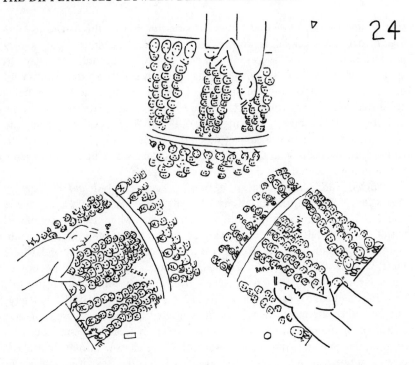

on plate 13, responses VLO and LVO on plate 19, and responses VOL and OVL on plate 24 are scored on this scale.

Of these, response VOL on plate 24 is a "popular" response; response VOL on plate 13 and VLO on plate 19 are "semi-popular" responses; and response OVL on plate 13, response LVO on plate 19, and response OVL on plate 24 are "rare" responses. All six responses are scored on the "a" variant; the semi-populars and rares are scored on the "f" variant; and only the rares are scored on the "d" variant. The cutting points for this scale are three for the "a" and "f" variants and two for the "d" variant, i.e., in order to be scored as extreme on the "a" or "f" variant of this scale it is necessary to give a response which ends with the hero being aggressed against on each of the three plates where such responses are possible, while in order to be extreme on the "d" variant, it is only necessary to give such responses on two of the plates if both responses are rare. Any individual who was extreme on at least one of these three variants was considered extreme on this personality characteristic.

Plate 13: Denial of aggressive press. The conviction that people are going out of their way to make trouble for you is, of course, frightening. One way of dealing with a frightening situation, albeit an inefficient way, is simply not to recognize that any such situation exists; this is the psychological defense mechanism known as denial. An individual who is very much afraid of being aggressed against, and who, in order to allay his anxiety, characteristically invokes the primitive defense mechanism of denial may manifest this on the PAT by denying that the hero is being aggressed against on plate 13. Picture L of that plate is commonly described as "The boss is bawling him out" or "The foreman's giving him hell." If, instead of this, a subject described the action as "The mechanic is telling him everything is OK" or "The boss comes and helps him again," the response is scored as a denial of aggressive press.

Scale 128:   High general aggressive need; delayed and negativistic aggression.   The natural reactions to being aggressed against are, on the one hand, fear and, on the other, anger. Even when fear is dominant, hatred is still felt. When, however, as in the case of a black person, counter-aggression is likely to meet with increased aggression, and where there is little doubt of the inevitable outcome, there is no hope but to stifle any impulse to fight back. One's own anger becomes a problem; this may be handled by suppression (that is, the person is aware he is angry, but he either attempts to control his anger or any actions based on that anger) or by repression (the anger is completely barred from consciousness, so that the person is no longer aware of being angry). Insofar as a black person *suppresses* his anger, we would expect the reactive increase in aggression to be reflected in the PAT not on the high general aggression scale, but as an increase in delayed expressions of aggression (aggression is aroused or expressed in the picture placed first, and then not expressed in the second, and finally expressed) or in negativism (mediation of another person stops work or leads to aggression). Two of the responses which make up this scale are LVO and VLO on plate 13; the former is an example of a delayed expression of aggression, and the latter is an example of a negativistic response.

Plate 4:   Denial of physical aggression.   It is reasonable to expect that a good deal of the defending against an extremely frightening problem about which no effective action is possible will be accomplished by means of unconscious mechanisms, that is, mechanisms of whose action the individual himself is unaware. We have already noted the increase in the use of the defense mechanism of denial with respect to aggressive press. This same massive defense is invoked in this test against the recognition of a situation involving blatant physical aggression. Plate 4 is commonly described as "(L) having a hot argument, (O) someone breaks it up, (V) all friends now," or "(V) telling jokes, (O) someone gets mad, (L) gets into a fight." If, instead of this, the action is described as "(O) looks to me like they're on a dance

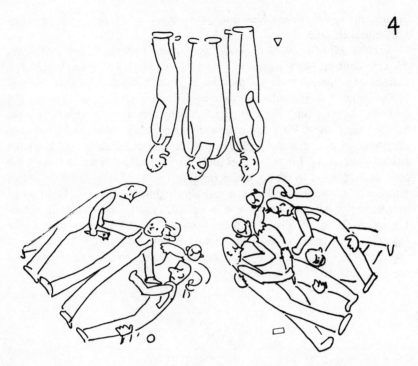

floor, (L) I don't know what to give here, (V) looks like they are at a party and are dancing and singing" or "(V) the men are talking, (O) the men are working, (L) the rest of the men are working, too," the response is scored as a denial of physical aggression.

Plate 13: Denial of symbolic aggression. Physical aggression is not the only kind of aggression, nor is it the only kind which is frightening. The retaliation for verbal or symbolic aggression ("symbolic" is used not in the psychoanalytic sense, but merely to indicate an act which does not directly inflict physical pain or suffering upon another person, but which is an expression of aggression because of its socially defined significance) may be as severe as the punishment for a physical assault. Even the feeling of anger and the thought of being angry may become so frightening that the impulse to be angry is subjected to a massive *repression*. In order to safeguard this repression, the defense of denial may then be invoked against any situation which is too closely related to the repressed impulse. Thus, on plate 13 the subject may deny that the hero feels angry. Picture O of that plate is commonly described as "He's just telling the supervisor where to go" or "He is hot under the collar and is thumbing his nose at the boss." If, instead of this, the action is described as "He is blowing his nose" or "He has cut his finger and can picture that guy bawling him out," the response is scored as a denial of symbolic aggression.

Plate 25: Denial of symbolic aggression. Pictures V and L of plates 25 are identical with pictures V and O of plate 13, respectively. The remaining picture of each set provides a context which influences the subject's reactions to the other two pictures. Picture L of plate 13 shows the foreman "bawling out" the hero; this is usually seen as the instigation for the hero's feeling angry. Plate 25 has no such instigation included in the pictures. For some subjects it is less frightening to express anger when there is no one around to retaliate; for others it is more frightening inasmuch as there is no obvious instigation to the aggression (and the feeling of anger therefore seems "irrational"); and for many it is equally frightening (or not frightening) irrespective of whether anyone else is around. Typical descriptions of picture L of plate 25 are "To heck with the foreman" or "Thumbs his nose at the foreman." If, instead of this, the picture is described as "He is waiting on somebody to come help" or "A friend is looking at him," the response is scored as a denial of symbolic aggression.

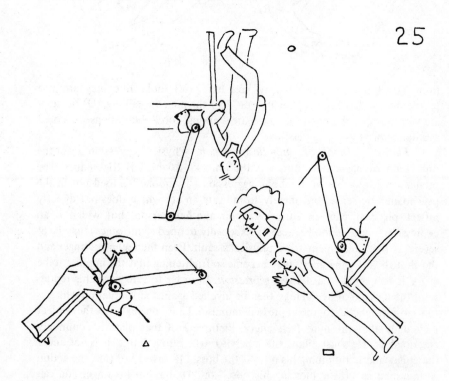

25

The use of denial

The psychological mechanism of denial is perhaps the most basic of the defenses. (Cf. Anna Freud.) It is a primitive and inefficient mode of coping with unpleasant reality which is called into play when a person is faced with an unpleasant situation about which he can do nothing. This defense mechanism is more frequently utilized by children than by adults, and more frequently utilized by pathological individuals than by normals. Denial is most frequently utilized by psychotic patients. The fact that we find, in the pilot study, an increase in the use of denial with respect to stimuli relating to every aspect of aggression measured by the PAT raises the possibility that, as suggested by Kardiner and Ovesey, blacks are more prone to use denial than other defense mechanisms. If, however, we consider denials of physical injury, both with and without serious consequences, we find that these denials are not significantly more frequent (at the 20 percent level) in the black sample. This result leads to the conclusion that blacks are not necessarily more prone to use denial than are whites, but they may have more problems for which denial is a more nearly appropriate defense, e.g., provocations toward reacting aggressively, of which they are afraid, and with which they feel powerless to cope.

Emotionality

Scale 195: General weak affect. When people are dealing with the problem of choking back anger, their whole emotional life may be seriously disrupted. One of the effects, according to Kardiner and Ovesey, is not an increase in either happiness or unhappiness, in the sense of awareness of feeling, but rather a general deadening of affect. This is manifested on the PAT by sequences which end with no emotion where it was possible to end with a strong emotion. Responses VOL, OVL, and LVO on plate 11 are examples of the sequences which make up this scale.

Scale 202: General labile affect. Still another consequence of anger which breaks through and must be choked back, both consciously and unconsciously, and yet may break through again, is that the whole affective life may become an extremely unstable equilibrium wherein an emotion may be immediately followed by its opposite. This emotional lability may be manifested on the PAT by sequences wherein moods change to their opposites quickly and without an intermediate neutral stage—i.e., sadness to happiness or vice versa, friendliness to anger, etc. Responses VOL, OVL, LVO, and LOV on plate 12 are examples of sequences which make up this scale.

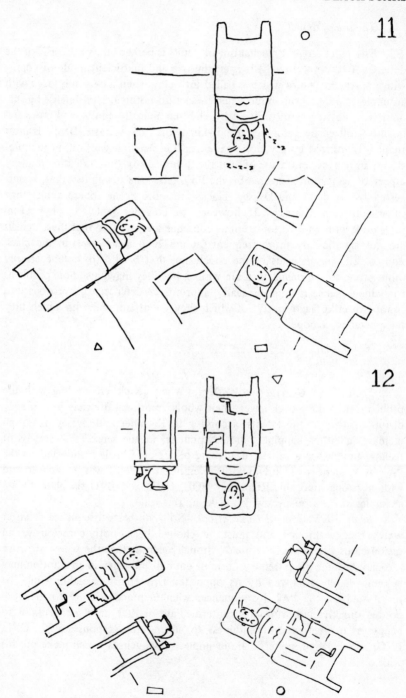

Attitudes toward work

Scale 227: Social facilitation a necessary but not sustaining condition of work (Externalized work motivation). An emphasis on work is a dominant characteristic of the American culture, and it is internalized to a greater or lesser extent by various segments of the population. But, as Myrdal and Frazier have pointed out, the southern black is not rewarded to the same degree as other segments of the population for working hard and saving, or for showing independence; in fact, such behavior is apt to be looked upon as getting "uppity." He is often rewarded for dependency rather than hard work. We should, therefore, expect him to be less likely than the northern white (or black) to internalize the emphasis on work which is characteristic of the American culture as a whole. In this sense, we may speak of the southern black as having "weak" internalized standards with respect to work. External stimuli may provide the motivation where internal stimuli are lacking. This is shown in PAT sequences where the hero receives praise, help, or aggression from a male authority figure, after which the hero goes to work, but the work is not sustained. Response LOV on plate 5 is an example of a sequence which is part of this scale.

Scale 232: Starting inertia followed by low endurance in work—works after distraction (Conflicting work motivation). Perhaps a clearer picture is given by considering the black as essentially a man in conflict: getting and holding a job, especially a decent job, remains his biggest problem, yet the apparent impossibility of accomplishing anything may make it difficult for him to maintain his motivation. Such a conflict may be manifested by sequences in which an interruption (or potential distraction) is followed by working, but ends in not working. This would seem to indicate an effort to counteract the distraction, but the motivation peters out. Response OVL on plate 1 is an example of a sequence which is part of this scale.

It is interesting to note that the black does not seem to be differentiated on scales which indicate either high or low work motivation, but only on scales which indicate conflict about work.

Interpersonal relations

Scale 120: Sociophobia—avoidance of physical contact with same sex person—masculine-masculine (Avoidance of male-male contacts). A feeling that people are potentially dangerous may lead one to avoid close contact with others when possible. This may be manifested on the PAT by sequences where the hero ends alone when there were possibilities for the hero to end in close physical contact with someone else. Such a tendency to avoid close physical contact was found in this pilot study for male-male situations, but not for male-female situations. Inasmuch as there are no female-female situations depicted in the PAT plates, the possibility cannot be precluded that the avoidance of male-male contacts represents a generalized avoidance of close physical contact between members of the same sex. Nevertheless, the most plausible assumption is that this is specifically an avoidance of close physical contact between men since these are the contacts most likely to erupt in physical aggression. Responses LVO and LOV on plate 5 are examples of sequences which are part of this scale.

The discriminant score

In order to be able to test in the later studies whether northern and southern blacks are discriminated by this set of eleven personality characteristics, and whether this discrimination may be accounted for by the background factors, other than the caste sanctions enforced against blacks, which differentiate the North from the South, each person was given a score of +1 on a personality characteristic if he was extreme on that characteristic, and a score of zero otherwise. The scores on each of these eleven personality characteristics were added up for each subject to form a crude discriminant score, which could vary from 0 to 11. (Seven was the highest score actually obtained by any person in any of the samples in this research.) The distributions on this discriminant score of NW, the northern white sample, and of SB-1, the southern black sample with which NW had been compared, are shown in Table VI-4.

The clear tendency for southern blacks to have higher discriminant scores than the northern white sample is, of course, a necessary consequence of the fact that the characteristics which make up the discriminant score were chosen on the basis of the differences between these two samples. However, we could now ask whether or not these differences were due to the effects of the extraneous background factors which differentiate the South from the North.

Of these characteristics, sex, rural-urban residence, population density of the general area, and degree of industrialization of the general area were found to be unrelated to the discriminant score, and therefore could not account for the differences. Age, education, and vocabulary, however, did seem to be appreciably related.

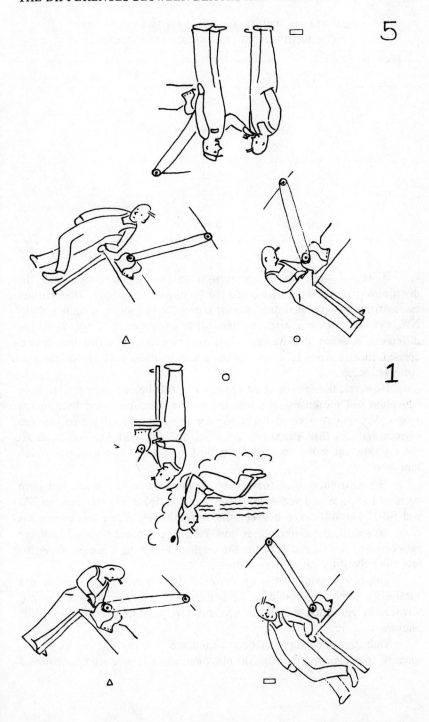

Table VI-4 DISTRIBUTION OF DISCRIMINANT SCORES
FOR SAMPLES NW (N=148) AND SB-1 (N=51)

Score	NW	SB-1
0	103	12
1	24	11
2	10	8
3	5	2
4	4	12
5	2	1
6	—	3
7	—	2
Average Score	0.57	2.31

Since, of these three, age seemed to have the greatest effect, the discriminant scores were first corrected for the effects of age. The distributions of the age-corrected discriminant scores for the northern white sample, NW, and the southern black sample, SB-1, are shown in Table VI-5. The difference between the average scores (or means) of the two samples decreased slightly from 1.74 for the uncorrected scores to 1.56 for the age-corrected scores.

However, the age-corrected scores were still appreciably related to both education and vocabulary, although less so than the uncorrected discriminant scores. Vocabulary seemed to be slightly more closely related to the age-corrected scores than education; consequently, the next step was to adjust the discriminant score for the effects both of age and of vocabulary simultaneously.

The distributions of these new discriminant scores, which had been corrected for age and vocabulary, are shown in Table VI-6 for samples NW and SB-1. The difference between the average scores of the two groups has again decreased; the difference is now 1.38 as compared with 1.56 for the age-corrected scores, and 1.74 for the original discriminant scores. Nevertheless, the bulk of the difference remains.

This new discriminant score, corrected for the effects of both age and vocabulary level, was found to be unrelated to education. Therefore, differences in education could not account for the differences between the samples.

Thus the possibility has been eliminated that the differences in personality characteristics between the black and white sample can be accounted

Table VI-5   DISTRIBUTION OF AGE-CORRECTED DISCRIMINANT SCORES
IN SAMPLES NW (N=148) AND SB-1 (N=51)

Score	NW	SB-1
0.0-0.4	6	1
0.5-0.9	30	7
1.0-1.4	70	6
1.5-1.9	10	6
2.0-2.4	15	5
2.5-2.9	4	4
3.0-3.4	3	3
3.5-3.9	2	1
4.0-4.4	3	4
4.5-4.9	3	6
5.0-5.4	0	2
5.5-5.9	0	1
6.0-6.4	2	1
6.5-6.9	0	2
7.0-7.4	0	0
7.5-7.9	0	2
Average Score	1.50	3.06

Table VI-6   DISTRIBUTION OF AGE- AND VOCABULARY-CORRECTED
DISCRIMINANT SCORES IN SAMPLES NW (N=148) AND SB-1 (N=51)

Score	NW	SB-1
0.0-0.4	0	0
0.5-0.9	1	0
1.0-1.4	17	6
1.5-1.9	50	7
2.0-2.4	43	5
2.5-2.9	12	7
3.0-3.4	11	2
3.5-3.9	2	4
4.0-4.4	4	2
4.5-4.9	3	2
5.0-5.4	3	7
5.5-5.9	0	3
6.0-6.4	0	1
6.5-6.9	1	1
7.0-7.4	1	0
7.5-7.9	0	2
8.0-8.4	0	2
Average Score	2.27	3.65

for on the basis of extraneous background factors—the ratio of men to women, how rural or urban a community they live in, how thickly populated or heavily industrialized an area they live in, their differences in age, or in vocabularly intelligence, or in education.

We are still left with the question of whether the differences in personality were due to chance, hereditary differences between blacks and whites, or the effects of the caste sanctions. For the answer to this question we have to await the outcome of another experiment.

THE DIFFERENCES BETWEEN
NORTHERN AND SOUTHERN BLACKS

If the caste sanctions have an effect upon human beings, and if the differences in personality between blacks and whites are caused by these social pressures, then northern blacks will differ from southern blacks on precisely the same characteristics, and in the same way, as do northern whites, although the magnitude of the differences may not be the same.

Of course, the differences must reach the generally accepted levels of statistical significance even after the background variables have been taken into account before it would be reasonable for us to conclude that the effects of the caste sanctions upon the human personality had been demonstrated.

A sample of northern blacks and a sample of southern blacks were compared to provide an answer to our question. These validation samples consisted of the 70 northern blacks (sample NB) from the Gallup sample, and the 52 southern blacks (sample SB-2) *who had not been used in the pilot study*. The geographical distributions of these two samples are shown in Table VII-1. The distributions of these samples by age, education, I.Q. (vocabulary), rural-urban residence, and sex are shown in Table VII-2.

Results of the validation

Each person in these two samples, NB and SB-2, was scored on each of the eleven characteristics which in the pilot study had seemed to differentiate northern whites from southern blacks. (It will be recalled that, in order to eliminate any bias in scoring the "write-ins," these two samples

137

Table VII-1 GEOGRAPHICAL DISTRIBUTION OF CASES

NB (N=70)		SB-2 (N=52)	
Maine	0	Maryland	2
New Hampshire	0	Virginia	6
Vermont	0	North Carolina	2
Massachusetts	1	Kentucky	0
Rhode Island	0	Tennessee	4
Connecticut	0	Oklahoma	4
New York	21	Texas	4
New Jersey	13	Florida	3
Pennsylvania	7	South Carolina	5
Ohio	10	Georgia	5
Michigan	0	Alabama	8
Illinois	11	Mississippi	5
Wisconsin	0	Louisiana	2
Minnesota	0	Arkansas	2
Iowa	1		
Nevada	0		
California	5		
Washington	1		

had been combined randomly with samples NW and SB-1 and all four samples scored on the six denial scores without the scorer knowing from which sample any test booklet had come.) The number of extreme cases in samples NB and SB-2 on each of the eleven characteristics is shown in Table VII-3.

To provide an overall test of the basic idea, or hypothesis, that northern blacks differ from southern blacks on the same personality characteristics and in the same direction as do northern whites, the discriminant score (D_i) for each individual was determined, as in the pilot study, by adding up for that individual the number of these characteristics upon which he was extreme. The resulting distributions of discriminant scores are shown in Table VII-4. The average scores, or means, of the two samples do in fact differ in the predicted direction. The basic hypothesis would seem to be confirmed unless this difference could be accounted for by the background variables or by chance.

To eliminate the effects of the background variables, the discriminant scores corrected for age ($D_{i \cdot a}$) and the discriminant scores corrected for both age and vocabulary ($D_{ia \cdot v}$) were computed for each person, using the formulas given in Chapter V. The resulting distributions of $D_{i \cdot a}$ and $D_{i \cdot va}$

Table VII-2   DISTRIBUTION OF NN AND OF SN-2
BY BACKGROUND FACTORS

	NB	SB-2
Age		
10-19	12	5
20-29	11	3
30-39	12	4
40-49	14	5
50-59	10	17
60-69	8	8
70-79	2	9
80-89	1	0
90-99	0	1
Education		
0	5	13
1-6 years	21	16
7-8 years	15	19
High school, incomplete	13	1
High school, complete	12	1
College, incomplete	3	2
College graduate	1	0
Nurses training	0	0
Trade school or beauty school	0	0
Business school or college	0	0
Intelligence (Vocabulary)		
Borderline and defective (Below 80)	13	13
Dull normal (80-90)	22	20
Average (90-110)	29	19
High average (110-120)	5	0
Superior (120 or above)	1	0
Rural-Urban Residence		
Farm	0	24
Non-farm under 2,500	6	9
2,500-10,000	5	1
10,000-24,999	1	11
25,000-49,999	2	0
50,000-99,999	9	2
100,000-499,999	7	4
500,000 and above	40	1
Sex		
Male	36	25
Female	34	27

Table VII-3   RESULTS FOR SAMPLES NB (N=70) AND SB-2 (N=52)

Differentiating variable	Number of extreme cases	
	NB	SB-2
Scale 124: High general aggressive press	2	4
Plate 13: Denial of aggressive press	13	25
Plate 4: Denial of physical aggression	9	14
Plate 13: Denial of symbolic aggression	19	28
Plate 25: Denial of symbolic aggression	22	26
Scale 128: High general aggressive need—delayed and negativistic aggression	7	5
Scale 195: General weak affect	4	7
Scale 202: General labile affect	6	10
Scale 227: Externalized work motivation	2	3
Scale 232: Conflicting work motivation	1	1
Scale 120: Sociophobia—avoidance of physical contact with same sex person—masculine-masculine	7	4

Table VII-4 DISTRIBUTION OF DISCRIMINANT SCORES
FOR SAMPLES NB (N=70) AND SB-2 (N=52)

Score	NB	SB-2
0	35	12
1	10	5
2	8	8
3	8	10
4	6	9
5	1	8
6	1	0
7	1	0
Average Score	1.31	2.44

are shown in Tables VII-5 and VII-6. When the corrections for the background variables had been carried out, the difference between the average scores of these two samples remained in the predicted direction but decreased in magnitude from 1.13 for the uncorrected discriminant scores to .92 for the age-corrected scores and to .85 for the scores corrected for both age and vocabulary.

Table VII-5   DISTRIBUTION OF AGE-CORRECTED
DISCRIMINANT SCORES IN SAMPLES NB (N=70) AND SB-2 (N=52)

Score	NB	SB-2
0.0-0.4	0	2
0.5-0.9	9	7
1.0-1.4	26	5
1.5-1.9	3	3
2.0-2.4	7	3
2.5-2.9	5	3
3.0-3.4	5	4
3.5-3.9	3	6
4.0-4.4	5	3
4.5-5.9	2	7
5.0-5.4	2	1
5.5-5.9	1	3
6.0-6.4	0	5
6.5-6.9	1	0
7.0-7.4	0	0
7.5-7.9	0	0
8.0-8.4	1	0
Average Score	2.26	3.18

Table VII-6   DISTRIBUTION OF AGE- AND VOCABULARY-CORRECTED
DISCRIMINANT SCORES IN SAMPLES NB (N=70) AND SB-2 (N=52)

Score	NB	SB-2
0.0-0.4	0	0
0.5-0.9	0	3
1.0-1.4	3	2
1.5-1.9	26	9
2.0-2.4	9	3
2.5-2.9	6	3
3.0-3.4	5	2
3.5-3.9	7	5
4.0-4.4	1	5
4.5-4.9	4	3
5.0-5.4	4	7
5.5-5.9	2	2
6.0-6.4	1	2
6.5-6.9	0	5
7.0-7.4	1	1
7.5-7.9	0	0
8.0-8.4	0	0
8.5-8.9	1	0
Average Score	2.90	3.75

It is now appropriate to ask whether this difference, .85, is large enough to preclude the possibility that it represents mere sampling error. The significance of this difference between the means (average scores) was tested conservatively, using Welch's modification of the t-test for the case where the two samples are drawn from populations which may have differing variances. This yielded a "t" of 2.62 with 97 degrees of freedom, which indicates that the difference between the means of the two samples is significant beyond the one percent level.

It is therefore reasonable to conclude that the basic hypothesis is confirmed: northern blacks do in fact differ from southern blacks in the same direction and on the same characteristics which differentiate northern whites from southern blacks, and these effects are not attributable to the background variables. This would seem to demonstrate rigorously that the caste sanctions do have an effect upon those human beings against whom the sanctions are enforced, and further, that these sanctions, and not heredity, account not only for the differences between northern and southern blacks but for the differences between blacks and whites as well.

A second pilot study

If the basic hypothesis had not been confirmed, these samples—NB and SB-2—would have been used in a new pilot study to derive ideas to be tested on other samples of northern and southern blacks to see if the caste sanctions had any effect, whether or not they accounted for the differences between blacks and whites. Since the basic hypothesis had been confirmed, the only point in undertaking such a pilot study was to see if any additional hypotheses might be located by the direct comparison of northern and southern blacks which were not predicted by the black-white comparison.

As in the original pilot study, the first step was to compare the two samples with respect to individual plate responses (sequences). The following responses were found to differentiate the two samples beyond the two-sided 20 percent level of significance:

1. More frequent among northern blacks:

   5-VOL, 8-VOL, 11-OLV, 12-OLV, 16-VLO.

2. More frequent among southern blacks:

   2-VLO, 6-OLV, 8-OLV, 12-LOV, 15-LVO, 22-OLV, 24-LOV, 25-VLO.

Thus, only 13 out of the 150 responses tested reached the 20 percent level of significance. (The tests are, of course, not independent.) From this it would not be suspected that anything other than sampling error was involved, and, if this were the original pilot study, it is probable that no attempt would have been made to score the scales, and we would never have discovered the scales which differentiate the samples.

When the denial scores were considered, the four denials of aggression reached the statistical criterion of differentiating the samples beyond the 20 percent level of significance, and the denials of physical injury, as in the other pilot study, did not reach this criterion. The number of extreme cases for each of the denials of aggression has already been given in Table VII-3. The approximate significance levels reached were as follows: denial of physical aggression, .12; denial of aggressive press, .006; denial of symbolic aggression (plate 13), .04; and denial of symbolic aggression (plate 25), .08. These represent the only characteristics which might have been considered had the northern vs. southern black comparison been the original pilot study.

It is clear that no new ideas are suggested by this direct comparison of northern and southern blacks. Thus, the black-white comparison revealed the effects of the caste sanctions more clearly than would this pilot study comparing two black samples, even though the differences between these samples were sufficient to validate these effects when we knew in advance of the experiment specifically which characteristics to examine.

Chapter VIII

NORTHERN VERSUS SOUTHERN BLACKS
–FURTHER STUDIES

The basic hypothesis that northern blacks differ from southern blacks on precisely the same personality characteristics as do northern whites seems to be confirmed. But how can we be sure?

Perhaps this was that one time in a hundred when the difference between the samples was significant by chance. Perhaps there was some flaw in the experiment, some factor which we did not take into account, which spuriously gave rise to our findings. How could we be sure that these findings should be taken at face value?

In view of the care with which the first experiment was planned and the solidity of its findings, these objections may seem unreasonable. But even such objections need not be cherished for long, nor need they be summarily dismissed. We can determine whether the same findings would occur again and again if the experiment were repeated, not only from the significance level of the first experiment, but by actually carrying out new, completely independent experiments testing the same hypothesis. We can then see directly whether, as the significance level of the first experiment indicated, we would obtain similar results.

The data necessary for two completely independent experiments testing the basic hypothesis that northern blacks differ from southern blacks on the same personality characteristics as do northern whites were available in the high school samples.

The first of these further experiments was originally planned to allow us to determine whether the caste sanctions had any effect upon personality, even if the differences between blacks and whites had proved to be innate. Since the black-white differences in personality were found to be due specifically to the caste sanctions, and since the direct comparison of northern and southern blacks had not given rise to any new ideas about the effects of these social pressures, the main purpose now served by this additional experiment was to possibly provide an independent confirmation of the findings.

This second validation, however, could provide a purer test of the basic hypothesis, since migrants could be eliminated from these samples. As mentioned earlier, the people interviewed for the Gallup sample had not been asked where they were born; consequently they were classified as "northern" or "southern" solely on the basis of where they were living when interviewed. Since there is relatively little migration into the South, eliminating migrants probably would not seriously affect the southern black samples. But roughly three out of five blacks living in the North are migrants who were born in the South. Insofar as the human personality bears the imprint of its life history and not just of the momentary forces which impinge upon it, these migrants might be expected to carry with them some of the effects of their previous way of life. Indeed, one of the facts which led us to suspect that there might be appreciable differences in the personality problems of northern and southern blacks was the marked difference in psychosis (insanity) rates in New York State between blacks born in that state and those who were migrants. If this susceptibility of migrant blacks to severe mental disorders was due to their experiences in the South, rather than the fact of being migrants, then the differences between northern and southern blacks should be even more striking when migrants were eliminated from the northern sample. However, even if their greater vulnerability to mental breakdown was not the result of having lived under the caste sanctions of the South, the fact that such a difference exists between migrants and other northern blacks would call for a purer test of the basic hypothesis—a test in which the people compared had spent their whole lives in the North or the South—and the difference specifically between northern and southern blacks should then be clearly revealed.

The samples for this validation were therefore chosen as follows: all black children in the ninth grade of one northern and one southern school who were born in the area (North or South as previously defined) in which they were now living. The northern and southern schools were selected on the basis of equivalence of testing conditions (and, of course, of there being a sizeable number of blacks in the student body). The time limits for the testing were identical for the northern and the southern schools which were selected: one and a half hours were allowed for all students, with an extra half hour for those who needed it.

There were 47 black children born in the North in the ninth grade of the northern school and 56 black children born in the South in the ninth grade of the southern school. These are the experimental samples and will be referred to as the North City and South Town samples, respectively.

North City is a northern industrial city with a population of a little more than 100,000. When the school system was segregated, only one of the five high schools was used by black students. Although segregation had been abolished for some years, the student population of this school remained approximately 80 percent black because of residential patterns. This was the school selected for the northern sample.

The southern sample came from the black high school in the segregated school system of South Town, a small rural community in the deep South. It will be recalled that rural-urban residence, in itself, was found not to have any appreciable effect upon the discriminant score, so that it is reasonable to compare samples which are not equated on this variable. Of course, sociologists have noted that in the South the caste sanctions are more severely enforced in the rural areas, so that the South Town sample consists of people living under extremely severe sanctions. The effects of this severity should be reflected in the discriminant scores.

Procedure

Unscoreable protocols (test booklets) are inevitable in any group administration, especially where a time limit is enforced. The first step, therefore, was to remove unscoreable protocols from the samples. A test booklet was considered unscoreable if it was incomplete, that is, if there was at least one plate for which the person had not indicated the sequence of the pictures or for which he had not written a description. Protocols were also considered unscoreable if they seemed to show a pattern or position preference. (Five successive plates in which the pictures were arranged in the same order by symbols, or five successive plates in which the pictures were arranged in the same order by position on the page were taken to be a pattern or position preference, respectively.)

The number and percentage of unscoreable protocols in these two samples are shown in Table VIII-1.

Insofar as the percentage of unscoreable cases reflects the testing conditions, the close agreement found would tend to support the judgment that the testing conditions were equivalent for these two samples.

The possible factors involved in producing incomplete protocols have been discussed in Chapter V. At this point it is sufficient to note that the samples were selected because of equivalent testing conditions, and the percentages of incomplete protocols were found to be extremely close. Therefore, the selective factors may be presumed to be operating equally upon

Table VIII-1   FREQUENCY AND PERCENTAGE OF
UNSCOREABLE PROTOCOLS

	North City		South Town	
	Frequency	%	Frequency	%
Incomplete	14	30	16	29
Pattern or position preference	3	6	3	5
Total unscoreable	17	36	19	34
Total scoreable	30	64	37	66
Total	47	100	56	100

Table VIII-2   DISTRIBUTIONS OF THE NORTH CITY (N=30)
AND SOUTH TOWN (N=37) SAMPLES BY AGE, SEX,
AND VOCABULARY (RAW SCORE)

		North City	South Town
Age:	14	11	2
	15	11	12
	16	7	9
	17	1	11
	18	0	2
	19	0	0
	20	0	0
	21	0	0
	22	0	1
Sex:	Male	14	14
	Female	16	23
Vocabulary:	0	0	0
	1	0	0
	2	0	0
	3	1	6
	4	2	1
	5	6	11
	6	5	8
	7	6	5
	8	5	5
	9	3	1
	10	1	0
	11	1	0
	12 or more	0	0

both samples, and it is proper to compare the scoreable protocols from each group. The distributions by age, sex, and vocabulary of these two high school samples (scoreable cases only) are shown in Table VIII-2.

Results of the second validation

To eliminate any possible bias during scoring, these two samples were randomly combined with each other and with the samples which were to be used for the matched sample experiment, and the four denials of aggression were scored blindly one at a time, as had been done with the samples from the Gallup data. The samples were then reassembled and scored on the seven remaining characteristics, the scoring for which is completely objective.

The number of extreme cases in the North City and South Town samples on each of the eleven personality characteristics is shown in Table VIII-3. Once more the discriminant score was computed for each person by adding up the number of these characteristics upon which he was extreme. The distributions of the discriminant scores are shown in Table VIII-4. The difference between the average scores is clearly in the predicted direction, as before.

The discriminant score corrected for age ($D_{i.a}$) and the discriminant score corrected for age and vocabulary ($D_{i.va}$) were again computed using the formulas given in Chapter V. The resulting distributions are shown in Tables VIII-5 and VIII-6.

Table VIII-3   RESULTS FOR THE NORTH CITY (N=30)
AND SOUTH TOWN (N=37) SAMPLES

		Number of extreme cases	
Differentiating variable		North City	South Town
Scale 124:	High general aggressive press	0	3
Plate 13:	Denial of aggressive press	3	22
Plate 4:	Denial of physical aggression	0	6
Plate 13:	Denial of symbolic aggression	2	21
Plate 25:	Denial of symbolic aggression	5	33
Scale 128:	High general aggressive need; delayed and negativistic aggression	0	3
Scale 195:	General weak affect	1	7
Scale 202:	General labile affect	1	5
Scale 227:	Externalized work motivation	0	1
Scale 232:	Conflicting work motivation	1	1
Scale 120:	Avoidance of male-male contacts	0	5

Table VIII-4   DISTRIBUTION OF DISCRIMINANT SCORES FOR THE
NORTH CITY (N=30) AND SOUTH TOWN (N=37) SAMPLES

Score	North City	South Town
0	21	1
1	6	5
2	2	10
3	1	10
4	0	7
5	0	2
6	0	0
7	0	2
Average Score	.43	2.89

Table VIII-5   DISTRIBUTION OF AGE-CORRECTED DISCRIMINANT SCORES
FOR THE NORTH CITY (N=30) AND SOUTH TOWN (N=37) SAMPLES

Score	North City	South Town
0.0-0.4	0	0
0.5-0.9	16	0
1.0-1.4	5	1
1.5-1.9	5	1
2.0-2.4	1	4
2.5-2.9	1	4
3.0-3.4	1	6
3.5-3.9	0	4
4.0-4.4	1	6
4.5-4.9	0	3
5.0-5.4	0	4
5.5-5.9	0	1
6.0-6.4	0	1
6.5-6.9	0	0
7.0-7.4	0	0
7.5-7.9	0	1
8.0-8.4	0	1
Average Score	1.36	3.89

The notion that the differences between northern and southern blacks
should stand out more clearly when the samples are confined to people who
have lived all their lives in the appropriate areas is strikingly confirmed. The
difference between the mean (or average) discriminant scores for the North
City and South Town samples is 2.46, which is considerably larger than the

Table VIII-6   DISTRIBUTION OF AGE- AND VOCABULARY-CORRECTED
DISCRIMINANT SCORES FOR THE NORTH CITY (N=30)
AND SOUTH TOWN (N=37) SAMPLES

Score	North City	South Town
0.0-0.4	0	0
0.5-0.9	0	0
1.0-1.4	1	0
1.5-1.9	20	1
2.0-2.4	0	0
2.5-2.9	6	5
3.0-3.4	0	0
3.5-3.9	2	10
4.0-4.4	0	0
4.5-4.9	1	10
5.0-5.4	0	0
5.5-5.9	0	7
6.0-6.4	0	0
6.5-6.9	0	2
7.0-7.4	0	0
7.5-7.9	0	0
8.0-8.4	0	0
8.5-8.9	0	1
Average Score	2.06	4.51

1.13 which was found using the Gallup data (which included migrants in the
northern sample). Because of the age distributions involved, this difference
does not decrease, but increases slightly to 2.63 for the discriminant scores
corrected for age ($D_{i \cdot a}$). For the discriminant scores corrected for both age
and vocabulary ($D_{i \cdot va}$), the difference decreases again to 2.45.

The statistical significance of this last difference was assessed as before,
using Welch's modification of the t-test of the significance of the difference
between two means. This conservative procedure yields a "t" of 8.40 with 55
degrees of freedom, which is far beyond any usual level of significance. (The
probability by chance is less than .0001.)

Thus a second completely independent test of the basic hypothesis of
this investigation confirms our previous findings: northern blacks are differentiated from southern blacks on the same characteristics and in the same way
as are northern whites. Further, this cannot be accounted for by either sampling error or the effects of the background variables. Therefore, it is reasonable to attribute these differences to the effects of the caste sanctions. Moreover, the fact that these differences are far more striking when the samples

consist of individuals who have spent their whole lives in the appropriate areas than when they include migrants seems to indicate that the effects of the caste sanctions upon human beings do not cease immediately upon a decrease in the sanctions themselves, but continue for some time thereafter.

The matched sample experiment

The findings in these experiments would seem to most of us to be conclusive. But there may be some people for whom the logic of the statistical corrections is not clear, and who may find a matched sample experiment easier to comprehend. Such an experiment was included, not primarily to test the overall hypothesis, but to help specify which of the eleven personality characteristics, considered separately, were most affected by the caste sanctions. Nonetheless, these matched samples could also be used to test the overall hypothesis, and this test would answer an important question, namely, whether the matched sample experiment would actually be of any use in examining the personality characteristics separately.

The possibility that the matched-sample experiment might not be of any use was raised by the fact that matching is a wasteful procedure. Consequently, the matched samples had to be taken from urban areas, where fairly large numbers of blacks had been tested, in order to end up with samples of reasonable size. But the cities of the South are characterized by far less severe caste sanctions than the rural areas. It would therefore be expected that those southern blacks who live in the cities would show considerably less of the effects of the caste sanctions.

Thus, it was possible that the differences between northern and southern blacks would not only decrease, but might even disappear, when the sample of southern blacks was chosen from a large city.

At the same time there was an advantage in using a southern community which was urban and relatively "enlightened," by northern standards. The difference between the results of these comparisons and those based on South Town, an area of severe caste sanctions, should provide us with some insight into the range of variation to be found in different parts of the South.

Metropolis and South City

The northern city, Metropolis, is one of the largest cities in the United States and one of the largest centers of black population. State law forbids asking or keeping any record in the school of whether a student is black.

Therefore, independent ratings of black physical characteristics were made surreptitiously by two raters not connected with the school system. These ratings were combined with the data only for the present study and do not appear on any permanent record. In addition, each student was asked not only for his own place of birth, but for the place of birth of each of his parents. Cases were selected for the sample only if they were born in the North, if their parents were born in the Continental United States, and if they were rated by both raters as having black physical characteristics. Each of the students who were selected for the black sample was found to have parents who were born in the South, which may be taken as additional support for the correctness of the classification.

The southern city, South City, is one of the larger cities in the South. Although it is a relatively large city for its region, it is by no means of the same order of magnitude as Metropolis. The caste sanctions are far less stringently applied in South City than they are in the rural areas of the South, and the segregated schools are, by southern standards, quite good. Only individuals born in the South were included in the sample.

In order to match the samples from these two cities, only ninth-grade students were used. The range of variation on age was examined. It was found that, except for one sixteen-year-old, all the cases in the Metropolis sample were fourteen or fifteen years old. The South City sample, which was nearly twice as large, included children ranging from twelve to eighteen. The first step in matching, therefore, was to discard all cases except those fourteen or fifteen years old. In vocabulary scores, the Metropolis sample ranged from 3 to 11, while the South City sample ranged from 2 to 12. The cases at score level 2 and score level 12 were removed, thus matching the two samples on the range of variation on age and vocabulary. At this point there were 57 cases remaining in the Metropolis sample and 87 cases in the South City sample. Each sample was now divided into four parts—dividing on age into fourteen-year-olds and fifteen-year-olds and dividing on vocabulary into low (3-6) and high (7-11) vocabulary scores. The number of cases, sex ratio, and mean vocabulary score of each subdivision of the two samples are shown in Table VIII-7.

The corresponding subdivisions of each sample were now matched with each other on sex ratio and vocabulary. In order to match samples it was, of course, necessary to remove cases. For example, in the South City sample there were nine female students who were fifteen years old and obtained a vocabulary score of 9. In order to produce the best match, only three of these cases should be included in the sample and six of them discarded. But which three? One could have drawn three cases at random. However, an alternative procedure was employed: each case was counted as a third of a case. This is

Table VIII-7   NUMBER OF CASES, SEX RATIOS, AND AVERAGE
VOCABULARY SCORES FOR THE FOUR SUBDIVISIONS OF EACH SAMPLE

	Number of Cases	Male	Female	Average Vocabulary Score
14-year-old, Low Vocabulary				
Metropolis	18	6	12	4.8
South City	17	7	10	5.3
15-year-old, Low Vocabulary				
Metropolis	8	4	4	5.3
South City	20	10	10	5.2
14-year-old, High Vocabulary				
Metropolis	21	9	12	8.0
South City	34	11	23	8.1
15-year-old, High Vocabulary				
Metropolis	10	3	7	8.3
South City	16	6	10	8.1

the same as drawing three cases at random, except that it represents the average of what we would obtain by using every possible combination of three people who might have been drawn from the nine cases. This same procedure of counting each case as a fraction of a case was used wherever it was necessary to discard cases in order to match the samples.

The matching was carried out in terms of the corresponding subdivisions of the two samples, and not in terms of the samples as a whole. In other words, each subdivision was matched with the subdivision of the other sample which corresponded to it: the fourteen-year-old, low vocabulary group of the southern sample with the fourteen-year-old, low vocabulary group of the northern sample; the fourteen-year-old, high vocabulary group with the fourteen-year-old, high vocabulary group; etc.

Although the effective number of cases in each of the four subdivisions is not the same in each sample, the samples are nevertheless matched since each of the four subdivisions was given equal weight irrespective of the number of cases in that subdivision. Thus, the average score for each sample was determined by computing the average score for each of the four subdivisions of that sample separately, adding these average scores together, and dividing by four.

The effective number of cases, the sex ratio, and the mean (average) vocabulary scores for each subdivision of each sample after matching are shown in Table VIII-8, as well as the sex ratio, age distribution, and the mean and standard deviation of vocabulary scores for the total samples (taking into

Table VIII-8   EFFECTIVE NUMBER OF CASES, SEX RATIOS, AND AVERAGE
VOCABULARY SCORES FOR THE FOUR SUBDIVISIONS OF EACH SAMPLE

	Number of Cases	Male	Female	Average Vocabulary Score
14-year-old, Low Vocabulary				
Metropolis	15	6	9	5.1
South City	17	7	10	5.3
15-year-old, Low Vocabulary				
Metropolis	8	4	4	5.3
South City	20	10	10	5.2
14-year-old, High Vocabulary				
Metropolis	21	9	12	8.0
South City	26	11	15	7.9
15-year-old, High Vocabulary				
Metropolis	8	3	5	8.1
South City	16	6	10	8.1

SEX RATIOS, AGE DISTRIBUTIONS, AVERAGES AND STANDARD
DEVIATIONS OF VOCABULARY SCORES FOR THE TOTAL SAMPLES
(SUBDIVISIONS WEIGHTED EQUALLY)

	Sex		Age		Vocabulary	
	Male	Female	14	15	Average Score	Standard Deviation
North	42.6%	47.4%	50%	50%	6.60	1.69
South	42.7%	47.3%	50%	50%	6.61	1.66

account the fact that the four subdivisions are weighted equally). It is evident
from this table that the technique of matching was extremely successful; the
samples are identical, or nearly identical, on all of these characteristics.

The discriminant scores were computed for the Metropolis and South
City samples. The difference between the average scores of the two samples
was the same for the uncorrected discriminant scores (D_i) as for the corrected
discriminant scores ($D_{i.a}$ and $D_{i.va}$). Table VIII-9 shows the average discriminant score corrected for age and vocabulary ($D_{i.va}$) for each of the experimental samples, including Metropolis and South City. The difference between
the means (average scores) of these two matched samples is .60. This is less

Table VIII-9   AVERAGE AGE- AND VOCABULARY-CORRECTED
DISCRIMINANT SCORE FOR ALL SAMPLES

North City, Ninth Grade	2.06
Northern White, Gallup Sample	2.27
Metropolis, Ninth Grade	2.44
Northern Black, Gallup Sample	2.90
South City, Ninth Grade	3.04
SB-1, Gallup Sample	3.65
SB-2, Gallup Sample	3.75
South Town, Ninth Grade	4.51

than the differences found in the previous North-South comparisons, but even this difference is clearly significant beyond the five percent level. Thus, the effects of the caste sanctions on human beings has again been confirmed.

A review

In surveying the findings for all the experimental samples, as summarized in Table VIII-9, it is clear that, as might be expected, all of the southern samples have larger average discriminant scores corrected for age and vocabulary than any of the northern samples. Thus, no matter which northern sample and which southern sample we had compared, the basic hypothesis would have been confirmed that the caste sanctions have an effect upon personality, and that the difference between the North and the South is reflected by appreciable differences in the personality structures of blacks.

Within the South, the average scores of the samples are in the order one would predict from the severity of the caste sanctions, that is, the two samples drawn from the Gallup data have essentially the same average scores, while South City, where the caste sanctions are least severe, has the lowest average score, and South Town, where the caste sanctions are most severe, has the highest average score.

The only northern black sample which has an appreciably larger average score than the white sample is that drawn from the Gallup data, which includes a presumably sizeable proportion of blacks who were born in the South and have lived there during the early part of their lives. The ninth-grade northern black samples turn out to have approximately the same average discriminant score as the white sample. Apparently the sanctions which these blacks have encountered have not affected them appreciably on these personality characteristics, despite the fact that the conditions under which they live are clearly substandard. Although this finding is puzzling, it is in keeping with the previously cited fact that psychosis rates in New York State are several times as high for blacks as for whites, but the increase is due entirely to blacks born in the South; blacks born in New York State have the same psychosis rates as whites born in that state. Whatever effects being black in the North has on a human being seem to be too subtle to be revealed by samples of this size, or to be reflected in gross mental breakdowns (in the 50's).

To shed light on the meaning of this surprising finding, we may return to Kardiner and Ovesey's intensive psychological and psychoanalytic studies of blacks which were summarized in Chapter II. It will be recalled that they studied at great length the personality structures of 25 blacks living in a northern community, Harlem. Although they did not call attention to differences between those who were born in the North and those born in the South, they did summarize their findings for each individual separately, and did report, as part of the case history, whether that person was born in the North or the South. If we now examine these case histories, we are struck by the fact that the only three individuals characterized as stable, effectively adapted, or essentially "normal" are all blacks born in the North. Further, those northern-born blacks who are maladjusted tend to have neurotic problems which Kardiner and Ovesey characterize as being essentially the same as those of neurotic whites.

Since more than half of the blacks studied were patients who came for psychotherapy, and who therefore must be neurotics, we cannot easily tell from their data whether or not northern-born blacks tend to be neurotic more frequently than whites; but we can confirm our own conclusion that northern-born blacks tend to be less disturbed than those who have lived part of their lives in the South, and that northern-born northern blacks tend to be more like northern whites in the personality problems that they do develop.

Chapter IX

THE PERSONALITY CHARACTERISTICS

The question of whether the caste sanctions enforced against blacks have any effect upon the personality structures of the people who feel them has been answered rigorously. The importance of being able to establish this basic conclusion is unquestionable, but it is not enough. The curiosity characteristic of science requires that we attempt to trace the specific nature of the repercussions these sanctions have within the personalities of the human beings who feel their effects. We know that the severity of the caste sanctions is reflected by an increase in the eleven personality characteristics which make up the discriminant score, and that, when these eleven characteristics are considered together, the increase is striking. But we do not know whether each of these characteristics is equally affected.

To answer such a question, each of the eleven personality characteristics must be examined separately to see if that particular trait shows the same tendency to increase among people living under more severe caste sanctions shown by all eleven characteristics when taken together.

When we say that we must examine each personality characteristic separately, this does not refer to the question of whether, holding all the other ten characteristics constant, there would still remain a relationship between a personality characteristic and the caste sanctions. That question, sometimes referred to as "examining each characteristic separately," is not one in which we are particularly interested at this point. We are simply interested in the question of whether there is a marked relationship between any one personality characteristic and the caste sanctions, whether that relationship is direct or indirect. We want to know whether the differences between the samples on any one personality characteristic considered by itself is so striking that we can be sure that that particular characteristic actually is more common among people who live under more severe caste sanctions. The difference between these two questions may be seen by considering what would happen if the difference on one personality characteristic were the result of the difference on another characteristic. If we had asked the first question, *neither* characteristic would be statistically significant, no matter how strongly related they both were to the caste sanctions; by asking the second question, both characteristics will be statistically significant if they are more frequent among people living under more severe sanctions.

It is entirely possible, of course, that the differences between the samples on the discriminant score might be statistically significant, without any one of the characteristics being significant by itself. What such a finding would mean is that there were real differences on these characteristics between the populations from which the samples were drawn, but that the differences were not large enough on any one trait to be statistically significant with this sample size. Such small differences, if not due to chance, might well cumulate to produce a consistently large and significant difference on the discriminant score. Thus, because of the limited data available, the conclusions for the personality characteristics separately may not be as clear-cut as they were for the whole group of characteristics taken together.

Nevertheless, in our present state of knowledge (or perhaps lack of knowledge) about the interrelationship of culture and personality in general, and of the effects of the caste sanctions in particular, even approximate answers are worth considering, and we are in a position to get some good approximate answers.

The first approximations were obtained by comparing, for one characteristic at a time, the proportion of people in each of the Gallup samples who were extreme, that is, who were characterized by that personality trait. Each of these comparisons could be tested for statistical significance.

The only problem with the resulting significance levels, aside from the relative insensitivity of small samples, is that they do not take into account the background variables of age and vocabulary level which have been shown to have a small but appreciable effect. For these Gallup samples, the difference on the discriminant score between the northern and southern black samples decreased when age and vocabulary were taken into account. When the North City and South Town samples were compared, however, the difference between the samples was essentially the same after as before correcting for age and vocabulary. Consequently, the difference between the North City and South Town samples in the proportion of extreme cases on each personality characteristic provides us with a second approximation which is considerably better than the first.

Since there was no way of knowing in advance that the background variables would make little or no difference for the North City vs. South

Town comparison, the matched sample experiment had been included in the research design to ensure that there would be at least one set of comparisons in which the background factors could not confuse the findings. This matched sample experiment, which used blacks from two large cities, now allows us to compare the effects of the caste sanctions in an area in the South that was relatively "enlightened," such as South City, with the effects of the caste sanctions in South Town, an area in which these sanctions were stringently enforced.

The separate personality characteristics

The eleven personality characteristics which make up the discriminant score are: the feeling that people are going out of their way to make trouble for you (high general aggressive press), not "recognizing" situations involving anger (the four denials of aggression), strong but consciously suppressed anger (delayed and negativistic aggression), deadened emotions (weak affect), emotions which change rapidly to their opposites (labile affect), conflicting work motivation, continuing to work only under the promptings of another person and not because of one's own inner standards (externalized work motivation), and avoiding close contacts between men.

Table IX-1 gives the percentage of each sample, including the pilot study samples, which were extreme on each of these eleven characteristics. No correction has been made for the effects of the background variables in Table IX-1, except for Metropolis and South City which are, of course, matched. The most meaningful way to look at Table IX-1 is to compare corresponding North-South samples.

The consistency of the comparisons is striking. Insofar as these personality characteristics reflect the effects of the caste sanctions, we expect them to be more frequent among the southern samples. Of the 33 comparisons between corresponding samples of northern and southern blacks, there are only four in which a characteristic is not more frequent in the southern sample, and on none of these traits does a reversal occur more than once.

To put it differently, there are seven personality characteristics for which the difference between northern and southern blacks is in the predicted direction in every one of the three independent experiments, while the difference between the northern and southern samples on the remaining four traits was in the predicted direction in two out of three comparisons. The seven personality characteristics which in every comparison were found to be more frequent in the southern sample are the feeling that people are going

Table IX-1   PERCENTAGE OF EXTREME CASES

	Northern Samples				Southern Samples			
	Northern Whites	Northern Blacks Gallup Sample	North City, Ninth Grade	Metropolis, Ninth Grade	SB-1	SB-2	South Town, Ninth Grade	South City, Ninth Grade
Scale 124: High General Aggressive Press	2.7	2.9	0.0	0.8	9.8	7.7	8.1	1.6
Plate 13: Denial of Aggressive Press	10.1	18.6	10.0	13.3	41.2	48.1	59.5	16.3
Scale 128: High General Aggressive Need; Delayed and Negativistic Aggression	3.4	10.0	0.0	0.0	15.7	9.6	8.1	5.1
Plate 4: Denial of Physical Aggression	3.4	12.9	0.0	0.4	15.7	26.9	16.2	1.3
Plate 13: Denial of Symbolic Aggression	16.2	27.1	6.7	29.9	47.1	53.8	56.8	35.6
Plate 25: Denial of Symbolic Aggression	12.2	31.4	16.7	26.0	52.9	50.0	89.2	68.7
Scale 195: General Weak Affect	2.7	5.7	3.3	2.4	9.8	13.5	18.9	0.4
Scale 202: General Labile Affect	3.4	8.6	3.3	0.8	11.8	19.2	13.5	1.4
Scale 227: Externalized Work Motivation	2.0	2.9	0.0	0.0	7.8	5.8	2.7	1.0
Scale 232: Conflicting Work Motivation	0.0	1.4	3.3	0.0	3.9	1.9	2.7	0.4
Scale 120: Avoidance of Male-Male Contacts	1.4	10.0	0.0	0.0	15.7	7.7	13.5	0.4

out of their way to make trouble for you, and the four denials of aggression, labile affect, and externalized work motivation.

It will be recalled that the percentage of a sample, a group of people whom we actually observe, always varies somewhat from the percentage of the population from which that sample was taken, and that, consequently, the difference between two samples will sometimes be larger and sometimes smaller than the difference between the populations from which these samples came. Indeed, the difference between the samples may even be in the opposite direction from the difference between the populations, especially if that difference is small. The statistical significance of a difference is the probability that a difference this large or larger could occur by chance, that is, when there was no difference between the populations from which the samples came. Since the probability of a difference between the samples when the populations differ in the opposite direction is less than the probability when there is no difference at all between the populations, we can conclude that the populations differ from each other in the same way as do the samples, if the probability by chance is small enough, for example, five or one percent.

The statistical significance of the difference in percentage for each characteristic was assessed by Mosteller and Tukey's graphical technique for the Gallup samples, by Fisher's exact test for the North City-South Town comparisons, and by the analysis of variance, as explained in Chapter V, for the matched-sample experiment. The resulting significance levels for the differences between corresponding samples are shown in Table IX-2.

It is clear that the rarity of extreme cases on some of these personality characteristics limits our ability to generalize from samples of the size used in this research. Of the 33 comparisons in Table IX-2, there were no less than nine in which all extreme cases occurred in the southern sample; yet, because of the small sample sizes, only three of these reached the generally accepted levels of statistical significance. If the samples had been sufficiently large, some, if not all, of the remaining six comparisons would undoubtedly have also been statistically significant.

Let us now consider each experiment separately. Our first approximation is given by the Gallup samples—Northern blacks vs. SB-2. The percentage of extreme cases is higher in the southern sample for all but two of the eleven personality characteristics (Scale 120: avoidance of male-male contacts, and Scale 128: high general aggressive need, delayed and negativistic aggression). Only four characteristics reach the five percent level of significance: the four denials of aggression. Labile affect (changeable emotions) reaches the six percent level. Since these samples are not comparable with respect to the background variables, we may immediately pass on to the other samples, while noting the fact that the use of the unconscious psychological defense mechanism of denial with respect to each of the aspects of aggression measured in the test seems to be striking.

In the North City-South Town comparison, where the differences in the background variables have little effect, the difference in the percentage of extreme cases is in the predicted direction for all but one of the personality

Table IX-2 SIGNIFICANCE LEVELS FOR THE DIFFERENCE IN THE
NUMBER OF EXTREME CASES FOR CORRESPONDING SAMPLES

	NB vs. SB-2	North City vs. South Town	Metropolis vs. South City
Scale 124: High General Aggressive Press	.17	.16*	.35
Plate 13: Denial of Aggressive Press	.0003	<.0001	.32
Scale 128: High General Aggressive Need; Delayed and Negativistic Aggression	.50†	.16*	.008*
Plate 4: Denial of Physical Aggression	.02	.02*	.28
Plate 13: Denial of Symbolic Aggression	.001	<.0001	.25
Plate 25: Denial of Symbolic Aggression	.03	<.0001	<.0001
Scale 195: General Weak Affect	.12	.05	.83†
Scale 202: General Labile Affect	.06	.15	.39
Scale 227: Externalized Work Motivation	.26	.55*	.14*
Scale 232: Conflicting Work Motivation	.44	.80†	.26*
Scale 120: Avoidance of Male-Male Contacts	.66†	.05*	.26*

* Significance level limited by small sample size, although all extreme cases in these comparisons occur in the southern sample.
† The difference between the samples is in the reverse direction for these comparisons from that predicted—the percentage of extreme cases is higher for the northern sample.

traits, and the reversal does not occur on either of the characteristics which showed a reversal in the comparisons of the Gallup samples. Scale 120 (avoidance of male-male contacts), which showed a reversal in the Gallup samples, is now significant beyond the five percent level. It is, in fact, as extreme as is possible with these size samples. The reversal in these comparisons is on Scale 232 (conflicting work motivation).

In this experiment, where the southern sample is drawn from an area of markedly severe caste sanctions, the use of denial with respect to every aspect of aggression measured by the test is even more striking than before. The difference reaches far beyond the one percent level of significance for all of these types of denial, except the denial of physical aggression, which reached the two percent level. Thus, the ideas of someone being angry at him, of a physical fight, of the subject's being angry when someone else is angry at him (plate 13), or of his becoming angry even when no one is around (plate 25), are all so frightening that the unconscious defense mechanism of denial is aroused, and he just does not recognize the threatening situations. Of these, the most frequently denied by the individuals in the South Town sample is symbolic aggression when no one else is around: apparently the most frightening idea of all seems to be that one might at times feel angry without any immediate cause. This contrasts with the usual finding in most normal groups, as in the northern white sample, that there are less denials when there is no one around (plate 25) than there are when there is another person in the other pictures (plate 13).

Apparently, for most people it is less frightening to feel angry when there is no one around, than it is to feel angry when there is someone around who may retaliate. For a southern black, however, feeling angry without provocation means that the anger inside of him has finally burst through, and he has lost control. This loss of control is far more frightening than feeling angry when provoked, or having someone angry at him, or getting involved in a fight, frightening as these ideas are. If you cannot control your own anger in a world where you are constantly being provoked, and where the direct expression of anger brings inevitable disaster, you have no chance.

In this area of severe caste sanctions, weak affect is now significant at the five percent level, indicating that, under severe caste sanctions, there is an increase in the number of people whose whole emotional life is deadened by the struggle not to be angry. Labile affect is not significant but reaches the 15 percent level. As to the other three characteristics—the feeling that people are making trouble for him (Scale 124), suppressed anger (Scale 128), and externalized work motivation (Scale 227)—the sample sizes are too small for us to come to any strong conclusions; they are as significant as is possible with this sample size, i.e., all extreme cases are in the southern sample, yet they do not reach the generally accepted levels of statistical significance.

If we now examine the matched samples, Metropolis and South City, we again find that all comparisons except one are in the predicted direction. The reversal, however, is on still a different characteristic. This time the reversal is on Scale 195 (general weak affect).

In this urban area where the caste sanctions are less severe, and where blacks have a greater sense of security, there are only two characteristics which are statistically significant—both beyond the one percent level. The most striking North-South difference is again the percentage of denials of symbolic aggression on plate 25. The unconscious defense mechanism of denial is not mobilized to the same extent in any of the other aspects of aggression on the test. The overwhelming fear of blacks in this relatively enlightened area is that they will lose control and thus, by their own lack of control, endanger the relative security they now enjoy. The other characteristic which is statistically significant is Scale 128 (high general aggressive need, delayed and negativistic aggression, that is, anger which is consciously held back). The small sample sizes involved in the South Town comparison prevented this characteristic from reaching statistical significance, but in both comparisons extreme cases on this trait were observed only in the southern samples. We may therefore conclude that high aggression (anger) which is consciously suppressed, plus a fear of losing control over one's anger, are the two personality traits which most characterize the effects of living as the inferior caste in a caste situation, and these traits are strikingly increased even in a relatively "enlightened" area.

Once again, the small sample size prevents us from coming to any conclusion about three characteristics which do not reach the generally accepted levels of statistical significance, but on which extreme cases occur only in the southern sample—Scale 227 (externalized work motivation), Scale 232 (conflicting work motivation) and Scale 120 (avoidance of male-male contacts). With respect to the last, there is a striking difference within the southern samples in the percentage of extreme cases between South City and South Town, which would support the idea that the avoidance of close contacts between men is a reflection of the fact that these are the contacts that are most likely to lead to physical aggression. The greater physical security of the South City blacks, as compared with South Town, accounts for the decrease in the percentage of extreme cases on this characteristic.

An even more striking difference between South Town, where the caste sanctions are severe, and South City, where the sanctions are marked by a lack of severity, occurs on Scale 195 (general weak affect). The comparison on this scale between the northern and southern samples is statistically significant for South Town, but there is no significant difference for the comparison involving South City. In fact, the percentage of extreme cases on "weak affect" was lower in South City than in Metropolis, although this difference is not significant. The considerable difference between South City and South Town in the frequency of this characteristic represents a real gain in emotional freedom, a notable improvement in the adjustment of blacks which results from living under less stringent conditions within the South. The importance of this difference in personality functioning should not be underestimated. A person who cannot feel emotions is a psychological cripple who lives, at most, half a life.

Chapter X

CONCLUSIONS

"I'd like to think that I'd have my problems no matter what I was, and sometimes I believe it. But sometimes I think it's all because I'm black. I can't be sure. I just don't know. Maybe you could tell me what it really means to be black."

This, in human terms, was the question this book set out to answer, and some clear-cut and solidly grounded answers were obtained. But the human problem was not what first prompted these experiments. Their original purpose was the general scientific goal of discovering the relationship between a set of social institutions, that is, recognizable patterns of regularities in the ways that people deal with each other in a complex western society, and the personality structures of the people who live in that society. It has been demonstrated that it is possible to investigate such relationships rigorously and without being misled by the effects of extraneous factors, even in a highly complex society.

The particular social institutions which were studied are the caste sanctions enforced against blacks in the United States in the 1950's—those social patterns which ensure that the children of blacks will be treated as blacks, that blacks will marry only other blacks, and, most important of all, that blacks will be treated as inferiors. Only the effects of these sanctions upon blacks, the people who are assigned the inferior status, have been examined.

An impressive body of knowledge concerning the black population in the United States has been amassed by sociologists. Almost every aspect of black life in this country, from the jobs which are open to them to the jokes they tell, has been painstakingly detailed by field observers, and compiled to provide a nearly exhaustive picture of the experiences which blacks undergo and to which they are subjected. It was the care and thoroughness of these descriptions which first suggested the experiments in this book, since no

165

other social institution in any complex society has been described with such detail and exactitude. Thus the problem of obtaining an adequate conception of the social pressures whose effects were to be studied had already been solved.

There were, of course, some answers to the question of what these effects might be even before these experiments. In one area of personality functioning, intelligence, there was a considerable body of research, and the results were unambiguous. On the average, the caste sanctions produce a considerable decrease in intelligence (as measured by intelligence tests). Undoubtedly, a large part of this effect is directly traceable to the restrictions on educational opportunities.

In the areas of personality functioning other than intelligence, however, no clear-cut differences specifically attributable to the caste sanctions had yet been rigorously established. Field observers had carefully described those characteristics of blacks which were readily observable. But for characteristics which were not so readily observable, there tended to be disagreements among the observers. There were also clinical studies of blacks, both normal and disturbed. These case histories provided accurate, insightful depictions of at least a number of black individuals. But were the findings typical only of these particular people, or of blacks in general?

As for experimental studies, there were none which were conclusive. The findings were inconsistent, and only rarely was any result found which reached the generally accepted levels of statistical significance. Further, even if differences in personality had been found, it would not have been rigorously established that they were the result of the caste sanctions since the problem of excluding alternative explanations, such as other social factors or heredity, had, for the most part, been given only superficial consideration.

Before more rigorous and therefore more dependable answers could be obtained, two problems had to be solved: measurement and research design. The problem of measurement was solved by using what had proved most satisfactory in previous studies of culture and personality, namely, the "projective" tests of personality which have been developed in clinical settings where they are used to obtain accurate psychological assessments of patients in a relatively short period of time, even for those aspects of personality which the patient is unwilling or unable to describe. The "projective" test used in these experiments was the Tomkins-Horn Picture Arrangement Test, which is particularly well suited to relatively large-scale research where group comparisons are to be made.

How the problem of research design was resolved has been described at great length. It was possible to design a program of research which would not only assess the statistical significance of the findings, but also determine whether these same findings would recur consistently from experiment to experiment, which would determine whether the differences between blacks and whites were hereditary or the result of the caste sanctions, and which would exclude the possibility that the differences in personality might be attributed to any of the plausible alternative explanations.

It has been clearly established that the caste sanctions have an effect upon the personality structures of the people who feel them, and that this effect is reflected in eleven characteristics. The fact that northern blacks differ from southern blacks on precisely the same characteristics and in the same way as do northern whites served to eliminate the possibility that these traits represented hereditary differences between blacks and whites. Thus, the caste sanctions not only have an effect upon personality, but these effects are sufficient to account for the differences in personality between blacks and whites.

The difference between the northern black sample which included a large but unknown proportion of migrants and the samples which were restricted to blacks born in the North indicated that the effects of the caste sanctions do not cease as soon as an individual leaves an area of severe sanctions, but persist in his personality structure for some time thereafter. The northern sample which included migrants was unmistakably more like the southern black samples and less like the white sample than either of the northern black samples which did not include migrants. Thus, a black who moves from South to North carries his past with him as reflected in these personality characteristics.

It will be recalled that the PAT scores are all dichotomous attributes, which either do or do not characterize a given individual. Therefore, when we say that a personality characteristic was found to "increase" in the southern black as compared with the northern white sample, we mean not that each southern black had a little bit more of that trait than did the northern whites, but that the percentage of southern blacks apparently characterized by that attribute is greater than the percentage of northern whites.

But what were these eleven personality characteristics which reflected the caste sanction? Six of them are directly concerned with the area of aggression. The first of these is the feeling that people will go out of their way to make trouble for you. Four of these traits involve the psychological defense mechanism of denial, which may be roughly described as being so afraid of an idea that one literally cannot bear to think about it. The ideas which seem to be so frightening were the idea that someone is making trouble for you, the idea of a physical fight, the idea of being angry in response to provocation, and the idea of being angry without provocation. The remaining characteristic relating to aggression was strong but consciously suppressed anger, the expression of which is, consequently, delayed or indirect.

These findings seem to confirm the widely held belief among social scientists that the most serious emotional problems of the black concern the handling of aggression.

The reason for the increase in these characteristics would seem simply to be that the caste sanctions are, in fact, ways in which people are making trouble for blacks; this trouble may mean not only inconvenience, discomfort, or humiliation, but also real physical danger. Against these problems, he may have no defense: any attempt to fight back seems likely to lead to vindictive and inescapable retaliation. He must therefore fight a continuing battle with his own feelings of anger, lest he lose control. In a rural deep South area where physical security for blacks is minimal, all of the aggression traits seem to increase. On the other hand, in a southern city, where blacks enjoy a good deal of physical security, this greater physical security is reflected in the fact that only two of the characteristics which concern aggression show striking increases over the North: strong but consciously suppressed anger, and denial of the idea of being angry without provocation. The increase in the latter seems to represent the fear of losing control and endangering the relative security he enjoys in this urban area.

Another characteristic which reflected the increased physical security of blacks in the urban area as opposed to the rural deep South area was weak affect. One of the consequences of choking back one's anger may be a complete deadening of one's emotions. This seems to occur only in the rural sample where a black is most insecure, but not where he enjoys the relative physical security of the urban southern area studied. The avoidance of male-male contacts is still another characteristic which showed a more striking increase for the rural sample than for the urban sample. This supports the notion that close contacts between men are avoided because these contacts are most likely to erupt in physical aggression.

The small sample size prevented us from being able to generalize with any great degree of certainty about the three remaining characteristics: labile affect, conflicting work motivation, and externalized work motivation.

It is striking that, with the exception of labile affect, all these characteristics are indicators of pathology, that is, they indicate disturbed individuals. This is clearly not an artifact of our procedure, since these characteristics were selected on an empirical basis from among all the possible traits measured by the Picture Arrangement Test—some of which, like these, indicate pathology, others of which indicate strengths, and the majority of which are simply descriptive. What this implies is that the impact of the caste sanctions on human beings is destructive, and the destructiveness varies with the severity of the sanctions.

On the basis of this evidence we are in a position to reject the previously plausible arguments that (1) the southern black, who lives in a self-consistent culture, is not disturbed by the caste sanctions which become a problem only for the northern black, who lives in an inconsistent culture; or (2) the conditions under which blacks live in the United States are at best so unpromising that the difference between North and South is not appreciable. It is clear that the difference between North and South is considerable in terms of human cost. Indeed, even within the South the difference between an area of severe sanctions and an area where they are less stringent is paralleled by an appreciable decrease in human cost.

The implications of these findings are obvious. Any of us who has had honest doubts about whether caste sanctions hurt blacks now has an objective answer. Those who have been sincerely convinced that the caste system was good for blacks, or that, at worst, it did them no harm, are now faced with the unpleasant alternatives of reappraising their view of the situation, or of simply shutting their eyes to the facts.

The most important practical implication of these results may be for those people who are actively trying to alleviate the burden of caste which has been laid upon American blacks. Such people hear all too frequently, "Why bother? What difference will it make? Don't you realize that there will always be prejudice, discrimination, and segregation, just as there will always be malice, hatred, and envy, simply because they are part of the very nature of human beings? You will never change human nature, and nobody will ever create a perfect world."

But it is clear that it is not necessary to create a perfect world; it is only necessary to create a perfectable one, in which things can be a little better than they are. Any partial improvement, it seems, will be reflected in a decrease in human cost.

Nonetheless, it is questionable whether a research study such as this has any truly practical implication. For blacks, it will come as no news that the caste sanctions hurt, although the scar may not have been as clearly delineated before. For those whites who oppose the caste system, these findings may confirm their feelings, but they see the issue primarily as a moral one involving simple justice and common humanity. From their standpoint, it is wrong to unjustifiedly attempt to hurt another, whether or not one succeeds. For many of those whites who support the caste system, the findings are also irrelevant. They, too, see the issue as a moral one, but this time involving loyalty to their own group as opposed to those who are outside it. From their standpoint, it would be better if blacks were helped by the caste system than if they were hurt by it, but the important consideration is not what it does to blacks, but what it does to whites, and it is their belief that the caste system is a good thing for whites. On that question, the Appendix sheds light. (However, economists and sociologists have suggested that, with the exception of particular individuals, such as the southern politician, southern whites suffer more than they benefit from the caste system, although they are usually unaware that their difficulties stem from their "privileges.") For many other whites, it is not a matter of evidence or moral conviction, but simply one of courage. If the neighbors feel strongly about something, why stick your neck out? For them, these findings are obviously irrelevant, until the day comes when they feel free to dissent. Thus, the most important accomplishment of this study was its original purpose: furthering our understanding of the nature of human beings.

The inconsistencies in a culture as a source of emotional problems has been increasingly emphasized by sociologists and psychologists in recent years. However, caste sanctions are an example of an *increase* in the inconsistency of the culture leading to a *decrease* in emotional problems. In the experiments reported in this book, caste sanctions seem to result in *no* apparent problem for the northern black who has lived all his life in the North, in an inconsistent culture. The northern black samples were not gathered from some ideal community where they would encounter no discrimination, but from cities where there happen to be sizeable black populations. These northern blacks have encountered a good deal of discrimination in their lives, and are living under substandard conditions. It is nearly inconceivable that this has had no destructive impact. Yet the average discriminant score, corrected for age and vocabulary, is the same as for northern whites. Further, this apparent lack of disturbance of northern blacks who have lived all their lives in the North is substantiated by the psychosis rates reported by other investigators.

What does this mean? It probably does not mean there are no effects. In part, it may mean that the effects on northern blacks are correlated with intelligence, and the corrections for intelligence may tend to mask these effects. More important, the sizes of the samples used in this study are still small enough so that only relatively large differences will be clearly revealed. Personality disturbances due to the caste sanctions may be present in the northern black, but to too slight a degree to be revealed with this size sample. It is also possible that milder caste sanctions lead to totally different kinds of problems from those which are the result of living under severe caste sanctions, in which case the traits located in comparing southern blacks with northern whites may not be the proper characteristics. Instead there may be traits which differentiate northern blacks from both northern whites and southern blacks. However, it will be recalled that the northern-born northern blacks studied by Kardiner and Ovesey tended to develop neurotic problems essentially the same as those of whites, and our own pilot study comparison of northern and southern blacks revealed no striking differences on any characteristics other than those which differentiated northern whites from southern blacks. Moreover, whatever characteristics there may be are clearly not such as to appreciably affect the rates of psychosis.

The contrast between northern and southern blacks is striking: we are led to ask what it is that protects the personality of the northern black. Perhaps the southern black, whose whole society told him he is wrong even to resent his treatment, can never be completely sure that he isn't wrong, nor can he bring himself to completely accept the treatment he receives. The northern black, on the other hand, may be made to suffer, but he felt that those who make him suffer are wrong, and he has a right to resent it. He is engaged in an unequal struggle that he may never win, but he knew he is engaged in a struggle that is not hopeless. Apparently, being able to face the fact that one is being mistreated preserves a sense of personal integrity which, in turn, serves to ward off much of the destructive impact of oppressive experiences. It would seem that when we face the truth, the truth really does, to a large extent, set us free.

THE PRICE OF PRIVILEGE: THE EFFECTS
OF THE AMERICAN CASTE SYSTEM
ON THE SOUTHERN WHITE

If black people are the victims of the American caste system, whites are its beneficiaries. This widely accepted assumption underlies any such system of discrimination. This view is at least as old as Aristotle, who held that some men must be slaves if any men were to be free, since physical labor destroyed the mind.

Similarly, the history of the pre-Civil War South has been mythologized (Sellers), and the benefits for the white of a slave system exaggerated. This was first pointed out by Mark Twain shortly after the Civil War, when he complained that southern history was largely plagiarized, without acknowledgment, from Sir Walter Scott. Indeed, the historical difference between North and South has been greatly magnified. It will be recalled that the first northern state to abolish slavery (Vermont) did not do so until 1775. Jefferson, certainly a Southerner and a slave-owner, nonetheless wrote an anti-slavery paragraph in his original draft of the Declaration of Independence. It was deleted over his objections.

While the mythology holds that the pre-Civil War South consisted of a culturally rich plantation aristocracy to which most whites belonged, the facts are that most southern whites never owned a single slave, who was, after all, expensive property. As late as 30 years before the Civil War, there were debates in the South Carolina legislature concerning the problem that the average white citizen of that state did not feel himself to be primarily a citizen of South Carolina or of the South, but of the United States, and consequently in the event of secession might remain loyal to the Union, slavery or not. Among measures taken to create a "southern" identity was a mythologized history.

A cultural aristocracy did have some semblance of reality in Virginia in such people as Jefferson and Washington, but this was not typical of the South. Contemporary southern references to slave and plantation owners, for the most part, reflect an attitude similar to that of Americans to used car salesmen: they are not doing anything illegal, but they're interested in making a "quick buck" and aren't too fussy about how they do it.

Obviously, the real psychological effects of the American slave system on whites, as well as on blacks, cannot be empirically determined because the people are no longer available for study. Luckily, the people involved in the American "caste" system were studied while that system was still clear-cut. Thus, psychologically speaking, the current state of knowledge about the effects of a caste system on the "lower" caste and the determinants of these effects has become far more sophisticated in the modern era, but the "benefits" of the "upper" caste have not been subjected to the same careful empirical examination.

The American caste system, once rationalized as also good for the black man, has, by careful empirical investigations such as those contained in this book, been consistently revealed as injuring the caste assigned the lower status. The degree of psychological injury varies directly with the severity of the caste sanctions. No such body of data yet exists on the system's effects on the white man.

Myrdal's classic study (1944) suggested that the southern white was at least as much a victim of the caste system as the southern black, but that the former was more pathetic because he did not know the source of his woes. Myrdal traced the distinctive economic, social, and political problems of the South to the indirect results of the caste system. But the psychological effects of such a system on the dominant caste have not been systematically investigated. Data from the representative nationwide Gallup sample who were administered the Tomkins-Horn Picture Arrangement Test (PAT) permit such an investigation. (Most readers, particularly those of limited statistical sophistication, will find it more meaningful to skip to the *Summary of Results* and *Discussion* before reading as much of the *Method* sections as is necessary to assess the soundness of the procedures which led to those conclusions.)

Method

For the purposes of studying the white, the country was divided into three regions—North, Border South, and Deep South—on the basis of the nature of the caste system in each state, and of the involvement of the white population in the maintenance of the caste system. Any state which, as of the time of testing (1954), met the following three criteria was classified as being part of the North: no law concerning segregation in the public schools, or a law which expressly forbade it; no law concerning segregation in any form of public transportation, or a law which expressly forbade it; and no valid (by state standards) law forbidding intermarriage between blacks and whites. In addition, states were classified as northern which may have had one of these legal restrictions (e.g., an antimiscegenation law), but in which the number of blacks was so small that the restrictions against them could be expected to have had little effect on the way of life of the white population. Thus, the bulk of the population of the United States was classified as living in the North, namely, individuals from the following states: Maine, New Hampshire, Vermont, Massachusetts, Rhode Island, Connecticut, New York, New Jersey, Pennsylvania, Ohio, Michigan, Illinois, Wisconsin, Minnesota, Iowa, Utah, Nevada, California, Oregon, and Washington.

States which, as of the time of testing, were the obverse of the northern states on all three criteria were classified as southern, i.e., states which had laws requiring segregation in the public schools or in some form of public transportation, and a law forbidding intermarriage between blacks and whites and prescribing a criminal penalty.

The South was further subdivided into two groups: Border South and Deep South, using Gallup's classification, which has proved useful in his public opinion studies. Some marginal states that he includes in the Border South were excluded because they did not meet the above three criteria of being classified as southern. The Border South was defined as Virginia, North Carolina, Tennessee, Texas, and Florida. The Deep South was defined as South Carolina, Georgia, Alabama, Mississippi, Louisiana, and Arkansas.

The meaningfulness of this distinction of Border and Deep South can be justified historically, as well as by Gallup's findings that they tend to respond differently in public opinion studies. Moreover, blacks generally constitute a smaller percentage of the population in the Border South, which would lead one to expect a lesser involvement of whites in maintaining the caste system. The attitudes of the populace and the state governments of the Border South toward desegregation following the Supreme Court decision were distinctively different from those of the Deep South. For example, the governor of Tennessee (Border South) called out the National Guard to preserve law and order when a beginning was made to desegregate the schools in Nashville, while the governor of Arkansas (Deep South) also called out the National Guard when a beginning was made on desegregation, but in order to prevent the desegregation.

Based on the history of the Deep South states, their status before and after the Civil War, their regulations concerning black-white relations, and the nature of their resistance to desegregation, it is clear that these states differed from the rest of the country and even from the rest of the South in that the degree of commitment of whites to a caste system was greatest.

(The states of Delaware, Maryland, West Virginia, Indiana, Missouri, North Dakota, South Dakota, Nebraska, Kansas, Kentucky, Oklahoma, Montana, Arizona, Colorado, Idaho, Wyoming, and New Mexico were not included in any of the three groups because they did not meet the criteria for being unambiguously northern or southern. These states represent only 17 percent of the population of the United States.)

There were 187 whites from the Border South in the Gallup sample, and 109 whites from the Deep South. Approximately one-third of each sample (60 and 36 cases, respectively) were chosen by means of a random number table to be used for the pilot studies (samples BS-1 and DS-1); the remaining two-thirds of the cases were used for validation samples (samples BS-2 and DS-2).

In the pilot studies, samples BS-1 and DS-1 were each compared independently with the national norms. If the number of extreme cases on the "a," "d," or "f" variant of a scale was significantly different from the national norms at the 20 percent level, the scale was selected for validation. As mentioned in Chapter V, this low level of significance is appropriate in a pilot study since one wishes to pick up even hints in the data, and no interpretation of any finding was to be made unless it replicated at the conventional levels of significance.

Of the 158 interpretable scales on the PAT, 18 were selected in the Border South pilot study and 15 were selected in the Deep South pilot study.

For each of the two southern white validation samples, a northern white comparison sample was drawn from the national sample. The northern whites were drawn so that for each individual in the southern sample there were two northern whites of the same age, education, and I.Q. (the three variables for which the data of Tomkins and Miner [1957] and of the main study of this book indicate that it is necessary to control), and of the same sex. If there were more than two appropriate cases, a random number table was used to make the selection. If there was no exactly appropriate individual, the available individual most close on the four variables was selected. In order to maximize the match by maximizing the cases available, the control groups for BS-2 and DS-2 were independently drawn from duplicate decks of IBM cards, so that some of the same individuals may have been in each control group.

Inasmuch as there was more than one hypothesis being tested in each validation study, and inasmuch as these hypotheses (scales) were partially dependent, it was necessary to show that the difference between the two validation samples was significant on the whole set of hypotheses taken together before taking seriously a statistically significant finding on any one variable. One simple appropriate procedure, used in the main part of the book, is to calculate a simple discriminant score for each person by assigning a score of +1 for each of the variables located in the pilot study on which he was extreme and a score of 0 if he is not extreme. (All variables located in these pilot studies were in the direction of an increase in the frequency of extreme cases in the southern sample.) Thus, scores could vary from 0 to 18 in the Border South replication and from 0 to 15 in the Deep South replication. Only if the samples were significantly different on the discriminant score would it be appropriate to interpret a significant difference on an individual variable as meaningful.

Border South

Since the difference on the Border South discriminant score between the Border South validation sample and its northern white control did *not* approach statistical significance, no further analysis was carried out on those samples.

Deep South

For the Deep South validation samples, the difference in the discriminant score was statistically significant; the individual characteristics comprising it were therefore examined. Those which were either significant or close to statistical significance were then subjected to further scrutiny to determine whether they were a function of variables—other than the caste system— which differentiate the South from the North, that is, rural-urban residence, population density, and degree of industrialization. (Age, education, vocabulary I.Q., and sex-ratio differences had already been held constant by the matching procedure.)

Any of the PAT characteristics which were significantly related to these background variables was then subjected to an analysis of variance or covariance to correct for that background characteristic and to obtain a more precise determination of significance.

Table 1 shows the distribution of the Deep South validation samples by state; Table 2 gives the distribution by age, education, vocabulary I.Q., sex, and rural-urban residence.

Table 1   GEOGRAPHICAL DISTRIBUTION OF CASES IN DS-2 AND NW

Deep South-2 (n = 73)	
South Carolina	10
Georgia	21
Alabama	10
Mississippi	7
Louisiana	20
Arkansas	5
NW (n = 146)	
Maine	8
New Hampshire	3
Vermont	0
Massachusetts	5
Rhode Island	1
Connecticut	3
New York	21
New Jersey	10
Pennsylvania	17
Ohio	15
Michigan	5
Illinois	12
Wisconsin	6
Minnesota	2
Iowa	8
Utah	2
Nevada	1
California	19
Oregon	3
Washington	5

Table 3 shows the distribution of the Deep South validation sample and its northern white control on the discriminant score.

As expected, the data reveal a clear tendency for higher scores on the discriminant function to occur in the Deep South sample. This means that the incidence of these 15 characteristics in the Deep South sample is more frequent. A t-test of the significance of the difference between the two means, using Welch's (1949) simple conservative technique to correct for the fact that the samples differ in variance, yields a "t" of 1.83, which is significant at the .03 level.[1] An alternate appropriate technique is a simple non-parametric test which examines the difference in extreme scores. Because of the distribu-

1 This is obviously an appropriately one-sided significance level, since it follows a pilot study and, consequently, findings in a direction opposite to the pilot study would have to be treated as due to sampling error.

Table 2   DISTRIBUTIONS OF SAMPLES DS-2 AND NW
BY BACKGROUND FACTORS

	DS-2	NW
Age		
10-19	16	32
20-29	13	26
30-39	11	22
40-49	11	22
50-59	14	28
60-69	7	14
70-79	1	2
	73	146
Education		
0	0	6
1-6	16	32
7-8	22	44
High school, incomplete	13	26
High school, complete	10	21
Nurses training	1	1
Business school or college	1	2
College, incomplete	4	8
College graduate	3	6
	73	146
Intelligence (Vocabulary)		
Borderline and defective (Below 80)	10	20
Dull normal (80-90)	14	28
Average (90-110)	23	46
High average (110-120)	17	34
Superior (Above 120)	9	18
	73	146
Sex		
Male	40	81
Female	33	65
	73	146
Rural-urban residence		
Farm	13	16
Non-farm under 2,500	29	36
2,500-9,999	9	14
10,000-24,999	2	15
25,000-49,999	2	11
50,000-99,999	4	13
100,000-499,999	9	10
500,000 and over	5	31
	73	146

Marital status
Married	43	86
Single	25	47
Widowed	5	11
Divorced	0	2
	73	146

Table 3   DISTRIBUTIONS OF DISCRIMINANT SCORES
IN SAMPLES DS-2 AND NW

	DS-2 (n = 73)	NW (n = 146)
0	40	87
1	19	35
2	5	21
3	3	1
4	1	2
5	3	0
6	1	0
7	0	0
8	1	0
Mean	.97	.60

tion, i.e., there are no scores below zero, which is the modal score in both samples, neither sample is more extreme at the lower end. At the high end, the five most extreme scores are in one sample (DS-2), and that sample is one-half the size of the other. The probability that the largest observation would occur in the smaller sample is one-third; the probability that the next largest observation will occur in that sample is a little less than one-third, and so on. These probabilities are independent. Therefore, the probability that the largest five observations are all in the smaller sample is less than $(1/3)^5$, or less than 1/243, that is, less than .004. Clearly the differences between Deep South sample-2 and its northern white control sample are not due to chance or sampling error.

Because the samples were matched on age, intelligence, education, and sex, these variables, too, cannot account for these differences.

The individual characteristic

For six of the 15 variables, the two samples either did not differ at all or differed in the opposite direction from that predicted by the pilot study. Obviously, these six variables tended to make the discriminant score difference not significant, or significant in the opposite direction. (Only one of the six variables showed a marked trend in the opposite direction. But even a statistically significant finding in the opposite direction obviously would not have been interpretable, since whenever a finding is statistically significant in opposite directions in the pilot and validation studies, it is uninterpretable. The most plausible and usual explanation of such findings is that opposed findings are due to sampling error. It will be recalled that findings due to sampling error must occur with the small probability specified by the significance level.)

It should be noted, however, that the procedure of testing the discriminant score first has already taken into account these negative findings in evaluating the overall significance of the data, and that the findings on the other variables must be very compelling for the overall test of the discriminant score to be significant despite the negative findings. But the overall test (of the discriminant score) was clearly significant in the validation study, and hence it is safe to take the individual findings (where the pilot and validation studies are consistent) seriously. Table 4 lists the nine variables on which the two samples differed in the direction predicted by the pilot study. Each of them was tested for statistical significance by itself, and they are listed in the order of their statistical significance.

The most striking findings at this point are on the variables of "Negativism" (as measured on the PAT, really "Compulsive negativism"—the neurotic need to do exactly the opposite of what the person you are with wants you to do) and "Low work endurance—work interrupted" (the continuous search for good reasons not to have to continue to work or strive). The next two variables also have to do with work motivation. They are "Low general work" (the need not to work) and "Negative social facilitation—others stop work" (the presence of other people is the signal for stopping work). These are the only variables which, considered individually, reach the generally accepted levels of statistical significance. Thus, it can be concluded that these differences are not due to chance or sampling error; nor are they due to the effects of age, intelligence, education, or sex, on which the samples have been equated.

The remaining scales are "Dependence—continuing support as end state—dominance and/or instruction" (Submissive authoritarianism), "High starting inertia followed by high enduring work—works after passivity," "General dependence—support a necessary and sustaining condition of work or optimism," "High general aggressive press," and "Passivity—tendency to sit and/or lean."

It will be noted that the only one of these variables which is the same as that found for southern blacks is "High general aggressive press," and the findings on this variable are hardly very striking. It can therefore be con-

Table 4   NUMBER AND PERCENTAGE OF EXTREME CASES IN SAMPLES DS-2
AND NW AND SIGNIFICANCE LEVEL OF THE DIFFERENCES FOR THE NINE
VARIABLES THAT ACCOUNT FOR THE SIGNIFICANCE OF THE
DISCRIMINANT FUNCTION

		No. of extreme cases		% of extreme cases		Signifi- cance level
Scale	Variable	DS-2 (n = 73)	NW (n = 146)	DS-2 (n = 73)	NW (n = 146)	
125	Negativism	9	3	11.0	2.1	.003[1]
233	Low work endurance–work interrupted	9	3	11.0	2.1	.003[1]
223	Low general work	9	4	11.0	2.7	.006[2]
226	Negative social facilitation– others stop work	7	3	9.6	2.1	.015[2]
142	Dependence–continuing support as end state–dominance and/ or instruction (Submissive Authoritarianism)	5	4	6.8	2.7	.14[2]
230	High starting inertia followed by high enduring work–works after passivity	5	5	6.8	3.4	.20[2]
130	General dependence–support a necessary and sustaining condition of work oɪ optimism	6	9	8.2	6.2	.35[2]
124	High general aggressive press	1	1	1.4	0.7	.40[3]
214	Passivity–tendency to sit and/or lean	6	10	8.2	6.8	.46[2]

[1] Computed by Fisher's exact test.
[2] Computed by chi-square. (Cochran [1954] has shown that chi-square, using Yates' correction for continuity, is appropriate even when one cell has an expected value less than 5, if the total n is greater than 40).
[3] Computed by binomial probability paper (Mosteller & Tukey, 1949).

cluded that the effects of the American caste system on the Deep South white were different from the effects of that system on the southern black.

It is also clear that the effects on the southern white were not benign. The four variables on which there were striking findings consist of Compulsive negativism and three variables which indicate an impaired attitude toward work. The meaning of these findings will be discussed later in some detail, but further statistical analyses are necessary in order to be able to draw unambiguous conclusions.

Rural-urban residence, population density, and
degree of industrialization

The South (Cash, 1941) was mainly differentiated from the North by the existence of a stringent caste system and by the consequences of that system. Nonetheless, as mentioned in Chapter II, it is clear that the sex ratio and the age distribution are somewhat different because of migration patterns. Moreover, the South is a less educated section of the country, and there is a tendency for Southerners to score lower on intelligence tests. The data of Tomkins and Miner (1957), as well as the research reported in this book, indicated that the important variables to control in interpreting the PAT were age, education, and intelligence. The samples have been matched on these three variables as well as on sex.

But there were other differences between the North and the South.[2] The South was also a more rural region, a less densely populated region, and a less industrialized region. While these variables did not appreciably affect the characteristics which increased among southern blacks, it remained to investigate empirically whether they were related to (and therefore might account for) the personality characteristics which were more frequent among Deep South whites.

To investigate these relationships, only the cases in the northern white sample were used, as before. It may be useful to repeat the rationale for this procedure. First of all, the northern white sample was larger and more diversified, and hence would permit a sensitive test of whether such a relationship exists, even without the southern cases. More important, it is the effects, for example, of rural-urban residence *per se* on these personality characteristics, and not the interaction of rural-urban residence with the caste system which should be eliminated. It is conceivable that whites who live in the city in the South are apt to be less involved with the caste system, and hence may show fewer effects of the caste system on their personalities. It was not intended to eliminate that kind of relationship from the study, but only to eliminate the effect of rural-urban residence *per se*. To put it more simply, we do not want to palm off the characteristics of country folk wherever they are, whether or not they are involved with the caste system, as being the effects of the caste system.[3]

Each PAT variable which had reached at least the 20 percent level of significance in the validation was examined individually for its relationship to

2 For a fuller description of these methodological problems, see Chapter V.
3 See Chapter V for a fuller description.

rural-urban residence, degree of industrialization, and population density. Percentage of those employed who were employed in manufacturing industries was taken as the index of degree of industrialization. Number of people per square mile was taken as the index of population density. The state was used as the unit of area for both degree of industrialization and population density. In order to test the significance of the relationship between the differentiating variables and rural-urban residence, population density, and degree of industrialization non-parametrically, Kendall's Tau coefficient of rank correlation (Kendall, 1955) was used. The results are shown in Table 5.

It is clear that, on the whole, the differentiating variables were not closely related to rural-urban residence, population density, or degree of industrialization. There are only two relationships which reach the generally accepted levels of statistical significance. PAT scale 233, Low work endurance, is significantly related to rural-urban residence, and scale 142, Submissive authoritarianism, is significantly related to population density.

To be on the safe side, it was decided to correct for any background characteristic which reached even the 10 percent level of significance. The findings will be presented for each variable separately.

Table 5   SIGNIFICANCE LEVELS OF THE RELATIONSHIP OF RURAL-URBAN RESIDENCE, POPULATION DENSITY, AND DEGREE OF INDUSTRIALIZATION TO DIFFERENTIATING VARIABLE IN SAMPLE NW

Scale	Variable	Rural-urban residence	Population density	Degree of industrial- ization
125	Negativism	.06	.83	.39
233	Low work endurance–work interrupted	.02	.38	.17
223	Low general work	.30	.25	.52
226	Negative social facilitation– others stop work	.07	.96	.10
142	Dependence–continuing support an end state–dominance and/ or instruction (Submissive Authoritarianism)	.79	.04	.10
230	High starting inertia followed by high enduring work–works after passivity	.47	.28	.30

Negativism

To be conservative, it was decided to correct for the effects of rural-urban residence, although its relationship with Negativism did not quite reach the 5 percent level of significance, and the difference between the North and South on Negativism reached the .0003 level of significance.

The data were grouped into the rural-urban residence categories shown in Table 2, but the three categories from 10,000 to 100,000 were combined into a single category so that there would be no category with less than five cases. This combination of categories seems appropriate, since in the three combined categories there was exactly the same percentage of extreme cases in each sample (exactly zero percent). The percentage of extreme cases in each category was then transformed by an arc sine transformation $(\sin^{-1}\sqrt{p})$ and an analysis of variance on the arc sines was computed. The resulting analysis of variance table is shown in Table 6. It was clear that the difference between the North and the South which was found in Negativism was still significant at the .025 level, even when tested in this conservative fashion.

Low work endurance

Low work endurance seems to be clearly related to rural-urban residence. To correct for the effects of rural-urban residence, an analysis of variance, exactly the same as that which was performed for the variable of Negativism, was calculated. The resulting analysis of variance table is shown in Table 7. It was apparent that a conservative statistical analysis, in which the effects of rural-urban residence were taken into account, still revealed that the difference between the North and South was extraordinarily striking.

Table 6   ANALYSIS OF VARIANCE FOR NEGATIVISM

Source	d.f.	Mean square
NW vs. DS-2	1	256.6875
Rural-urban residence	5	112.0375
Interaction	5	67.1357
Error	∞	66.9275

$F_{1,\infty} = 3.84$ $p = .025$

Table 7   ANALYSIS OF VARIANCE FOR LOW WORK ENDURANCE

Source	d.f.	Mean square
NW vs. SW-2	1	706.6021
Rural-urban residence	5	24.5282
Interaction	5	109.2072
Error	∞	66.9275

$F_{1,\infty} = 10.56$ $p = .0007$

The mean squares for rural-urban residence and for interaction were not significantly different from the error mean square, as indicated by the appropriate "F" ratios. There seemed to be a tendency for Low work endurance to be more frequent among urban residents in the northern sample, but this tendency was not clear in the southern sample. When the two samples were considered together, there was not a significant relationship between Low work endurance and rural-urban residence; nor was the difference between the northern and southern sample in the degree of relationship with rural-urban residence significant either, as indicated by the non-significant "F" ratios. The significance level for the North-Deep South main effect, however, was now even higher (.0007).

Low work

The variable of Low work was not clearly related to rural-urban residence, population density, or degree of industrialization, as can be seen from Table 5. The significance levels did not come anywhere near the 5 percent level; hence no correction was necessary for these background factors. The significance of the difference between the northern and southern sample appropriately remained .0006.

Negative social facilitation—others stop work

From Table 5 it is clear that this variable was not significantly related to these three background factors. However, the relationship with rural-urban residence reached the .07 level, and the relationship with degree of industrialization reached the .10 level.

To be conservative and correct for the effects of rural-urban residence, an analysis of variance was carried out as before. The resulting analysis of variance table is shown in Table 8. As might be expected, given that the

Table 8   ANALYSES OF VARIANCE FOR NEGATIVE SOCIAL FACILITATION –
           OTHERS STOP WORK

Source	d.f.	Mean square
NW vs. SW-2	1	295.91402
Rural-urban residence	5	58.4240
Interaction	5	115.6884
Error	∞	66.9275

$F_{1,\infty} = 4.42$ $p = .018$

		Error of estimate mean square
NW vs. SN-2	1	1418.0774
Rural-urban residence	7	512.8127
Degree of industrialization[1]	1	447.7150
Residual	66	372.1113
Error	∞	821.

$F_{1,\infty} = 1.73$ $p = .10$

[1] Variance due to regression within North-South and rural-urban categories.

relationship with rural-urban residence was not significant in the first place, the significance level of the North-South difference has not been appreciably altered. It was originally .015, and the analysis of variance yielded .018.

To be very conservative and to take into account both degree of industrialization and rural-urban residence, even though the former relationship only reached the .10 level of significance, an analysis of covariance was carried out, using Degree of industrialization as a control variable and thus refining the analysis of variance performed above. It should be noted, however, that it was not possible to group the cases within each rural-urban residence category, and hence arc sines were determined for samples as small as one. When the N is less than 5, the theoretical estimates of variance do not really hold and the resulting approximation is not as precise as we would like. However, an analysis of covariance was carried out, and the following were the results. Using the theoretically derived estimate of error, $F_{1,\infty}$ was found to be 1.73 for the North-South difference. This was significant at the .10 level. However, the residual error (which should be an empirical estimate of the theoretical error term) was significantly smaller than the theoretically derived error term, the F ratio ($F_{\infty,66}$) being 2.21, which is significant at the

.02 level, 2-sided. Using the residual error term to evaluate the North-South difference yields an $F_{1,66}$ equal to 3.81, which is significant at the .05 level. However, if the theoretical error estimate does not hold, there are problems in estimating the error from the data, inasmuch as the error variance differs for differing subclasses of the samples. Because of these statistical problems, it is probably better to use the most conservative figure and to state that the significance level was at least .10.

Submissive authoritarianism

Submissive authoritarianism seems clearly, from Table 5, to be related to population density, in that it is more frequent in more densely populated areas. This relationship reaches the .04 level of significance. There is also a suggestion (at the .10 level of significance) of a relationship with Degree of industrialization.

To correct for population density, an analysis of covariance of the arc sines was carried out. The regression lines for the North and for the South were not significantly different from each other in terms of slope. Therefore, a pooled estimate of the regression line was determined. The analysis of covariance for Submissive authoritarianism, correcting for the effects of population density, is shown in Table 9. The resulting F ratio for the North-South differences, $F_{1,\infty}$ equals 4.29, and this is significant at the .02 level. As before, the empirically estimated error variance is smaller than the theoretical estimate of error, so that if there is any inappropriateness of the statistical model, it is on the conservative side, and the significance level is at least .02.

Thus, when the effects of population density have been taken into account, the difference between the North and South on Submissive authoritarianism now became clearly significant, where it was not before. Thus, in both the North and the South there was a tendency for Submissive authoritarianism to be more frequent in more densely populated areas. When this

Table 9   ANALYSIS OF COVARIANCE FOR SUBMISSIVE AUTHORITARIANISM

Source	d.f.	Error of estimate mean square
NW vs. DS-2	1	3,518.1830
Population density (regression)	1	3,507.1978
Residual	22	669.6943
Error	∞	821.

$F_{1,\infty} = 4.29$ $p = .02$

relationship had been taken into account, the difference between the North and the South became even more striking than it was before.

The background variable of Degree of industrialization also showed a tendency to be related to Submissive authoritarianism. However, when population density had been taken into account, this relationship disappeared. The product-moment correlation coefficient becomes .008, which is as close to zero as one would ever hope to see. Therefore, no further correction was necessary.

High starting inertia followed by high enduring work—works after passivity

It is clear from Table 5 that this variable was not related to rural-urban residence, population density, or degree of industrialization. It was therefore unnecessary to perform any corrections for this variable. The original significance level stands, as before, at .20.

Summary of results

There was *no* statistically significant difference between the Border South whites and northern whites, but there were for the Deep South whites. Table 10 shows the six variables which differentiated the Deep Southern white sample from the northern white sample at at least the 20 percent level and the significance level of these findings as they were originally, when only the background characteristics of age, sex, education, and intelligence were controlled, and the modified significance level after the additional background characteristics of rural-urban residence, population density, and degree of industrialization have been taken into account. The only major differences are that Negative social facilitation of work is less striking than it was before and Submissive authoritarianism is now considerably more striking. Our most striking findings, then, are increase in the frequency of the following characteristics among Deep South whites: Compulsive negativism, Low work endurance, Low general work, and Submissive authoritarianism.

Discussion

It is surprising at first glance that there was not a replicable difference between Border South whites and northern whites. In part this may be due to the insensitivity of the measuring instrument and to the size of the samples.

Table 10   SIGNIFICANCE LEVELS BEFORE AND AFTER TAKING INTO
ACCOUNT RURAL-URBAN RESIDENCE, DEGREE OF INDUSTRIALIZATION,
AND POPULATION DENSITY

Scale	Variable	Uncorrected significance level	Corrected significance level
223	Low work endurance—work interrupted	.003	.0007
233	Low general work	.006	.006
142	Submissive authoritarianism	.14	.02
125	Compulsive negativism	.003	.025
226	Negative social facilitation— others stop work	.015	.10
230	High starting inertia followed by high enduring work—works after passivity	.20	.20

But the same measuring instrument and even smaller samples were more than adequate to reveal differences between Deep South whites and northern whites, as well as to reveal differences between northern and southern blacks.

How is this to be explained? It could be argued that the Border South was healthy or that the North was sick. Probably both statements were true. The Border South of the 1950s obviously had more of a problem of black-white relations than did the North. But everyone in the Border South knew it was a problem. It was out in the open, and everyone knew that there would be changes. While the North had less of a caste system than the Border South, the white population of the North was trying to pretend that no problem existed at all.

Subsequent events demonstrate clearly that, on a social level as well as on a personal level, the worst way to handle a problem is to pretend it doesn't exist.

The Deep South, of course, had more of a caste system than the Border South. Nonetheless, Deep South whites were trying to pretend it did not have a problem. Thus, it might be expected that there would be findings, as indeed there are.

The psychological characteristics which were most strikingly increased among Deep South whites were Low work endurance, Low work, Submissive authoritarianism, and Compulsive negativism. It is striking that none of these represents an asset. The psychological effect of being a member of the dominant caste in a caste situation, therefore, seems to be destructive. It should be noted that these findings were derived from a purely mechanical selection on the basis of significance levels from among all the variables measured by the PAT. While some PAT variables represent pathology, others represent positive functions, and the bulk are merely descriptive without being obviously positive or negative. There was nothing about the procedure which required that the findings represent pathology; yet that is what each of the findings represent. This pathology seems to concern two areas of functioning: the area of work and the area of interpersonal relations. It is worthwhile to consider each of these separately.

The "horse-driver" phenomenon

The increases in the incidence of Low work endurance and Low work represent an increase in the frequency of people who are continuously seeking legitimate reasons for not having to continue to work and strive if they are already working, and an increase in those who are seeking not to work whether or not they are working.

This is different from the work problems of southern blacks which did not involve the low (avoidance of) work scales but, rather, Conflicting work motivation and Externalized work motivation. Nor were those work problems of southern blacks anywhere near as clear as the work problems of southern whites.

It has been argued that the so-called Protestant ethic typical of the United States as a whole—the belief that the way to get ahead is to have good ideas and work hard—is less deeply imbued in the southern culture, where the way to get ahead has been to find someone to exploit, as illustrated by the master-slave or landlord-sharecropper relationships. While there is obviously a good deal of truth in this view, there is a more general problem.

This problem is work motivation, which I have termed the "horse-driver" phenomenon. It is one of the consequences which always occurs as a function of an ascribed status situation, that is, in a situation where one's status is simply assigned but is not directly earned as a clear result of achievement. The "horse-driver" phenomenon occurs in those to whom the superior status is assigned.

One sees it in the armed services, where commissioned officers frequently have the feeling that if they did not have their ascribed status and had to compete as equals with noncommissioned officers, they could not.

One sees it in Orwell's description of British colonial troops in North Africa: "How long can we fool them into thinking we are superior?"

One sees it in the British upper classes who forbade any man who had ever worked with his hands from competing in the Diamond Sculls. It is as if they were saying that an aristocrat could be a champion athlete only as long as he didn't compete with supposedly physically stronger working men. (Yet it is obvious that sculling is such a specialized skill that this belief is, in general, not true.)

One saw it in the barrier which for so long barred blacks from professional sports in the U.S.A. The implicit belief was that white men could be star athletes only as long as they didn't compete with blacks.

But perhaps the clearest description of this phenomenon, from which the term "horse-driver" phenomenon was derived, was given by a foreman in the garment industry in New England. In describing what he felt to be the secret of his success on the job, he said, "If you ever let the horse know how strong he is, he'll grab the whip out of your hand and say, 'Goddamnit, you pull the wagon.' So you mustn't let the horse know how strong he is." (Interestingly enough, the men who worked under his supervision did not agree, but attributed his success as a foreman to his fairness in dealing with them, which was probably a more accurate understanding of the situation.)

Just as the ascribed status situation was more nearly ubiquitous in the South than elsewhere, so the horse-driver phenomenon was more widespread. The feeling that if one had to compete on merit with blacks, one couldn't, saps the drive to work as the road to success.

The relationship to authority

The Deep South of the 1950s was a highly structured society. The same social institutions which controlled the southern blacks served to control the whites as well. There was less room for dissent or toleration of controversy than in other sections of the United States. The political, economic, and social controls were great. This was reflected in the increase in Submissive authoritarianism. These are people who want a strong leader to tell them what to do. This is not to argue that there were more potential Hitlers in the Deep South, but that there were more potential followers of a potential Hitler. (Note that while the increase in incidence was striking compared to other groups of Americans, it was still a minority.)

The other finding is the increase in Negativism or, properly speaking, Compulsive negativism, since, as measured by the PAT, it indicates an all-pervasive need to do the opposite of what the person you are with wants you to do. This again is a reaction to the structured and controlled social system of the Deep South. It is the inner response of an individual who is continuously trying to prove that he isn't controlled because, indeed, he never really feels free. As Dr. Harold Schiffman aptly described it, "People generally talk the most about the problems they have never really solved. Perhaps,

ALLPORT, G. W.: Personality. New York, Henry Holt, 1937.

ALLPORT, G. W.: The nature of prejudice. Cambridge, Addison-Wesley, 1954.

ASHMORE, H. S.: The Negro and the schools. Chapel Hill, University of North Carolina, 1954.

BAUGHMAN, E. E.: Black Americans. New York, Academic Press, 1971.

BECK, S. J.: Rorschach's test. New York, Grune & Stratton, 1949.

CASH, W. J.: The mind of the South. New York, Knopf, 1941.

CAYTON, H. H.: The psychology of the Negro under discrimination. In A. Rose (Ed.), Mental health and mental disorder. New York, Norton, 1955, 371-388.

CLARK, K.: Effect of segregation and integration on children's personality (with discussion by K. Morland and B. Karon). In W. B. Brookover (Ed.), School Integration. East Lansing, Michigan, Bureau of Educational Research, Michigan State University, 1964, 1-26.

CLARK, K. B.: Dark Ghetto: Dilemmas of Social Power. New York, Harper, 1967.

CLEAVER, ELDRIDGE.: Soul on Ice. New York, Dell, 1968.

COCHRAN, W. G.: Some methods for strengthening the common X^2 tests. Biometrics, 1954, *10*, 417-451.

COOK, R. A.: Identification and ego defensiveness in thematic apperception. J. proj. Tech., 1953, *17*, 312-319.

DAI, B.: Some problems of personality development among Negro children. In C. Kluckhohn and H. A. Murray (Eds.), Personality in nature, society, and culture. New York, Knopf, 1948, 437-458.

DAVIE, M. R.: Negroes in American society. New York, McGraw-Hill, 1949.

DAVIS, A., AND DOLLARD, J.: Children of bondage. Washington, American Council on Education, 1941.

DAVIS, A., GARDNER, B. B., AND GARDNER, MARY R.: Deep South. Chicago, University of Chicago, 1941.

DAVIS, A., AND HAVIGHURST, R. J.: Social class and color differences in child-rearing. In C. Kluckhohn and H. A. Murray (Eds.), Personality in nature, society, and culture. New York, Knopf, 1948, 252-265.

DOLLARD, J.: Caste and class in a southern town. New Haven, Yale, 1937.

ERIKSON, ERIK H.: Childhood and society. New York, Norton, 1950.

FENICHEL, O. H.: The psychoanalytic theory of neurosis. New York, Norton, 1945.

FISHER, R. A.: Statistical methods and scientific inference. New York, Hafner, 1956.

FRAZIER, E. F.: The Negro family in the United States. Chicago, University of Chicago, 1939.

FRAZIER, E. F.: The Negro in the United States. New York, Macmillan, 1949.

FREUD, ANNA: The ego and the mechanisms of defense. New York: International Universities, 1966.

GOODMAN, MARY E.: Race awareness in young children. Cambridge, Addison-Wesley, 1952.

GRIER, W. H., & COBBS, P. M.: Black Rage. New York, Bantam, 1968.

GRIER, W. H., & COBBS, P. M.: The Jesus Bag. New York, Bantam, 1971.

GULLIKSEN, H.: Theory of mental tests. New York, Wiley, 1950.

HANFMANN, EUGENIA, AND GETZELS, J. W.: Studies of the sentence completion test. J. proj. Tech., 1953, 17, 280-294.

JENSEN, A. R.: Educability and Group Differences. New York, Harper, 1973.

JOHNSON, C. S.: Growing up in the black belt. Washington, American Council on Education, 1941.

KARDINER, A.: The individual and his society. New York, Columbia, 1939.

KARDINER, A., AND OVESEY, L.: The mark of oppression. New York, Norton, 1951.

KARON, B. P. & O'GRADY, P.: Quantified judgments of mental health from the Rorschach, TAT, and Clinical Status Interview by means of a scaling technique. J. Consulting & Clin. Psychol., 1970, 34, 229-235.

KENDALL, M. G.: Rank correlation methods. London, Griffin, 1948.

KILPATRICK, F. P., (Ed.): Human behavior from a transactional point of view. Hanover, N. H., Institute for Associated Research, 1953.

KING, M. L.: Why We Can't Wait. New York, Harper, 1964.

KLINEBERG, O.: Part II. Tests of Negro intelligence. In O. Klineberg (Ed.), Characteristics of the American Negro. New York, Harper, 1944, 23-96.

KLINEBERG, O.: Part III. Experimental studies of Negro personality. In O. Klineberg (Ed.), Characteristics of the American Negro. New York, Harper, 1944, 97-138.

KLOPFER, B., AND KELLEY, D. M.: The Rorschach technique. New York, World Book, 1942.

KLUCKHOHN, C., AND MURRAY, H. A., (Eds.): Personality in nature, society, and culture. New York, Knopf, 1948.

LONG, F. J., & KARON, B. P.: Rorschach validity as measured by the identification of individual patients, J. Proj. Techn. & Pers. Assess., 1969, 33, 20-24.

McLEAN, HELEN V.: Psychodynamic factors in racial relations. Ann. Amer. Acad. Polit. Soc. Sci., 1946, *244*, 159-166.

MALINOWSKI, B.: The dynamics of culture change. New Haven, Yale, 1945.

MALZBERG, B.: Mental disease among American Negroes. In O. Klineberg (Ed.), Characteristics of the American Negro. New York, Harper, 1944, 371-399.

MANGRUM, C. S.: The legal status of the Negro. Chapel Hill, University of North Carolina, 1940.

MARSHALL, W. W.: A large-sample test of the hypothesis that one of two random variables is stochastically larger than the other. J. Amer. Statist. Ass., 1951, *46*, 366-374.

MINER, J. B.: Intelligence in the United States. New York, Springer, 1957.

MORRIS, F. L.: The Jensen Hypothesis: Social Science Research or Social Science Racism. Los Angeles: Center for Afro-American Studies. University of California, 1971. (Monograph series, no. 2).

MOSTELLER, F., AND TUKEY, J. W.: The uses and usefulness of binomial probability paper. J. Amer. Statist. Ass., 1949, *44*, 174-212.

MURRAY, H. A., *et al.*: Exploration in personality. New York, Oxford, 1938.

MURRAY, H. A., *et al.*: The thematic apperception test manual. Cambridge, Harvard, 1943.

MURRAY, PAULI: States laws on race and color. Cincinnati, Women's Division of Christian Service, 1950.

MYRDAL, G.: An American dilemma. New York, Harper, 1944.

PARKER, S., & KLEINER, R. J.: Mental Illness in the Urban Negro Community. New York, Free Press, 1966.

PARSONS, T.: The social system. Glencoe, Free Press, 1951.

PARSONS, T., *et al.*: Towards a general theory of action. Cambridge, Harvard, 1951.

PITMAN, E. J. G.: Significance tests which may be applied to samples from any population, II. The correlation coefficient test. Suppl. J. Roy. Statist. Soc., 1937, *4*, 225-233.

POWDERMAKER, HORTENSE: The channeling of Negro aggression by the cultural process. In C. Kluckhohn and H. A. Murray (Eds.), Personality in nature, society, and culture. New York, Knopf, 1948, 478-484.

ROSE, A. M.: The Negro in America. New York, Harper, 1944.

ROSE, A. M.: The Negro's morale. Minneapolis, University of Minnesota, 1949.

ROSE, A. M.: Mental health and mental disorder. New York, Norton, 1955.

SELLERS, C. G.: The Southerner as American. Durham, University of North Carolina, 1960.

SHOCKLEY, W.: Discusses "Shockleyan" Genetics with William F. Buckley. Firing Line, WKAR, July 19, 1974 (phonotape).

SHOEMAKER, D., (Ed.): With all deliberate speed. New York, Harper, 1957.

SUNDBERG, N. D.: The acceptability of "fake" versus "bona fide" personality test interpretations. J. abnorm. soc. Psychol., 1955, *50*, 145-6.

TOMKINS, S. S.: The thematic apperception test. New York, Grune & Stratton, 1947.

TOMKINS, S. S.: The picture arrangement test. Trans. N. Y. Acad. Sci., Series II, 1952, *15*, 46-50.

TOMKINS, S. S., AND MINER, J. B.: The picture arrangement test. New York, Springer, 1957.

TOMKINS, S. S., AND MINER, J. B.: PAT Interpretation. New York, Springer, 1959.

U.S. BUREAU OF THE CENSUS: U.S. census of the population: 1950. Vol. II, Characteristics of the population. Washington, U.S. Government Printing Office, 1953.

WECHSLER, D.: The measurement of adult intelligence. Baltimore, Williams and Wilkins, 1939.

WELCH, B. L.: Further note on Mrs. Aspin's tables and on certain approximations to the tabled function. Biometrika, 1949, *36*, 293-296.

WHITING, J. W. M., AND CHILD, I. L.: Child training and personality. New Haven, Yale, 1953.

WILLIAMS, R. M., AND RYAN, MARGARET W.: Schools in transition. Chapel Hill, University of North Carolina, 1954.

X (LITTLE), MALCOLM: The Autobiography of Malcolm X. New York, Grove, 1965.

Adaptation, 10
  defensive, 45
  middle and upper class blacks
    and, 47
  problems of, 4
  warped childhood and, 32
AFL-CIO, 29
Aggression, 47, 48, 159, 163-164,
    167
  handling of, by blacks, 123-128,
    168
Agriculture, blacks and, 10-11, 27,
    36
Alexander, Irving E., x
Allport, G.W., 53, 193
Anger, xiv, xvi, 43, 44, 46, 47, 126,
    127, 128, 129, 159, 162-
    163, 164, 167-168
Anxiety, 43, 45, 126
Aristocracy, 11, 172, 173, 191
Aristotle, 172
Ashmore, H. S., 25, 193
Aspirations, 43
  symbolic substitutes for, 46
Authoritarianism, submissive, 187-
    188, 189, 191
Avoidance of male-male contacts,
    131
Awareness of being black, 3

Beck, S. J., 54, 193
Binet, Alfred, 49
Birth control, blacks and, x
Black pride, v
"Block-busters," xiii
Boas, Franz, 42
Brutality, 10, 22, 24
Businesses, black-owned, 29, 36

Cantril, Hadley, x
Cash, W. J., 182, 193
Caste sanctions, 2-6, 7, 19, 165,
    166-171
  definition of, 2
  economic, 27-29
  North and, 4
  personality characteristics and,
    157-164
  political, 22-27
  South and, 5, 6
  study of effects of, 74
Caste system, American, 7-40, 173
  effect of, on whites, 169-170,
    172-192
Cayton, H. H., 51, 123, 193
Chance, personality differences
    and, 76-82
Change, 11, 33

Characteristics of blacks, 45-51
Child, I. L., 3, 195
Child rearing practices, 33
Civil rights movement, 18, 34
Civil War, 8
Class structure, 29-30
Clement, Governor (Tennessee), 38
Clinton, Tennessee, riots in, 38
Cochran, W. G., 181, 193
Concubines, black, 15
Conversation, between blacks and
        whites, 19-20
Cook, R. A., 72, 193
Courts, blacks and the, 23-24, 29,
        51
Culture
    of the South, 11
    problem of, 3-6

Dai, B., 33, 123, 193
Dancing, interracial, 15, 19
Dating, interracial, xv
Davie, M. R., 8, 193
Davis, A., 33, 44, 193
Democracy, vii, 40
Denial, defense mechanism of, 47,
        48, 126, 127, 128, 129,
        143, 162-163, 167
Depression, 43
Desegregation, 38, 174-175
Desertion, 31
Design, experiment, 72-112
Determinants, universal, 57-58
Determinism, 57
Differences
    between northern and southern
        blacks, 45, 48-49, 50, 76,
        137-156, 167, 171
    black-white, 42-48, 49, 75, 113-
        136

chance and, 76-82
    significance of, 77
    specific natures of, 90-96
Discriminant score, 132-136, 138,
        148-150, 155, 157, 159,
        170, 180
    adjusting the, 107-109
Discrimination, xv, xvi, 10, 14, 34,
        35, 170, 172
    economic, 27-29
    effects of, 43
    patterns of, xiv
    politics and, 22-27
    See also Caste sanctions
Distribution, geographical, of blacks
        in U.S., 14
Dollard, J., 193
Dream interpretation, 54
Drinking, interracial, 18
Drinking fountains, separate, for
        blacks, 18

Eating, ritualism and, 18
Economic sanctions against blacks,
        27-29
Education, xv, 3, 11, 14, 27, 30,
        32, 34, 35, 37-40
Educational Testing Service, x
Eisenhower, Dwight D., 39
Emancipation, 8-10
Emotional life of blacks, 45-51,
        129, 159, 164
Employment, blacks and, xv, 27-
        29, 35, 36
Equality, 9, 12, 24, 27, 33, 35, 36
Erikson, Erik H., 3, 193
Estevan, Donald P., x
"Etiquette of race relations," xiv,
        18-21, 35
Experiment, design of an, 72-112

Exploitation, xv, 8, 10, 11, 12, 15, 43, 190
Extramarital relations between blacks and whites, 15

Family structure, 30-32
Farmers, black, 10-11, 27-28, 36
Fear, vii, 43, 126, 163
  freedom from, vii
Fenichel, O. H., 193
Fisher, R. A., 73, 161, 181
Flamboyance, 46
Fourteenth Amendment, 6
Frazier, E. F., x, 8, 9, 49, 51, 131, 193
Free association technique, 54, 56, 58
Freud, Anna, 129, 194
Freud, Sigmund, 57
Frustration, xv, 43, 44

Games, color barrier in, 19
Gardner, B. B., 193
Gardner, Mary, 193
Genocide, birth control as, xv
Geographical distribution of blacks, in U.S., 1 4
Getzels, J. W., 72, 194
Goldfarb, W., 45
Goodman, Mary E., 3, 194
Gulliksen, H., x, 56, 194

Haddon, A. C., 42
Handshake, interracial, 20-21
Hanfmann, Eugenia, 72, 194
Havighurst, R. J., 33, 44, 193
Hedonism, 43, 47

Heredity, personality differences and, 75, 167
Homicide, xvi
"Horse-driver" phenomenon, 190-191
Hospital services, xiii-xv
Hostility, vii, 43, 45, 46
Housing, xii-xiv, 3, 4, 29, 30, 34-35
  segregation and, xii, 28
Huxley, J. S., 42

Illegitimacy, 30, 31
Immigrants, 11
Income, blacks and, 27
Inferiority of blacks, alleged, 3, 6, 19, 20, 35, 40, 42, 49, 50, 165
Integration, 38-39
Intelligence, 41, 46, 49-50, 75, 85, 86, 166, 170
  black-white differences in, 49, 75
Intelligence tests, 45, 49-50, 75, 85, 86, 166, 182
Intermarriage, 14-15, 24, 174
Interpersonal relations, 131-132
  between blacks and whites, 14-15, 18-21

Jefferson, Thomas, 172, 173
Jensen, A. R., 50, 194
Jim Crow laws, 5, 35-36, 37
Jobs, *see* Employment
Johnson, C. S., 194
Jury duty, 3, 23

Kardiner, Abraham, viii, 3, 4, 9, 28, 30, 33, 42-43, 44, 46, 47,

Kardiner, Abraham *(Cont.)*
    48, 5 2, 123, 129, 156,
    170, 194
Kelley, D. M., 54, 194
Kendall, M. G., 104, 105, 106, 183,
    194
Kilpatrick, F. P., 58, 194
Klineberg, O., 42, 49, 50, 51, 52,
    78, 194
Klopfer, B., 54, 194
Kluckhohn, C., 3, 194

Labor, 11
Labor unions, blacks and, 11, 29,
    35, 36
Law, blacks and the, 3, 4, 22-24,
    33, 51
Little Rock, Arkansas, desegrega-
    tion issue in, 38-39
Long, F. J., 72, 194
Lord, Frederic M., x
Lynchings, 23, 37

McLean, Helen V., 194
Male-male contacts, avoidance of,
    131
Malinowski, B., 194
Malzberg, B., 49, 194
Mangrum, C. S., 194
"March-on-Washington," 26
Marriage, *see* Intermarriage
Marshall, W. W., 105, 106, 194
Migration, black, to the North, 13,
    14, 26, 31-32, 34, 50-51,
    145, 167
Miner, J. B., 5, 57, 60, 62, 63, 66,
    67, 68, 85, 86, 88, 89, 91,
    94, 104, 116, 117, 175,
    182, 194, 195
Minority groups, blacks differenti-

ated from other, 8
Miscegenation, *see* Intermarriage
Montgomery, Alabama, blacks of,
    37
Morris, F. L., 50, 195
Mosteller, F., 122, 161, 181, 194
Murray, H. A., 3, 55, 194
Murray, Pauli, 24, 25, 194
Myrdal, G., 8, 10, 15, 26, 29, 51,
    99, 131, 173, 194

NAACP, *see* National Association
    for the Advancement of
    Colored People
Nashville, Tennessee, desegregation
    issue in, 38
National Association for the Ad-
    vancement of Colored Peo-
    ple (NAACP), 34, 37, 38,
    39
National Guard, 38, 39, 174
Negativism, 126, 180, 181, 184,
    188, 189, 191
Neurosis, 45, 156
"No social equality" theory, 35
North, the
    black migration to, 13, 14, 26,
        31-32, 34, 50-51, 145, 167
    black-white relations in, 10-13,
        33-35
    caste sanctions in, 4
    Civil War and, 8
    developing situation in, 33-35
Northern blacks, differences be-
    tween southern blacks
    and, 45, 48-49, 50, 76,
    137-156, 167, 171

O'Grady, P., 72
Orwell, George, 190

Ovesey, Lionel, viii, 3, 4, 9, 28, 30,
    33, 42-43, 44, 46, 47, 48,
    52, 123, 129, 156, 170

Parsons, T., 3, 7, 195
PAT, see Tomkins-Horn Picture Ar-
    rangement Test
Personality, 7
  black, conflicts in, 9
  characteristics, caste sanctions
    and, 157-164
  definitions of, 53
  differences in, 42-48, 75
  measurement of, 52, 53-57
  problem of, 3-6
  theories of, 54
Picture Arrangement Test, see Tom-
    kins-Horn Picture Arrange-
    ment Test
Pilot study, 80-81, 82, 84, 91, 92,
    95, 99, 113, 123, 129,
    137, 171, 175, 176, 179
  second, 142-143
Pitman, E. J. G., 106, 195
Plessy vs. Ferguson, 5, 6, 27
Police
  black, 36
  blacks and the, 23-24
Political rights, 4, 6, 22-27
Political sanctions against blacks,
    22-27
Poll tax, 25
Population, black, in U.S., 8, 12, 14
Poverty, 11
Powdermaker, Hortense, 123, 195
Prejudice, racial, 34, 40
Pride, black, xiv
Primary, white, 27, 40
Princeton University, viii
Probability, 77, 78, 81

Professions, blacks and, 29, 36
Projective tests, 54-72, 166
  use of, with black subjects, 72
Prostitution, 15
Protestant ethic, 190
Protocols, incomplete, problem of,
    101-104, 146, 147
Psychology, black, 45-51
Psychosis rates, 49, 145, 171
Psychotherapy, xv, xvi, 41, 43, 156
Public Health Service, U.S., x
Public Opinion Surveys, Inc., 67

"Race pride," blacks and, 15
Race relations, patterns of, xiv
Rage, 43, 46
Randolph, A. P., 26
Rebellions, slave, 8
Reconstruction, 10
Repression, 126, 127
Restaurants, segregation and, 18
Restrictions, see Caste sanctions
Restrooms, separate facilities for
    blacks, 18
Riots, race, xiv, 23, 24, 38
Ritualism, 18, 20
Rorschach, Hermann, 54
Rorschach tests, 45, 46, 47, 52, 54-
    55
Rose, Arnold M., viii, 3, 8, 23, 24,
    25, 40, 51, 195
Ryan, Margaret W., 195

Sadism, 22
Samples
  description of, 113-114
  matched analysis of, 111-112,
    151
  selection of, 96-98

Saunders, David, x
Schiffman, Harold, 191
Schockley, W., 50
Schools, 5
    segregation and, 24, 25, 27, 28,
        36, 37-40, 174
    See also Education
Scorer reliability, 56
Scott, Sir Walter, 172
Segregation, 3, 5, 6, 12, 18, 20, 21,
        24, 27, 36, 40, 174
    housing and, xii, 28
    restaurants and, 18
    schools and, 24, 25, 27, 28, 36,
        37-40, 174
    transportation, public, and, 24,
        25, 27, 37, 176
Self-determination, xv
Self-esteem, low, of blacks, 43, 44
Sellers, C. G., 172, 195
Sentence Completion Test, 72
"Separate but equal" doctrine, 27,
        35, 36
Separate facilities, 5-6, 18, 27, 37
Separatism, xv
Sex training, 44
Sexual behavior, blacks and, 33
Sexual maladjustment, 46, 47
Sexual relationships, interracial, 9,
        15
Sharecroppers, 27, 51, 190
Shoemaker, D., 195
Significance levels, 77-78, 80, 106,
        111, 158, 175, 183, 189,
        190
Sitting, rituals concerning, 20
Skin color, importance of, 3, 30, 33
Slavery, 8-10, 13, 172-173
    abolition of, 8, 9, 10, 172
Slaves, status of, 8-10
Social institutions, ix

defined, 2
    interrelationship between per-
        sonality structures and,
        3-4
Society, Universalistic-Achievement
        oriented, 7
Sociophobia, 131-132
"Solid South," 12
South, the
    black-white relations in, 10-13,
        35-40
    caste sanctions in, 5, 6
    Civil War and, 8
    culture of, 11
    developing situation in, 35-40
    pre-Civil War, 172
South Carolina, 40, 172
Southern blacks, differences be-
        tween northern blacks
        and, 45, 48-49, 50, 76,
        137-156, 167, 171
Sports, color barrier and, 19, 191
States' rights, 11, 15
Statistics, 73-74
Status of blacks, 5, 8-10, 14, 27,
        29, 35, 36, 37
    as slaves, 8-10
Stereotypes, 3, 11, 18
Subculture, 7, 8
"Success phobia," 44
Sundberg, N. D., 195
Suppression, 126
Supreme Court, U.S., 5-6, 14, 27,
        37, 38, 39, 40, 174
Swimming, mixed, 15

Taney, Roger B., 27
TAT, *see* Thematic Apperception
        Test
Terrorism, 10, 26

Tests
  intelligence, 45, 49-50, 75, 85, 86, 166, 182
  picture arrangement, *see* Tomkins-Horn Picture Arrangement Test
  projective, 54-72, 166
    use of, with black subjects, 72
  Rorschach, 45, 46, 47, 52, 54-55
  Sentence Completion, 72
  Thematic Apperception (TAT), 47, 48, 52, 55-57, 58, 72
  Thorndike-Gallup Vocabulary, 66, 86
Theatres, seating in, 20
Thematic Apperception Test (TAT), 47, 48, 52, 55-57, 58, 72
Thorndike-Gallup Vocabulary Test, 66, 86
Toilet training, 33, 44
Toilets, public, separate facilities for blacks, 18
Tomkins, S. S., vii, ix-x, 5, 52, 55, 57-72, 85, 88, 89, 91, 94, 104, 116, 117, 175, 182, 195
Tomkins-Horn Picture Arrangement Test, 5, 52-72, 73-136, 166, 167, 168, 173, 175, 176, 180, 182, 190, 191
  administration of, 66-72
  advantages of, 52-53
  design of an experiment, 73-112
  disadvantage of, 53
  rationale of, 57-63
  testing materials, 64-66
Tradition, 11
Transference, 54, 58
Transportation, public, segregation

and, 24, 25, 27, 37, 174
Tucker, Ledyard R., x
Tukey, J. W., x, 122, 161, 181, 194
Twain, Mark, 172

Unempolyment, blacks and, 29, 35
Unions, *see* Labor unions
Universal determinants, 57-58
Universalistic-Achievement oriented society, 7
Urban League, 34

Vagrancy laws, 51
Variables, background, 104-107
Veterans, black, 37
Violence, vii, xii, xvi, 22-23, 26, 37, 38
Vocabulary Test, Thorndike-Gallup, 66, 86
Voting rights, 3, 12, 24-26, 37

War veterans, black, 37
Waring, J. Waties, 40
Washington, George, 173
Wechsler, D., 86, 195
Welch, B. L., 110, 142, 150, 195
"White supremacy," 10, 14, 29, 37
Whites
  attitude toward blacks, 9, 13, 15, 22
  effect of American caste system on, 169-170, 172-192
Whiting, J. W. M., 3, 195
Williams, R. M., 195
Women, black
  employment and, 29, 31
  family and, 30-32
  special problems faced by, xv

Women, black (*Cont.*)
   status of, as slaves, 9
Work, attitudes toward, 131, 159,
       168, 180, 181, 184-185,
       190

Yates, F., 181
Youth, black, 32